How to Do *Everything* with Your

Digital Camera

WITHDRAWN

How to Do *Everything* with Your Digital Camera

Dave Johnson

Osborne/**McGraw-Hill**

New York Chicago San Francisco
Lisbon London Madrid Mexico City
Milan New Delhi San Juan
Seoul Singapore Sydney Toronto

Osborne/**McGraw-Hill**
2600 Tenth Street
Berkeley, California 94710
U.S.A.

To arrange bulk purchase discounts for sales promotions, premiums, or fund-raisers, please contact Osborne/**McGraw-Hill** at the above address. For information on translations or book distributors outside the U.S.A., please see the International Contact Information page immediately following the index of this book.

How to Do Everything with Your Digital Camera

4567890 DOC DOC 01987654321

ISBN 0-07-212772-4

Publisher	Brandon A. Nordin
Vice President &	
Associate Publisher	Scott Rogers
Acquisitions Editor	Megg Bonar
Project Editor	Madhu Prasher
Acquisitions Coordinator	Alissa Larson
Technical Editor	Rowena White
Copy Editor	Judith Brown
Proofreader	Pat Mannion
Indexer	Valerie Robbins
Computer Designers	Lauren McCarthy, Kelly Stanton-Scott and Tara Davis
Illustrator	Michael Mueller
Series Design	Mickey Galicia

This book was composed with Corel VENTURA™ Publisher.

For Newt

About the Author

Dave Johnson writes about technology from his home in Colorado Springs, Colorado. He's Senior Editor for mobile and desktop computing at Planet IT, and writes frequently for magazines like *Home Office Computing* and *Family PC*. He's the author of 14 books that include *How to Use Digital Video* and *How to Do Everything with Your Palm Handheld* (with Rick Broida).

Dave started writing professionally in 1990, before anyone had a chance to talk him out of it. Prior to that, he had a somewhat unfocused career that included flying satellites, driving an ice cream truck, managing weapons at an Air Force base, stocking shelves at Quick Check, teaching rocket science, photographing a rock band, and writing about space penguins. He's still not playing bass in a psychedelic band, but at least he's found steady work.

Contents at a Glance

Contents

Acknowledgments

Thanks to all the great folks at Osborne who are always fun to work with—especially folks like Megg Bonar, Cindy Wathen (who unfortunately has moved on to bigger and better things), and Madhu Prasher.

One of the best things about writing this book was having the chance to play with a variety of digital cameras. A very warm thanks to Karen Thomas and the fine folks at Olympus for lending me an Olympus e10 (what a camera!). And thanks to Katrina Laine and the Kodak team for the loan of a Kodak DC4800 and all the trimmings.

Special thanks are due to the following people for their help in securing images for this book's cover:

Epson America Inc., and Becky Aoanan and Kylie Ware at Walt & Company

Eastman Kodak Company and Katrina Laine at Weber Shandwick Worldwide

Olympus America Inc., with thanks to Chris Sluka for his help and to Gina Prescia at Thomas PR

Ricoh Company Ltd., and Lisa Christopher at Future Works, Inc.

Finally, let me thank all the selfless models who posed for me as I shot picture after picture for this book—including Kris, Evan, Marin, Mysti, and Tumanna.

Introduction

Welcome to *How to Do Everything with Your Digital Camera*. This is not your typical book on digital photography—I wrote it to answer all the questions I had about digital cameras and photography techniques when I was starting out. I've been a photographer for about 20 years, and in that time I've read a lot of books and magazines about the art and science of photography. I figured that this was a good time to write a book that would hopefully explain it all in the space of a few hundred pages.

A tall order, I know.

Nonetheless, I know what it feels like to have a new digital camera and search fruitlessly for the answers to seemingly obvious questions. I've read too many books that make passing references to "control your depth of field with the aperture" without explaining what either the aperture or depth of field actually is. Or mention that you need a lot of pixels to print an 8x10-inch picture without ever telling you how many pixels you actually need.

So when I wrote this book I mapped out all of the things I thought you might need to know. I went right to the beginning and decided to cover photography techniques like lighting, composition, and close-ups. And hopefully you'll find that the book walks you through the key steps of using a digital camera—from working with memory cards, to file formats, to editing images on a PC, to printing, and finally, to sharing your images.

The world of digital photography is changing fast. It's still in its infancy in many ways. But this is a great time to purchase and use a digital camera, and I hope that some of my enthusiasm for the digital medium comes through. I love the freedom and flexibility that a digital camera gives me; armed with my Olympus D-620L or e10, I can take pictures without worrying about buying film or using it before it expires. I can instantly preview my work and download just the images I want to keep. And I particularly like the fact that I can print 8x10- or 13x19-inch enlargements exactly the way I want without trying to convey imprecise instructions to a tech in a photo shop. I've even started using a Nikon CoolPix 990 underwater when I scuba dive, and that, too, is a whole new and exciting world of photography that is made dramatically easier by digital cameras.

I wrote this book so that you could sit down and read it through like a novel if you'd like to—but I realize few people will actually do that. If you're looking for specific information, I've organized the book so topics should be easy to find. Part I kicks things off with the basics of using your camera. I begin by explaining how to shop for a digital camera and how to operate the most common controls on digital cameras. From there, I delve into stuff you need to know no matter what kind of camera you have—stuff like composition, lighting, close-ups, and how to take advantage of the special features on your camera.

Part II of the book is all about getting the images from the camera into your PC. I talk about how to use file formats like JPG and TIF, and how to care for the memory cards that come with your camera. For those of you who want to scan traditional film prints into your PC, I've dedicated a chapter to selecting and using a scanner.

I'm guessing that most of you will be keenly interested in Part III—at least that's one of the most exciting parts for me. This is where you can learn how to edit digital images as if your PC were a sort of digital darkroom. Sure, there are simple techniques in here like how to crop and resize images, but I also write about cool special effects—adding text, changing images so they look like they were painted, and even creating Hollywood-style "bluescreen" effects.

Finally, the book ends with Part IV, a few chapters that explain how to print and share your images. I tell you exactly what you need to know to get great results—like optimizing your printer, using the right paper, and calculating how large you can print your image based on how many pixels it has. And then you can learn how to share your images—on the computer screen, in email, on the Web (even without any programming), and in devices like Palms and digital picture frames.

To help you along, you can find special elements to help you get the most out of the book:

- **How-To**   These special boxes explain, in a nutshell, how to accomplish key tasks throughout the book. You can read the How-To box for a summary of what the chapter at-large is explaining.

- **Notes**   These provide extra information that is handy for trivia contests but isn't essential to understanding the current topic.

- **Tips**   These tell you how to do something a better, faster, or smarter way.

- **Sidebars**   These talk about related topics that are pretty darned interesting, but you can skip them if you prefer.

- Within the text, you'll also find words in special formatting. New terms are in italics, while specific phrases that you will see on the screen or need to type yourself appear in bold.

Want to email me? You can send questions and comments to me at:

cameraquestions@bydavejohnson.com.

My Web site is located at bydavejohnson.com, and you're welcome to visit there and check out other books or my photography anytime you like. Thanks, and enjoy reading the book!

Part I

Your Camera

Chapter 1

Welcome to the Future

How to…

- Navigate around your digital camera
- Distinguish between point and shoot and professional camera features
- Pick a camera resolution based on print size
- Conserve battery power
- Tell the difference between a digital and optical zoom
- Shop for a new digital camera
- Choose gear and accessories for a digicam

This chapter is called "Welcome to the Future," and I mean it. I'm convinced that digital photography is, without doubt, the best way to take pictures, and the technology just keeps getting better all the time.

With a digital camera, it's possible to take photos and review them instantly—while they're still stored in the camera—to see if they turned out the way you like. From there, you can transfer them to a computer and easily crop them to size, adjust their color and brightness, and then print the final result to exactly the size you like for a frame in your living room. Then take the same picture and email it, post it to a Web site, or show it to friends from your handheld organizer. The beauty of digital imaging is its immediacy and versatility—just try to do those things with a 35mm or APS camera.

So if you've recently bought a digital camera, congratulations—you've made the right choice. In this chapter, we'll take a quick look at your camera and digital cameras in general. And if you're still shopping for your camera, flip to the end of this chapter, where I tell you what to look for when you head off to make your purchase.

A History Lesson

When I was a kid, my dad bought a darkroom kit so he could develop his own photographs. I clearly remember that box—as if it were yesterday—and how it sat, untouched, on top of a hall closet. For years. Why did my dad never get around to setting up his darkroom? In a nutshell, it was just too much trouble.

Darkrooms require, well, darkness. You have to have a room that you can dedicate to the task and trust that people won't come barging in while you're developing film (or hang their wet bathing suit in there when you're not actively using the room).

And then there are the chemicals. Film processing is all about using nasty, toxic chemicals that, if you were running a business, would probably get the attention of OSHA. When I worked in the space launch business, I'm sure that some of the fuels we used weren't as frightening as the chemicals that home darkroomers routinely expose themselves to. Who wants to muck around with that stuff?

Oh, yeah—and it isn't all that easy, either. Black-and-white processing isn't really brain surgery, but working with color film is tough. It's not a hobby you can master in a few weeks, to be sure. And the whole point of having your own darkroom is so you can get better results than the corner store delivers, right?

No wonder my dad never got too far with his darkroom kit.

These days, digital photography gives you the same flexibility as those old chemical darkrooms—the ability to brighten or darken an image, crop it down to generate a better composition, and print enlargements in a variety of sizes—but without the chemicals, without the steep learning curve, and without dedicating a part of your house to nothing but photography. How did we get here?

A Slow Evolution

These days, some digital cameras can compete with the best 35mm SLRs in terms of resolution and image quality. Obviously, it hasn't always been this way.

When you consider the first digital cameras, it's a miracle that anyone used them at all. They were strictly for early adopters, since they offered very limited resolution and substandard optics to boot. Early digital cameras generated low-resolution images, like 320x240 pixels—not even enough to fill a computer screen when set to the lowest Windows resolution.

Those early digital cameras typically also had plastic lenses, and their digital film was a component called a Complementary Metal Oxide Semiconductor (CMOS) chip. CMOS chips are popular because they are cost effective and require very little power, but they create fuzzy pictures. Because they are cheaper than the Charged Coupled Devices (CCDs) almost universally in use today, CMOS chips, consequently, found their way into many of the first cameras. See Figure 1-1 for an example of the difference between an image taken with a CMOS chip (on the left) and a CCD (on the right).

As time went on, Video Graphics Array (VGA) resolution became something of a standard. Digicams came equipped with CMOS or CCD chips capable of capturing 640x480-pixel images, which is perfect for VGA monitors. That was fine for posting images to Web pages or inserting them in email, but you can't really print such a picture. On a typical inkjet printer, you get a photograph that measures just three inches across.

Then came *megapixel*. "Mega" means million, and the term simply refers to the resolution of the camera. A megapixel camera can create an image with a million pixels, for example, 1000x1000 or 860x1200 or any other pixel dimension that adds up to at least a million. The first megapixel cameras raised the bar for everyone. Like owning last year's laptop with a slow processor, no one wanted to own a VGA camera. That started the race we're still in the midst of today.

Today, a typical digital camera captures anywhere from 2 to 3.3 megapixels. Some higher-end cameras capture more pixels—as many as 6 million. Why the fuss over pixels? Well, as I alluded to earlier, the more pixels you have, the larger your pictures can be printed. If you'd like to print a digital photo at 8x10 or larger, for instance, a VGA camera simply won't cut it—each pixel will be the size of a postage stamp. Take a look at Figure 1-2. On the left is a detail from a picture

FIGURE 1-1   Cameras with CMOS chips typically offer lower image quality than those with CCDs.

taken at 640x480 pixels. On the right is the same detail, but it's cropped from a 3.3-megapixel image. As you can see, the smaller image has fewer pixels to work with, and that's why it looks

FIGURE 1-2   The more resolution that you begin with, the more quality you will end up with in your final image.

so grainy. Obviously, you need lots of pixels to print pictures at a large size, and that's why each year we see larger-resolution digital cameras hitting store shelves.

The Future of Digital Cameras

And there's no end in sight, at least for a while. The goal of most camera manufacturers has traditionally been to elevate the resolution of digicams to the same level as what film cameras offer today. But not all film cameras are the same, and serious photographers always want more resolution. More resolution—or more pixels per picture—allows photographers to blow up images to larger sizes and to crop images and enlarge just one small section of a photo without sacrificing resolution as well.

Today's 3.3-megapixel cameras are adequate for making 8x10-inch enlargements. But if you want larger pictures—11x17 or 13x19 (well within the ability of some desktop inkjet printers)—you need more pixels. A few top-of-the-line digicams can generate 6-megapixel images. That's an important number because that resolution is equivalent to what a 35mm SLR can do with fine-grained slide film.

Unlike chemical film cameras, digital cameras have no resolution limits—they can take pictures as large as their CCDs and storage cards allow. Film cameras are limited by the physical standards set in place. So while it would be great to take a wall-sized picture with your 35mm SLR, that's simply impossible. 35mm slides and negatives are far too small; if you enlarge them, the grains start to become readily visible once you get past 8x10-inch prints. The only way to get larger prints is to start with a larger negative, and that means switching to medium- or large-format photography.

So what's next? No major camera makers have yet announced 8- or 10-megapixel cameras, but it's just a matter of time. Heck, the first 8-megapixel cameras may be on their way to market by the time this book is hitting the shelves of your local bookstore. The industry is evolving that fast. Evolution of camera resolution will probably slow down after everyone starts to gravitate around the 6-megapixel mark, but eventually, digital cameras will no doubt come in formats that allow photographers to work with huge prints like those from large-format cameras.

In the meantime, we'll see another trend in digital photography. Right now, there are two main kinds of digicams—point and shoot cameras (which constitute the majority of digital camera sales) and Single Lens Reflex (SLR)–like pro cameras. Point and shoot models appeal to casual photographers and look like 35mm point and shoot models (see Figure 1-3), while pro-level cameras like the Nikon D1 feature interchangeable lenses, snap-on, powerful flash units, and a wealth of manual controls. The D1, seen in Figure 1-4, is one of the most popular pro cameras around, but it costs a hefty $5000. As digital cameras get ever more integrated into the mainstream, we'll see more of these cameras that give photographers all the power and flexibility of SLR cameras with the immediacy of the digital medium, and their prices should drop rapidly. I predict that within two years, the future equivalent of the Nikon D1 will retail for perhaps $2000, about the same as the Nikon F100, today's popular pro-level 35mm SLR.

FIGURE 1-3 A point and shoot digital camera, also known as a digital rangefinder camera

FIGURE 1-4 The Nikon D1 is an expensive yet powerful tool for serious photographers.

Features, Gadgets, and Goodies

No two digital cameras are the same. Each camera maker is known to some greater or lesser extent for implement-specific kinds of features—like interchangeable lenses, swivel bodies, and movie recording features. If you cut through all those goodies, though, you'll find that most cameras share many of the same fundamentals. Let's start at the top and cover your camera's fundamentals.

The Optical System

At the heart of every camera, no matter how it stores its images, is an optical system, as you can see in Figure 1-5.

As you can see in Figure 1-5, most digital cameras have two distinct viewfinders—an optical one and a digital one. The optical viewfinder is composed of a glass or plastic lens that shows you your subject directly. The digital viewfinder is an LCD display that reproduces what the camera's CCDs are actually seeing.

Which one should you use? Whichever one you like. You'll get better results, though, if you understand the difference between the two. The majority of digital cameras are rangefinder designs, also known as point and shoot cameras. With a rangefinder, you do not actually see what the camera sees when you look through the optical viewfinder. The optical viewfinder is a parallax-inducing viewfinder, a popular low-cost mechanism that dates back almost all the way to the invention of the camera itself. No doubt you have a point and shoot camera lying around the house with just such a viewfinder.

The optical viewfinder is essentially a window that cuts through the camera case parallel to the lens assembly. When taking pictures from a distance, the viewfinder and lens see essentially the same thing. Close up to your subject, though, they clearly see two different things (as you can see from Figure 1-6). The concept of parallax—and what it means to your photographs—is discussed in detail in Chapter 5.

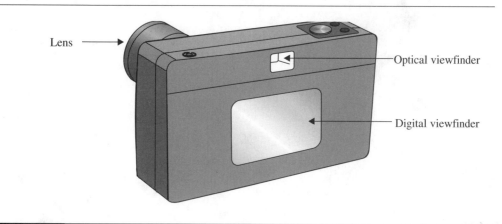

Lens

Optical viewfinder

Digital viewfinder

FIGURE 1-5   All digital cameras rely on a similar optical system.

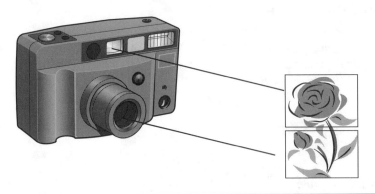

FIGURE 1-6   The optical viewfinder and the camera's lens don't always look at exactly the same thing.

The digital viewfinder, on the other hand, shows you exactly what the camera sees, and thus is the most accurate gauge of your potential photograph. You won't want to use your digital viewfinder all the time, though. For starters, it uses a lot of power, and you can get a lot more mileage out of your camera's batteries by using the optical viewfinder instead. In addition, the LCD display can be very difficult to see in certain lighting conditions, like outside in midafternoon.

Some cameras allow you to turn off the LCD display to conserve power. Leave the display off most of the time to get more battery life.

TTL Viewfinders

Not all cameras are rangefinders with parallax-inducing viewfinders; some have TTL (Through-the-Lens) optical systems. These TTL viewfinders trace a light path through the lens, which means they show you exactly what you're going to photograph (as illustrated below). They come in especially handy with zoom lenses. While SLR-style cameras like the Nikon D1 have a TTL viewfinder (and a $5000 price tag to boot), more affordable cameras occasionally include this feature as well. The Olympus D-620L is one such example.

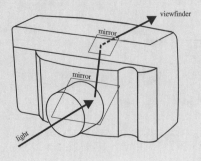

Power Systems

It shouldn't surprise you terribly to learn that your digital camera takes batteries. Most—but not all—digital cameras rely on four AA batteries, just like the ones in the Epson camera seen below. Some cameras, like the Olympus D-490, also accept a special single-use Lithium battery or some other kind of power, like rechargeables.

Power management is discussed in more detail in Chapter 6, but for now heed this sage advice:

- Insert batteries according to the diagram on the camera body—make sure you align the battery's positive and negative ends correctly.
- Don't leave batteries in the camera for an extended period of time. If they leak, your camera can be ruined.
- Don't mix and match fresh and used batteries, or batteries of different kinds.
- When you can, run your camera using AC power.

That last bullet is particularly important. Some digital cameras come with their own AC adapters, while for others it's an optional accessory. Check the camera body for an AC adapter connector (as in Figure 1-7). If you can connect the camera to a wall outlet, especially during image transfers to the PC, you can significantly extend the length of your battery's life.

Memory Storage

If I had to pick one element that most differentiates digital cameras today, I'd probably choose memory storage. Digital cameras use computer-style memory like traditional cameras use film. The more memory your camera has, the more images it can store. Chapter 8 includes an in-depth discussion of the various memory formats available, but for now suffice it to say that your camera includes a memory card with some memory capacity (such as 8MB or 16MB) that, when inserted in the camera, stores images. When it's full, you can remove this card and insert

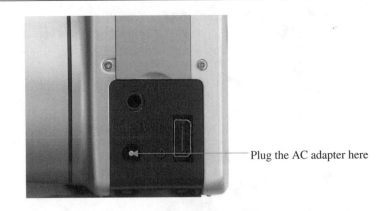

Plug the AC adapter here

FIGURE 1-7   Some digital cameras feature a port for wall power from an AC adapter.

other cards for additional storage. Some memory cards can be inserted into the PC with the help of adapters (see Figure 1-8), or you can use a cable of some kind to transfer the data on those cards from the camera to your computer.

There are three main kinds of memory cards in use today:

- Smart Media
- Compact Flash
- Memory Stick

FIGURE 1-8   Smart Media cards can be inserted in your computer's floppy drive, while Compact Flash cards require bulkier transfer solutions.

In addition to each of those, some cameras—specifically Sony Mavica cameras—use a floppy disk or a recordable CD for storing images.

Only very inexpensive or old digital cameras do not include removable storage at all. Such cameras rely exclusively on the memory that's built into the camera to store images.

Camera Controls

Perhaps the most subjective of digital camera features, the controls are also among the most important. I can't really tell you which is best; you need to experiment with a few cameras to see which you like the best. Try handling cameras in the store whenever you can.

Digital cameras typically feature two distinct control systems: on-body buttons and dials plus on-screen menus. Figure 1-9 shows some body controls, such as a diopter dial (for adjusting the eyepiece to your personal eyesight), shutter release button, and zoom controls. The on-screen menu (seen in Figure 1-10) is commonly used to adjust less frequently used controls, like resolution settings, exposure compensation, and special effects filters. That's not alway the case, though, as you can see in Figure 1-11. There, the Epson PhotoPC 850 uses buttons to change the resolution without resorting to a menu system.

You need to take the time to review your camera manual to find out how to operate all your camera controls. Without knowing how to operate your camera, you can't really learn to take great pictures.

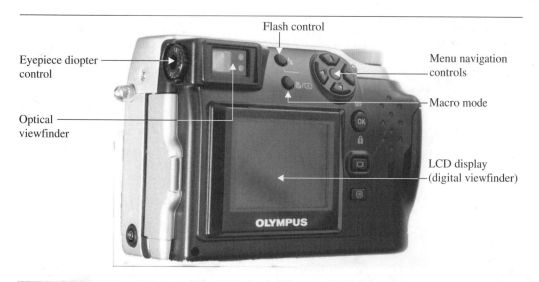

FIGURE 1-9   Most of these controls are common to all digital cameras.

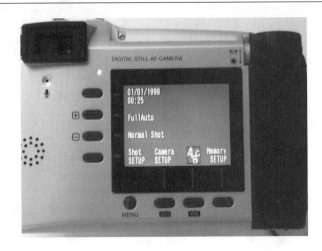

FIGURE 1-10   Digital cameras use a menu system in the LCD display to control advanced features.

Choosing Your Own Digital Camera

If you haven't yet made your digital camera purchase—or if you are planning to upgrade—you're in luck. The field has never been more crowded with excellent choices, and as I mentioned earlier, technology advances keep making these cameras better each year.

Even though the camera field is evolving all the time, the basics really don't change. The next few sections cover the most important elements to consider when shopping for a camera.

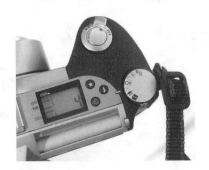

FIGURE 1-11   The star is used to change resolution modes on this camera.

The Upgrade Race

Do you need to get a new camera next year just because the megapixel bar has been raised—or some other cool new features have surfaced?

No, you don't. Just like your desktop computer, a digital camera isn't obsolete just because a new model came out with more memory or horsepower. It's only obsolete when it no longer does what you want it to do.

Consider my main digital camera. Although I get to see and play with a large number of cameras every year, I've stuck with what you'll surely consider to be an ancient model—the several-year-old Olympus D-620L. I like this camera because it has a TTL viewfinder and an excellent macro mode. The downside? It's a mere 1.4 megapixels. That's so Twentieth Century. That's OK, though—I use the camera to take screenshots for books, magazines, and Web sites. I rarely need anything much bigger than 1024x768 for those applications, and that's well within the capability of this venerable old camera. If I found another TTL digital camera that captured 3.3- or 6-megapixel images—and didn't cost a small fortune—I'd upgrade. But for now I stick with the D-620L for most of my photography.

The bottom line? Find a camera you like and stick with it. Digital cameras are a costly investment, and they won't "pay for themselves" in film savings if you replace them every year or so with a newer model.

Resolution

First and foremost, figure out how much resolution you need. This should be the very first decision you make, since it determines what cameras you will be evaluating. Use this handy little guide to decide what megapixel range you need:

Megapixels	Print Size
Sub-megapixel (VGA)	On-screen only (Web, email)
1 megapixel	3x5-inch prints
2 megapixel	5x7-inch prints
3 megapixel	8x10-inch prints
6 megapixel	13x19-inch prints, prints from small crop areas of the original image

Remember that even if you choose a 6-megapixel camera, you can set it to capture lower-resolution images—even a mere 640x480 pixels—making your camera quite versatile. Or you can capture a high-resolution image and reduce its size on the PC in an image editing program. (I explain how to do this in Chapter 12.) The higher the resolution, the fewer pictures you can store at a given time, so there is a bit of a trade-off. If you buy a camera with too little resolution, though, you can't ever add information to a picture, and trying to "blow it up" to print beyond its ideal size will generate a pixely, grainy mess.

Optics

It is a camera, after all—not a computer. Don't forget to weigh the optics carefully. What kind of pictures do you want to take? A fairly wide angle lens is good for landscapes, indoor shots, and general-purpose photography. If you want to take portraits or wildlife shots, a longer reach is important. Many digital cameras announce their focal length in "35mm equivalents"—in other words, if this digital camera were a 35mm camera, its 9.3mm lens would give you the same picture as a 50mm camera, for instance. But you can't generally go into a digital camera shop and ask for a camera with the equivalent of a 100mm lens. Most salespeople just aren't savvy enough to know the equivalence between digital and 35mm cameras.

That can be a pain, I know, so you can use this formula I've concocted to convert digital camera focal lengths to their 35mm equivalents, where FL is the actual focal length of the digital camera's lens, usually a small number like 5mm or 10mm:

35mm equivalent focal length = FL / .186

So if the camera has a 6.5mm lens, for instance, you can run it through this handy little equation and determine that it will work like a 35mm lens.

If you don't have your calculator handy, use the following table instead. It shows you what common 35mm focal lengths correspond to in the digital world, and what they're generally good for:

35mm Focal Length	Digital Camera Focal Length	Common Photo Apps
24	4.5	Wide-angle photography, outdoor landscapes
35	6.5	Landscapes, indoor photos
55	10.2	"Normal" photography; since this is the same as your eyes' focal length, this captures images the way your eyes see things
100	18.6	Portraiture
200	37.2	Telephoto; great for pulling in distant scenes

This guide works fine for many point and shoot digital cams. If you are working with an SLR-style digital camera, though, you need to use whatever focal length guide the camera maker recommends. The Kodak DCS520, for instance, uses 35mm lenses, but considering the difference in size between the camera's CCD and ordinary 35mm film, you need to add 15% to the focal length of the lens. Also, this calculation is sensitive to the actual size of the camera's CCD, so it may not be accurate with all cameras.

Choosing a Zoom

Of course, few digital cameras come with a fixed focal length lens. The focal length is a measure of how much the camera magnifies the image, and zoom lenses are known for their ability to let you zoom in and out of a scene for the perfect composition. In general, the greater the zoom the better. You'll commonly see 2x, 3x, and perhaps even 5x zooms. With some simple finger pressure, you can use your camera to go from a normal or wide-angle view to telephoto. The effect of a 3x zoom is apparent in Figure 1-12, taken with the Olympus D-620L at both ends of its zoom range.

Beware, though, of a camera's digital zoom. While optical zooms move the lenses around to actually magnify the image, a digital zoom simply grabs an array of pixels in the middle of the scene and processes them to make the image look enlarged. Since the result is pixely, I suggest that you ignore digital zoom ratings when evaluating a camera and just look at the optical zoom ratings.

Memory

The more memory your camera holds, the more pictures you can take. It sounds simple, but don't forget that cameras come with all different kinds of memory solutions. Smart Media cards, for instance, usually start at 8MB and top out at 64MB. They can't hold as much memory as Compact Flash cards, but Compact Flash is accordingly more expensive. Likewise, Smart Media

FIGURE 1-12   Zoom lenses are common because of their flexibility when composing pictures.

is more convenient because you can slip the card into a floppy drive with a floppy disk adapter—Compact Flash is too thick for that kind of arrangement.

Bottom line: if you want to take a lot of high-resolution images in the same session and you don't want to keep swapping memory cards, look for a camera that accepts high-capacity memory, like Compact Flash or Type II PC Cards. If your images are all low resolution or you don't mind swapping cards a lot, then it doesn't matter what you buy.

Flash

Almost all digital cameras come with a built-in flash these days. The real issue is how well the flash works. Check to see what the maximum range of the flash is and if it works when the camera is in macro, or close focus, mode. You might also want a flash with special features like these:

- **Red eye reduction**   This mode preflashes the subject to try to minimize reflected light from the pupil known as *red eye*.
- **Force/fill**   Force or fill flash is used to reduce shadows outdoors or in otherwise adequate lighting when the flash might not fire.
- **Rear curtain flash**   This mode fires at the end of a long exposure. It comes in handy at night so that light trails precede the main subject, illuminated by the flash.

Some cameras also come with sync ports or hot shoes that allow you to connect more powerful, external flash units.

Special Effects

Since digital cameras are part computer, they can be programmed to do some neat tricks that were inconceivable with traditional 35mm cameras. Few of these effects are necessary; in fact, I'd choose a camera based on solid features like the zoom, lens quality, and overall handling before I looked too hard at whether the camera included a video mode or sepia tint. Nonetheless, these are some of the effects you may see:

- **Panorama mode**   This feature takes wide-screen-style images either by automatically cropping the top and bottom off an image or by letting you stitch together several pictures to create one oversized one.
- **Movie mode**   Some cameras can capture short, low-resolution video clips as well as still images. Don't confuse this with real high-quality digital video, though—the results are strictly for Web pages.
- **Tint modes**   With special settings, you can take black-and-white or sepia-tinted stills. Remember, though, that you can achieve the same effect in an image editor on the PC after the picture is taken, so you aren't losing anything if your camera lacks this feature. In fact, I'd say it's better to start with a full-color image; that way you can do whatever you like to it later and always have the high-quality original to fall back on.

Transfer Mechanism

Getting images out of your camera is just as important as taking the pictures to begin with. If you like to view your freshly shot images on a television or want to record them, slide show style, directly to a VCR, then you should definitely consider a camera with a video-out port. Using an ordinary RCA-style composite video cable, you can connect the camera to a TV, VCR, or some other video display unit.

For computer connection, I recommend USB. USB allows you to transfer images painlessly, especially compared to the more traditional serial cable.

Some cameras include even more elaborate solutions, like adapters that accept the removable media card and connect to the computer directly. The advantage with these devices is that you can transfer images without draining the camera batteries, and transfers are often easier to do, since you avoid using arcane transfer software and instead just drag and drop images from a folder on the Windows desktop.

Gear You'll Need

Every hobby has its accessories. I sometimes joke that my dive buddy only became interested in scuba diving after she discovered that scuba gear was a whole new way to spend money.

While there's no doubt some truth to that, it's also true that there are some things you really need to buy to accompany any activity, and digital photography is no exception. Here's a short shopping list of things you might consider buying as you get more into shooting digitally:

- ■ **A camera**   It goes without saying that you need a camera, but don't rush into the purchase. You can even use a 35mm camera to begin with, and scan the images into the PC for editing and printing. If you've read the previous sections of this chapter and decided what features are important to you, you can shop like a pro.

- ■ **An adequate PC**   Crunching data to process digital images takes a bit more horsepower than you might be used to when working with Word or Excel. I suggest using a Pentium II–class PC with no less than 128MB of RAM. If you want to work with really big images—like 6-megapixel pictures—then consider 256MB of RAM.

- ■ **Batteries**   Digital cameras are power hogs. I highly recommend buying two sets of NiMH rechargeable batteries, since they'll pay for themselves before you can say "alkaline." If you can, also get an AC adapter to power the camera when you're transferring images to the PC.

- ■ **Memory**   Buy the biggest memory card you can afford. The measly 8MB memory card that came with your camera won't last a day when you're on vacation, so having a 64MB or 128MB card is almost essential. A spare card, if it's in the budget, can keep you going when you fill up your main card far away from your PC.

- ■ **Image editing software**   Your camera probably came with some rudimentary image editor, but it may not be up to the task. Try a few out, and buy the image editor that you like the best. I typically use Paint Shop Pro, for instance.

■ **Printer**   Get a good color inkjet printer and premium photo paper. Don't skimp on this step—when the time comes to print your pictures, why bother having a good camera, this book, and taking the time to improve your photo skills if you're going to print pictures on a budget printer with lousy paper?

■ **Tripod**   If you want to extend your photography into the world of close-ups or long-range telephoto images, a tripod is a necessity. It needn't be large or heavy, since most digital cameras are significantly lighter than their 35mm counterparts.

■ **Lenses and filters**   The time may come when you want to take pictures—like extreme close-ups, wide-angle shots, or extreme telephotos—that are beyond the range of the lens that came with your camera. Likewise, you might want to reduce glare or add other special effects to your images. If that's the case, you want lenses and filters for your camera. You may not need them right now, but consider them an advanced purchase for later on.

■ **Camera bag**   Choose a bag that lets you arrange your camera and accessories in a way that they're protected from theft and damage, but easy to use when the time comes to shoot a picture.

How to ... Choose a Digital Camera

When you're shopping for a digital camera, make a checklist of features and capabilities you want based on these criteria:

■ **Resolution**   Decide how large your finished images need to be, and look for cameras that can take pictures in the appropriate "megapixel" range.

■ **Optics**   Consider the lens quality, optical zoom range, and the possibility of adding lenses or filters for more capabilities.

■ **Flash**   Consider the flash range and special features like red eye reduction. For serious flash photography, look for cameras that accept external flash units.

■ **Special effects**   If you want goodies like movie modes or panoramic capture, worry about that now after the essentials are out of the way.

■ **Transfer mechanism**   One last issue to consider is how the camera transfers images to the PC—this is a convenience issue.

Chapter 2

Understanding Exposure

How to...

- Tell the difference between analog and digital camera operation
- Distinguish between slide and negative photography
- Pick ISO settings for a digital and film camera
- Match aperture and shutter speed settings for correct exposure
- Use the Sunny 16 Rule
- Modify the Sunny 16 Rule based on ISO and lighting conditions
- Adjust exposure manually
- Tweak exposure with your camera's EV settings
- Choose metering modes for better pictures
- Use exposure lock to optimize exposure
- Tell when to ignore the camera and make your own exposure decisions

Some people think that photography is akin to magic. They turn on the camera, snap a picture, and a day or two later they've got a mystical re-creation of the scene they saw in the viewfinder. With a digicam, it's even more magical—the pictures are available instantly! How does it work? Who knows?

The problem with the Abe Simpson approach to photography (which I've so named based on an episode of *The Simpsons* in which someone took a picture of old Abe and he shouted feebly, "You stole my soul!") is that you can never really improve if you don't know what your camera does or why—and if you don't know how you can influence the camera yourself to improve your shots. This chapter, consequently, walks you through the exposure process. Here you'll learn what constitutes a proper exposure and how to get it yourself—even on cameras that are mostly automatic.

How Cameras Take Pictures

The best place to start is often right at the beginning—how on earth does a camera take a picture, anyway?

All cameras, regardless of type, work more or less the same way—as depicted in the illustration below. They open their shutter for a brief time, allowing light to enter. That light then interacts with a sensitive photo-receptor (like film, or perhaps a computer chip), and an image is recorded. Let's start by looking at a traditional 35mm camera to give us a little perspective.

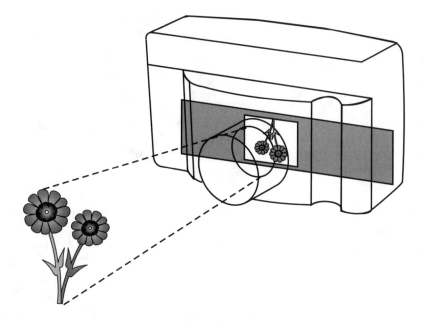

Inside a 35mm Camera

Traditional cameras rely on good old-fashioned film. But what is film, really? It's just a strip of plastic that has been coated with a light-sensitive chemical. The chemical soup on the film is loaded with grains of silver halide. When exposed to light, the silver halide reacts, and that is the essence of photography. The longer the film is exposed to light, the more the silver is affected.

There are two kinds of film in common use today: negative and slide film. They work a little differently, but the end result is similar. When you use color negative film, also referred to as reversal film, the film itself becomes a "negative" image of the scene you photographed. After processing—which includes letting the film sit in a chemical bath that coaxes the grains of silver to visually materialize on the film—the negative is used to create positive prints of the scene. It's a two-step process, and one that is highly subjective. When creating prints from negatives, photo-finishers often tweak the picture to improve its appearance. Of course, what the corner shop considers an "improvement" may not be what you were trying to achieve, and that explains why your pictures never seem to benefit from filters, exposure changes, or any of the other corrections you try to make when taking pictures.

But I digress. The other kind of film is simple slide film. This is a color positive development process—after fixing the slide film in its chemical bath, the film becomes slides that can be held up to the light to display images.

The Moment of Exposure

Depending upon the kind of camera, the events at the moment of exposure can be quite complicated. In a modern 35mm SLR, for instance, microprocessor-controlled sensors determine the exact amount of light needed to expose a picture at the moment you press the shutter release. The lens automatically adjusts the size of its opening to admit the correct amount of light, the mirror mechanism that usually lets you look through the viewfinder flips up and out of the way, and the aperture opens for the programmed amount of time. Point and shoot cameras, in contrast, don't use mirror mechanisms to let you see through the lens before the shot, so there are fewer moving parts at the moment of exposure.

No matter what kind of film you have, it eventually needs to be exposed to light. When you take a picture, you obviously press the shutter release. The shutter release instructs the camera to open a diaphragm in the lens for a brief period of time and then close again. If all went well, that was just long enough to properly expose the film.

If you want to shoot with 35mm film, scan the results, and then edit and print the results on your PC, you might want to work with slide film. Slides are more exacting—they require you to nail the exposure fairly precisely, as I explain in Chapter 11—but they'll better represent what you actually photographed instead of the local photo shop's vision of what you photographed.

How and Why Film Varies

As you no doubt know by shopping for film, not all canisters of 35mm film are alike. Film is differentiated principally by its speed, or ISO number.

A film's ISO number refers to how sensitive it is to light. The lower the number is, the less sensitive—requiring long exposures or very bright scenes.

ISO stands for International Organization for Standardization, and that's the group that helped establish how the number scheme works. Film around the world uses ISO numbers, so you can buy it anywhere, and it'll all work the same. In the United States, photographers used to call this system ASA, which stood for the American Standards Association. That term was essentially abandoned about 20 years ago, so if you want to be considered a gristled old geezer, you can refer to ISO numbers as "ASA."

A fairly typical ISO number for ordinary daylight photography is ISO 100. Increasing the ISO to 200 doubles the sensitivity of the film; dropping back to an ISO of 50 halves the sensitivity of the film.

This has a tangible effect on the mechanics of photography. To see why, look at Figure 2-1. This diagram shows a typical camera body as a picture is taken. The lens is equipped with a diaphragm—called an *aperture*—that has a certain diameter and consequently is designed to

FIGURE 2-1   Every camera—no matter what it uses for film—controls light with some sort
of aperture.

allow a specific amount of light through to the film. With ISO 100 film in specific lighting
conditions (say, at midday) the shutter might need to open for a 250th of a second (1/250) to
adequately expose the picture.

But what happens if we instead try to take the same picture with ISO 200 film? The film is
exactly twice as sensitive to light as the previous roll of film. And that means, all other things
being equal, that we only need to leave the shutter open for half as long (a 500th of a second, or
1/500) to take the same picture.

That's not all. Suppose you're trying to take a picture in late afternoon—when there isn't
as much light available? You might need to leave the shutter open for 1/30 in that situation to
gather enough light. That shutter speed is a bit on the slow side, though. Not only might you
jiggle the camera as you're taking the picture (it's hard to hold a camera steady for 1/30), but
your subject might move as well, causing a blurry picture. You can probably guess what the
solution is—stepping up to ISO 200 film will enable you to grab that picture at a much more
reasonable 1/60, and ISO 400 would halve the shutter speed yet again, to a crisp 1/250.

The F/stop Ballet

So far so good—but there's one other aspect to consider, and that's the fact that camera lenses
can change the diameter of their aperture, thus letting in more or less light as needed.

The size of a camera's aperture at any given moment is called the *f/stop*, or sometimes
referred to as the *f number* of the lens. F/stops are represented by numbers that start with "f/"—
like f/2, f/5.6, and f/11. The larger the number, the smaller the opening, so an f22 is very, very
small (not much light gets through to the film), while a lens set to f/1.2 is a huge opening that
literally floods the film with light. Every "whole" f/stop, such as from f/5.6 to f/8 or f/11 to f/16,
increases or reduces the light by 100%. If you adjust a lens from f/8 to f/11, for instance, you've
reduced the light by half.

We'll talk about this in more detail in Chapter 3 (it's really important, yet really simple), but
for the moment take a look at Figure 2-2. This diagram shows the relationship between f/stop
and shutter speed. As you reduce the shutter speed, you need to increase the diameter of the
aperture in order to have enough light to take a properly exposed picture.

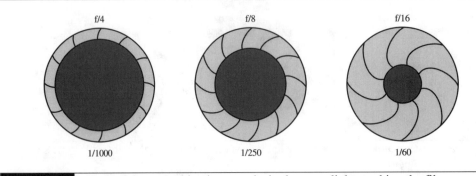

f/4	f/8	f/16
1/1000	1/250	1/60

FIGURE 2-2 Each of these combinations results in the same light reaching the film.

Of course, there's a link between aperture, shutter speed, and your film's ISO rating. Look at Figure 2-3. At a given film speed, you can take a picture with a specific aperture/shutter combination. If you double the film speed without changing the lighting conditions, though, you have to adjust the aperture and shutter speed so that you still get a properly exposed picture. And perhaps most importantly for us, suppose you are in the situation described below.

You want to take a picture of frolicking lions at the zoo near dusk. The aperture is wide open at f/2—it won't open any farther. Nonetheless, your camera needs to use the relatively slow shutter speed of 1/15 second to take the shot. You know the image would be a blurry mess at that sluggish shutter speed, so what is there to do? Take a look at your film speed. It's ISO 100 film. Well, you might be in luck. If you're willing to pop the film out of your camera and put in film that's two f/stops (often, just called "stops") faster, you can keep the aperture at f/2 and change the shutter speed to 1/60. That's probably good enough to get the shot. Just do it quickly—it isn't getting any brighter out, and if you dally, you might find you need to increase the speed by three stops by the time you get the film loaded and ready to go.

> *You probably don't need to know this, but it might come in handy during a trivia game some day. Mathematically, f/stops are the ratio of the focal length of the lens divided by the diameter of the opening of the diaphragm. Thus, when you divide the focal length of the lens by a very small opening, you get a large number, while dividing the focal length by a comparatively large diameter gives you a smaller number.*

How Digicams Are Different

All that talk about f/stops, shutter speed, and ISO settings may seem irrelevant to your digital camera, but it's not—all cameras use these concepts, even though they're sometimes disguised fairly well. The main difference between a digital camera and a chemical film camera, of course, is the fact that digicams don't use film. That means you never load anything that has a specific ISO value into the camera. So how does the camera actually work?

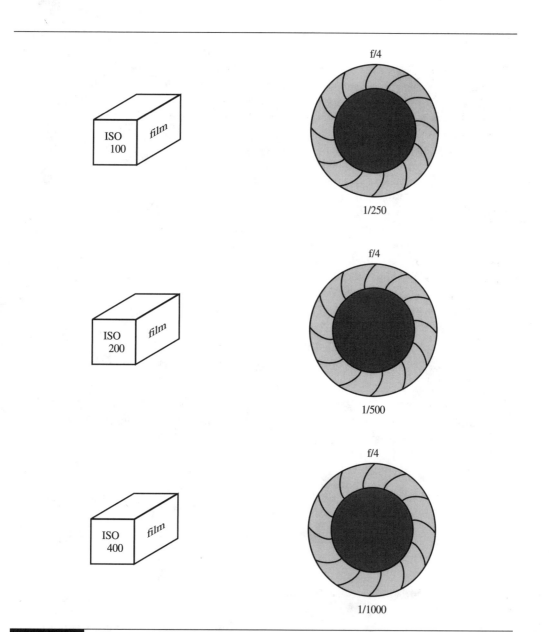

FIGURE 2-3   Film speed—known as ISO—also affects shutter speed and aperture.

Simple. When light enters the camera at the moment of exposure, it doesn't hit light-sensitive silver halides that are fixed in a chemical broth. Instead, the light hits a computer chip called a CCD (which stands for Charge Coupled Device). The CCD is light sensitive, and each of its many pixels register changes in light just like the film's many grains of silver react individually to light (see Figure 2-4). In other words, the silver grains in film and the pixels in a CCD are essentially the same thing. They contribute to your picture in the same way, and both are the smallest components that make up your picture.

The CCD makes a picture by noting the variation in light rays that travel through the camera lens. The CCDs pass this information on to the camera's microprocessor in the form of varying electrical charges. The image is transformed into digital bits and stored on a memory card.

Your camera's CCD functions like the film in a 35mm camera, except that it differs in one important way—you can't swap the CCD out of your camera and insert one with more light sensitivity for low-light photography. The CCD is a permanent part of the camera. Camera makers understand that you might need to change the camera's light sensitivity on occasion, though, and that's why many cameras can have their ISO rating "adjusted" on the fly, whenever you want. In essence, what this does is allow you to "turn up" your camera's sensitivity to light.

Use ISO for Exposure Control

You can use the ISO control built into your digital camera to vary its sensitivity to light and thus mimic the effect of using different grades of 35mm film. This can come in handy in a number of situations, such as when you're shooting in particularly high or low light levels. Remember a few key facts about your camera's ISO ratings, though:

- It's not a real ISO adjustment, in the sense that your camera doesn't have real film. Each camera maker has a somewhat different way of implementing this feature, but they all

190	200	210	210	200
180	160	100	120	190
160	150	100	153	160
170	160	90	110	110
130	125	90	120	110
125	100	88	120	110
	100	90	92	

FIGURE 2-4   A digital camera uses a huge grid of pixels on the CCD in place of chemically reactive grains of silver.

use ISO numbers since that's comparable to 35mm film, which most people are at least somewhat familiar with.

■ Don't leave your camera set at the highest ISO all the time. Some folks think that by setting their cameras to the highest sensitivity, they'll be prepared for anything all the time and won't have to muck with the camera menu when they're on the go, trying to take pictures. In reality, boosting your CCD's sensitivity to light also increases the amount of digital noise you're capturing. (You can see an example of this kind of noise in Figure 2-5.) More ISO means more fringing, artifacts, and digital detritus. Sometimes that's unavoidable, but stick with the lowest ISO value you can get away with most of the time.

Change the ISO Setting

If you find yourself in a situation in which the lighting isn't quite right for your picture, it's time to bump up the camera's ISO value. Remember that not all cameras come with ISO adjustments, so review your user manual to see if this applies to your particular model. Figure 2-6 shows a typical ISO adjustment; you'll probably find it in the on-screen menu system, displayed in the LCD screen on the back of your camera.

FIGURE 2-5   CCDs can generate digital noise when there's too much or too little light in a scene.

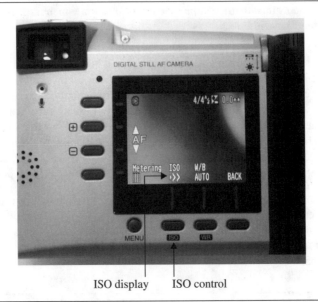

ISO display   ISO control

FIGURE 2-6   A typical ISO adjustment on a digital camera

Here are some situations in which you might need to increase the ISO:

■ You're shooting in a low-light situation, such as early evening or indoors. Natural-light photos have a certain appeal, and by increasing the light sensitivity of your camera you may be able shoot a picture without using the flash at all. Using natural light can eliminate harsh shadows and produce more natural colors.

■ Your subject is too far away for the flash to have any effect. During the day you might be outdoors and want to take a picture of something, but there's not quite enough light— such as in winter or during very overcast conditions. Your camera wants to use a flash, but your subject is just too far away. As you'll see in Chapter 4, the flash on your digital camera has a very limited range. So to properly expose your picture, you need to use "faster film"—that is, increase the camera's ISO setting.

■ You're shooting at night. Most digital cameras have very little ability to take pictures at night or in near total darkness. A few models can extend the shutter to about half of a second, but that's about it. As a result, if you want to capture anything at all with a night shot, you'll need to increase the camera's light sensitivity to maximum.

If night photography interests you, investigate an SLR-style digital camera. These professional models are better equipped to deal with very low light such as you'll encounter at night. They have manually adjustable shutter speeds that facilitate long exposures for light trails, glowing illuminated signage, and other special effects.

Perfecting Shots with Aperture and Shutter

Let's return to the idea of aperture and shutter speed again for a moment. As we observed earlier in this chapter, they're essential ingredients to creating good pictures. Of course, with most digital cameras, you rarely have to worry about setting shutter speed and aperture size at all for typical photography.

How Cameras Choose Aperture and Shutter Speed

Here's what usually happens: when you apply pressure to the camera's shutter release, the camera's microcomputer samples the scene in front of the lens and determines how much light is needed to adequately expose the scene. With most digicams, the camera selects a shutter speed and aperture combination that is sufficient to get the job done. But, you might be wondering, how does it choose? After all, there are a lot of shutter speed/aperture pairs that will work. To take the same properly exposed picture at ISO 100, any of these combinations should be exactly the same:

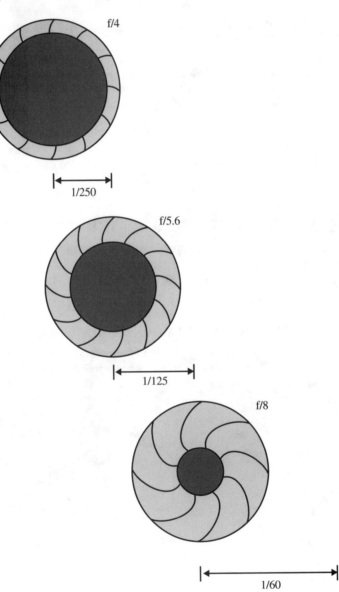

2

In most cases, the camera uses the following logic:

The photographer wants to take a picture using the fastest available shutter speed to minimize camera shake and motion blur from objects moving inside the picture.

Though there are some exceptions, most cameras tend to choose the combination that allows for the highest available shutter speed, limited only by how small they can make the aperture given the current lighting conditions and ISO setting.

This isn't always what you want your camera to do, though, and in fact you might sometimes want to choose a slower shutter speed, overexpose the image, underexpose it, or perhaps base the exposure on a completely different part of the picture. That's why you might want to investigate your camera and look for controls that let you tweak the shutter speed and aperture.

The Truth About Shutters

Though I talk quite a lot about shutter speed in this book, the reality is that few digital cameras have a real shutter in the sense that 35mm cameras have shutters. The 35mm cameras usually have a physical barrier that blocks light from entering the chamber where the film is stored. This mechanism—the shutter blade—moves lightning fast, able to deliver shutter speeds as fast as 1/8000 of a second. That's fast.

Digital cameras, in comparison, rarely have actual shutters. You can tell this yourself with a simple experiment: When you press the shutter release on a 35mm camera, you can hear the quick, metallic click of the shutter blade opening and closing. A digital camera may not make any noise at all. Or it might make an obviously fake "click" sound through the camera's speaker (Kodak cameras tend do this) or some other very quiet sound. It can, in fact, be quite difficult to discern whether a picture has been taken at all until you get used to the way digital cameras work. When I had my first digital camera, I actually had to look at the LCD display on the back of the camera to see if the picture was captured, or if for some mysterious reason the camera was still waiting to grab the shot.

So if there's no shutter blade, how is the picture actually taken? Often, the CCD is simply turned on long enough to expose the picture. Since the CCD is an electronic component that acts as the camera's film, it can be actuated electronically for whatever exposure time is needed. In addition, the camera's aperture may close completely to keep light from reaching the CCD—prolonged exposure to sunlight can damage this sensitive part of the camera. But the aperture needn't spring open and closed as quickly as the shutter blade in a 35mm camera, so the sound it makes isn't as dramatic. You'll hardly notice it at all.

Adjust Exposure Manually

The most basic manual exposure control you can exert over your camera involves setting both the aperture and shutter speed. Some digital cameras allow you to set these controls as if you had a fully automatic 35mm SLR. There are two kinds of cameras you may run into with this capability:

- **Rangefinders** Most point and shoot digicams that include manual settings for aperture and shutter speed require you to use the LCD display to make on-screen menu changes. The Epson PhotoPC 850Z, for instance, uses the + and - buttons on the side of the screen to adjust shutter speed, while you need to use the ISO and White Balance buttons to change the aperture settings (as seen below). It isn't hard to do, but you need to remember first to set the camera to its Manual Exposure mode, then remember which buttons do what for fine-tuning exposure.

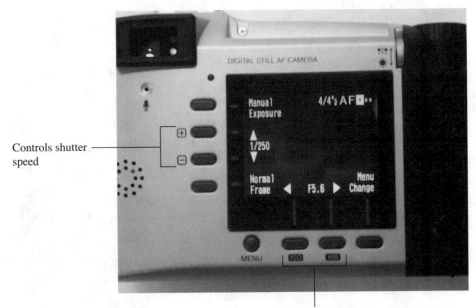

Controls shutter speed

Controls aperture

- **SLRs** A few digital cameras—professional SLRs, for the most part—use traditional SLR controls for making manual adjustments to exposure. Specifically, you can turn the aperture ring on the lens to change the f/stop or use a control on the camera to accomplish the same thing, as you can see below. Shutter speed is likewise affected with a dial on the camera body, and you can look through the viewfinder to keep tabs on the setting.

Controls shutter speed and aperture

To set exposure manually, you must choose a shutter speed and aperture combination that will properly expose your scene at a given ISO. This is a great exercise for new photographers who are serious about learning photography theory.

Use the Sunny 16 Rule

At an ISO of 100, which many digital cameras use for general-purpose photography, you might want to rely on the traditional "Sunny 16 Rule" for a starting point. The Sunny 16 Rule is very old—it dates back to the earliest days of analog photography—and it suggests that when shooting outdoors in bright sunlight, choose an aperture of f/16 and a shutter speed that's equivalent to your film speed. Since few cameras offer the ability to choose 1/100, most photographers that rely on this rule use 1/60 or 1/125 when shooting with ISO 100 film. Here is a chart that identifies other acceptable combinations. (All of these add up to the same overall exposure.)

Shutter Speed	Aperture
1/1000	F/4
1/500	F/5.6
1/250	F/8
1/125	F/11
1/60	F/16
1/30	F/22

Keep in mind that these recommendations are just a starting point. Here are some tips that can help you zero in on your ideal exposure:

■ Your camera will recommend an ideal exposure, which you can accept or reject. If the camera considers your setting out of bounds, you'll see something like this in the viewfinder or LCD display:

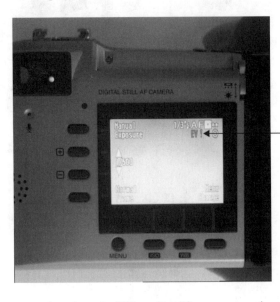

Indicates the camera believes the manual exposure is wrong

■ Adjust your exposure based on the ISO setting. If your camera is set to an equivalent of ISO 200, for instance, the Sunny 16 Rule would call for a shutter speed of f/16 and a shutter speed of 1/250.

■ Make adjustments for brighter or darker scenes. If you're shooting in a dark room, for instance, the Sunny 16 Rule doesn't really apply—but it's a good starting point. Open the aperture or lengthen the shutter speed to account for the reduced light.

Use Shutter or Aperture Priority Adjustments

Instead of relying on an all-automatic or all-manual exposure system, you can compromise and use your camera's shutter or aperture bias, if it has one. The idea with these controls is that you select either an aperture or a shutter speed, and the camera automatically selects the other half of the exposure for you.

Aperture and shutter priority modes are discussed in more detail in Chapter 3. These settings are usually used to find the right balance between freezing (or blurring) motion in a picture and focusing attention on the subject by sharpening (or blurring) the background of an image.

Tricky Lighting Situations

Not all lighting situations are easy to shoot; that's why photography is both an art and a science. Specifically, it's fairly easy for real-life scenes to trick your camera's exposure sensor and consequently under- or overexpose a picture. You can fix that tendency to some degree on the PC afterwards (and we'll talk about how to do that in Chapter 12), but it's much better to expose the picture correctly to begin with. That's because an over- or underexposed image is missing information about colors, texture, and detail that can never be restored afterwards; only the moment of exposure can ensure that all the information will be in your image.

What are some examples of tricky photos? There are many, but just a few problems tend to surface most frequently. Take a look at Figures 2-7 and 2-8 for common examples.

FIGURE 2-7   A very lightly colored subject convinces the camera to reduce the exposure for the overall image, which happens to be darkly colored. That results in an overall underexposure, with a penguin in the background that's hard to see.

FIGURE 2-8   A very dark subject like this penguin tricks the camera into adding too much
light to the scene. The subject is properly exposed, but the brightly colored
animals are washed out.

There are several solutions to these kinds of problems, and you can experiment to see which
works best for you in various situations. Here are some ways you can correct your exposures
when you see a problem in the viewfinder:

- **Use exposure compensation**   Use the EV control on your camera to intentionally under-
  or overexpose your pictures beyond what the camera's exposure sensor recommends.

- **Switch metering modes**   You can use a different kind of exposure meter to account for
  very contrasty images like the examples in Figures 2-7 and 2-8.

- **Use exposure lock**   Lock your exposure on a different part of the image, and then
  recompose the picture and shoot.

To see how to use each of these exposure techniques, keep reading.

2

Use Exposure Compensation

Most digital cameras come equipped with an exposure compensation control, usually referred to as the EV adjustment. The EV control allows you to lock in and use the camera's recommended automatic exposure setting, but then adjust that value up or down based on factors that you're aware of but the camera may not be smart enough to see. Each Exposure Value (EV) corresponds to changing the exposure by one stop, such as going from 1/60 to 1/30 (this is a change of +1 EV since it doubles the exposure) or 1/15 to 1/30 (this is -1 EV since it reduces the exposure by half).

Take Figure 2-9, for example. In the original picture (on the left), the bright cat toy in the middle of the scene has confused the camera, making it think the scene was properly exposed when, in fact, it is horribly underexposed. The penguin in the background is almost invisible. As you can see, the background is dark and murky, since the camera tried using the central object as the average light entering the scene. When the camera is set to overexpose the scene by one stop or EV, however, the scene is much better exposed. The image was saved, as you can see on the right side of Figure 2-9.

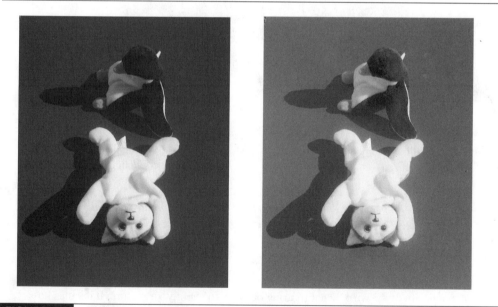

 FIGURE 2-9   The EV control lets you use your own judgment about exposure values instead of relying exclusively on the camera's meter.

To use the EV control on your camera, do this:

1. Size up the scene you want to shoot. Decide if it calls for over- or underexposure.

2. If you need to add light to a scene to properly expose it, add exposure by setting the EV control to +1. If you instead need to underexpose the scene, set the EV control to -1.

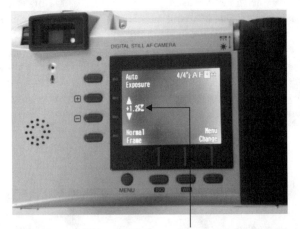

This camera is set to overexpose by 1.2 EV

3. Take the picture and review the picture in the LCD display. If you don't like the result, adjust the EV and shoot it again.

Most cameras allow you to adjust exposure by up to three EVs, either positive (overexposed) or negative (underexposed), and some models also allow you to set the EV in increments of one half or one third of an EV at a time for more fine control over your scene.

You have a digital camera at your disposal, so frame your picture and take the shot. If you don't like the results, take it again with different settings!

Switch Metering Modes

As I mentioned earlier, it's really the camera's exposure sensor—known as an exposure meter—that does the majority of the work when figuring out how to shoot your picture. It decides how much light is needed to adequately expose your picture. So it should come as no surprise to learn that cameras distinguish themselves by the kind of meter they use. Some meters are better than others at metering a scene and applying the right exposure.

Center-Weighted Meters

In the old days, most cameras came with a simple center-weighted light meter. This meter measures the light throughout the image, but applies more weight, or importance, to the central part of the scene in the viewfinder. The assumption—usually a good one—is that you are most interested in the stuff in the front of the picture, so the camera tries to get that part of the scene exposed properly. You can see a center-weighted light meter in Figure 2-10. Most digital cameras rely on this for ordinary picture taking.

Matrix Meters

A new innovation in photography is a kind of sensor that has been around in 35mm SLR photography for a decade or more. Called matrix metering, this system is most prevalent in Nikon models, all the way from the CoolPix 950 to the high-end D1. The matrix meter, seen in Figure 2-11, is famous for its ability to properly expose tricky scenes by balancing the lighting needs of five or more discrete regions within a picture. Instead of concentrating primarily on the middle, matrix meters gauge the light in many parts of the scene at once. If your camera has a matrix meter mode, you should use it most of the time.

Spot Meters

The last major kind of light meter is called a spot. The spot meter is never the only kind of meter in a camera; instead, it's an option that you can switch to if the center-weighted or matrix meter fails you. As you can see in Figure 2-12, the spot meter measures light exclusively in the center one percent of the screen, ignoring the rest of the frame completely. That can come in handy on occasion, but a meter that only measured the light in the central one percent of the frame would typically take very poor pictures—either highly under- or overexposed depending upon the situation.

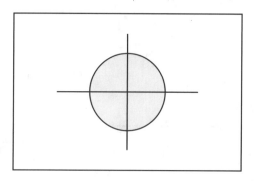

FIGURE 2-10   Most digital cameras use a center-weighted meter like this one.

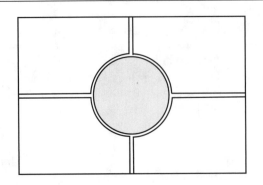

FIGURE 2-11 The matrix meter is more accurate because it uses information from several distinct regions of the picture with a sophisticated algorithm for deciding which are most important.

So when should you use the spot meter? Any time you are trying to photograph a scene in which a small subject must be exposed properly for the picture to work—and its lighting is different enough from the rest of the scene that you're worried it won't come out right otherwise.

Varying the metering mode—especially the spot meter—is best used in conjunction with the third technique, exposure lock.

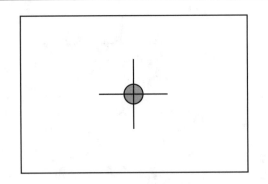

FIGURE 2-12 The spot meter is great for taking an exposure reading from one small part of a picture.

Use Exposure Lock

The exposure lock feature in most digital cameras is borrowed from 35mm camera technology, and it is one of the handiest tricks you can learn and master. Exposure lock is almost always achieved by applying slight pressure to the shutter release—not enough to activate the shutter and take the picture, but enough that you feel the button move and the camera itself respond. Here's what happens when you take a picture:

1. Apply slight pressure to the shutter release button.

2. As you feel it depress slightly, the camera's autofocus lens locks the current subject into sharp focus.

3. At the same time, the camera's exposure meter measures the light and locks in an exposure.

4. Apply more pressure to the shutter release to press it in all the way. The camera then takes the picture and saves it to memory.

> *Cameras that use a fixed focus lens often do not include an exposure lock feature, or they use a separate button to lock the exposure. Inexpensive "budget" cameras may fall into this category. Refer to your camera's manual to see if it has exposure lock, and how to use it.*

The magic of exposure lock is that as long as you continue applying light pressure to the shutter release, the camera will use that "locked-in" exposure information regardless of where you later point the camera. You can lock in exposure information for the sky and then point the camera at your feet and snap the shutter release all the way. You'll take a picture of your feet using the sky's exposure data. You probably wouldn't want to do that since the result will be totally underexposed, but it gives you an idea of the potential.

Exposure lock is a great tool for telling the camera that you'd like to take a picture with the exposure data from one specific part of the scene. Imagine, for instance, a scene like the one in Figure 2-13. Here we have a boy at the beach, standing in the water at sunset. The image can be dramatic, but only if exposed properly. We'd like to capture the overall dark tones inherent in a sunset scene, with exciting splashes of color to light up the subject in a subtle way. Just pointing the camera at the scene might result in the camera averaging the bright and dark bits of the picture, generating an image that might as well have been captured at midday. That would be quite ordinary and not at all what we want.

Instead of taking the average picture, here's what you should do, step-by-step:

1. Frame the scene in your viewfinder so you know what you want to photograph.

FIGURE 2-13 This kind of shot begs for you to tweak the exposure to capture the setting sun in all its glory.

2. Before actually taking the picture, point the camera up into the sky. Include the brightest part of the sky that doesn't also include the sun—that might be overkill. Sounds like guesswork? It is, a little. This is art, not science. You can take the picture, see if you like the result, and reshoot as necessary.

3. Press the shutter release partway to lock in the exposure information. You should sense that the camera has also locked the focus at the same time.

4. Recompose your picture. When you're happy with the scene in the viewfinder, press the shutter release all the way to take the picture.

Obviously, you could also choose the spot meter (if your camera has one) and lock the exposure with that instead of the default center-weighted or matrix meter in step 2. It's up to you. Take a look at Figure 2-14. This is a real challenge for most cameras, since the subject is a wolf sunning itself in an isolated patch of light. A center-weighted camera would probably average the light in the darker surrounding areas and determine that it needed to select a fairly wide-open aperture to add light to the scene. But that would wash out the poor little wolf. Instead, the best solution is to select the spot meter, frame the wolf carefully, and press the shutter release partially to lock in exposure on the bright subject. Then reframe the picture and shoot.

FIGURE 2-14   This wolf is lit very differently than the rest of the scene, so the only way to capture it properly is with a spot meter.

As you become more confident with your ability to visualize compositions and exposures, you can try different things to get the desired effect.

When to Take Control

As I mentioned at the outset, you may often be perfectly satisfied with the results you can get from the automatic exposure controls in your camera. But there will be times when you can do better on your own. Keep your eyes peeled for situations like those described next.

Very Bright Sunlight

Very bright sun can overwhelm your camera, especially if the scene is filled with brightly colored clothing, reflective surfaces, or other tricky subjects. You can reduce the exposure for better effects. Underexpose the scene by EV -1 for starters, and see if that helps.

Backlit Subjects

If you are taking a picture of someone or something and the sun is behind the subject, you're usually in trouble—the bright background will cause the camera to underexpose the scene. That means the subject itself will look like it's in shadow. You'll get this if you follow the old (and very wrong) rule to put the sun behind the person you're photographing. The best way to shoot an outdoor portrait is to put the sun over your shoulder. Nonetheless, if you find the sun behind your subject, overexpose the scene, such as with an EV +1.

Low Light

In low light, such as at night, indoors, or under thick cloud cover, you can often get better results by overexposing the scene slightly, such as with an EV +1. Vary the EV level depending on how dark the scene actually is.

How to ...   Consider Exposure When Taking a Picture

Most of the time, you can just compose your shot and press the shutter release. But don't forget to adjust the exposure when necessary. Use this decision process:

1. Do I need to adjust the depth of field—that is, make the background more or less sharp compared to the foreground? If yes, then adjust the aperture/shutter or use the aperture priority mode, discussed in detail in Chapter 3.

2. Do I need to change the shutter speed to depict motion in the picture? If yes, then again try to adjust the aperture/shutter, or instead use the shutter priority mode, discussed in detail in Chapter 3.

3. Is the scene significantly brighter or darker than the camera is designed for? If it is, under- or overexpose the scene.

4. Is the subject backlit, such as with the sun behind? Overexpose the scene.

5. Is the subject especially bright, such as on fresh, bright snow? Try underexposing.

6. Do I want to expose the scene based on the lighting in a specific part of the scene? If so, use a spot meter or just lock in the exposure for that part of the picture and recompose the scene.

Chapter 3

Composition Essentials

How to...

- ■ Use the rules of composition to take compelling photos
- ■ Take less cluttered snapshots by emphasizing a focal point
- ■ Take interesting photos with the rule of thirds
- ■ Avoid cropping out important pixels by filling the frame
- ■ Use lines and symmetry for artistic images
- ■ Break the rules for more engaging photos
- ■ Understand the relationships among shutter, aperture, and depth of field
- ■ Employ depth of field for pictures that emphasize the subject
- ■ Zoom a lens to achieve the right field of view
- ■ Apply rules of composition to common photographic situations

What does it take to take a good picture? Certainly, it requires more than a mastery of your camera's various controls. If that were all you needed, anyone who knew how to read a camera manual could be Ansel Adams. No, taking good pictures demands a little creativity and a touch of artistry. Perhaps more importantly, though, it takes a solid understanding of the rules of photographic composition and some knowledge—which you can acquire as you get better at photography—of when it's OK to break those rules.

Composition is all about how you arrange the subjects in a picture and how you translate what is in your mind's eye—or even right in front of you—into a photograph. After all, the camera sees things very differently than you do, and in order to take great photographs you have to understand that and learn how to see the world the way your camera sees it.

Taking a picture with a digital camera is really no different from taking a picture with a 35mm camera. That's why in this chapter we will be talking about the rules of composition: what they are, how to use them, and how to break them. If you are already an accomplished photographer and you're reading this book to make the transition to digital photography, you may not need most of what I offer in this chapter. But if you're not an expert, I welcome you to study this chapter. It is only through an understanding of composition that your images will go from snapshots—the ones that bring comments like "What a nice picture of a cat!"—to potential works of art.

Why Composition Is Important

Have you ever been on vacation, pulled out your camera upon seeing a picturesque view, and then been somewhat underwhelmed with the final results? If so, you just learned the first rule of photography: reality, as seen by your camera, is quite different from what you see with your own eyes. If you frame all of your pictures without taking that into account, you will always be disappointed.

3

There are a few reasons why what your cameras sees is different from what you see. First of all, your eyes aren't little optical machines that function in a vacuum. Instead, all that you see is supplemented, enhanced, and interpreted by your brain. In a sense, when you see a majestic landscape while hiking through the backwoods of Kauai, some of the splendor of the scene is actually being added by your mind. Lift the camera to that same view, and you get a totally objective representation of the scene, without any intelligent enhancements. That's because the camera actually is a little optical machine. And it does not have a brain.

And then there's the fact that a camera has a much more limited range of focus, exposure, and composition than you do. When you look at a scene like the Hawaiian landscape I just mentioned, you might think you're seeing a fairly static scene with your eyes. But that's not really the case. In fact, as your eyes dart around, you are constantly recomposing the scene, since you can dynamically change the visual "frame" in which you are viewing the scene. To make matters worse, the aperture of your eyes, called the pupil, changes size constantly in response to changing lighting conditions and where you're looking. The result? You don't realize it, but your eyes, working in conjunction with your brain, are creating a visual feast that is difficult, if not impossible, to reproduce on paper.

In comparison, it's amazing that we can get good pictures at all with a camera. Film—and by film I mean both 35mm and digital—has a much narrower exposure range than your eyes because the aperture freezes a single instant in time with a fixed set of lighting conditions. And unlike the magical pictures in the *Harry Potter* series of books, real photographs cannot change their composition or framing on the fly. What you see in the viewfinder is, unfortunately, what you are stuck with forever.

What We See

Look around. What do you see? If you look carefully, you'll notice that your field of vision is a rectangle with rounded corners—almost a wide ellipse. In other words, we see the world panoramically. While there are some cameras and some techniques for creating panoramic photographs, most of the time this is not the kind of shot we take.

Nope—our job as photographers is to take the panorama that we see with our own eyes and translate it into an attractive photograph using the laws of photographic composition. As you can see in Figure 3-1, there's often more than one way to frame a picture; it's really your job to decide which works best for the kind of photograph you are trying to achieve. In this situation I had an extremely rare opportunity to photograph endangered monk seals, so I shot many different compositions.

Rules of Composition

For a few pages now I have been alluding to the rules of composition. I hope that you're curious what they might be. In truth, the rules of composition are no more rigid than rules of etiquette or the rules of Web page design. Certainly, those rules are important, but they're simply guidelines

FIGURE 3-1   Though we see the world as a panorama, we have to condense that view into something that looks good in a typical photographic frame.

to help us get the job done. If you violate any of these rules, nothing awful happens (unless you're still living at home when you break the rules of etiquette). And that's why we'll be able to break these rules later on. To begin with however, we need to learn the rules and apply them.

Isolate the Focal Point

I know what you're wondering: what is the focal point? The *focal point* is the main subject of your picture, such as a building or perhaps a person. In other words, the focal point is the main point of interest that the viewer's eye is drawn to when looking at your picture.

You should always strive to consider what the focal point of your picture actually is and then plan your photos accordingly. In my experience, the single biggest problem with photographs taken by new photographers is that they fail to consider what their subject actually is. When you don't know what you're taking a picture of, it's hard to emphasize that element in the final composition. That leads to muddy, confused arrangements in which there is nothing specific for the viewer to look at. Take a look at Figure 3-2, for instance. In this image, there is no real focal point, and thus there is nothing for the viewer to concentrate on. The photographer should have decided what the subject was and then rearranged the image to emphasize that.

FIGURE 3-2   Without a focal point, your eye wanders aimlessly, looking for something of interest.

When your subject is simply too expansive to be considered a focal point in and of itself, try to contrive a focal point that adds some relief for your viewer. You might try an approach like this when you are photographing a mountainous landscape, for instance. In fact, landscapes really benefit from this approach. A tractor, a mountain cabin, or a gaggle of hikers near the horizon allow the viewer's eyes to rest on something familiar, even though the real subject fills up most of the frame. Technically, this is called a secondary focal point. You can see how I used this technique in Figure 3-3 to give the viewer a visual resting spot when looking at the backdrop of mountains. Remember: photography is subjective, and I did not intend for the cabin to be the photo's subject. Instead, the mountains were the subject, but by themselves they would make a terrible photograph.

As a general rule, you only want a single focal point in your photograph. More than one main subject is distracting, and viewers won't really know where to look. If I show you a photograph in which several objects have equal visual weight, you probably won't like it, even though you may not be sure why. It is certainly possible to include multiple focal points in an image, but you should do it with care, and only after you have mastered the basics.

FIGURE 3-3 Secondary focal points add interest to landscapes.

Use the Rule of Thirds

Many snapshot photographers don't really think much about the organization of what they see through the viewfinder, so the *rule of thirds* helps restore some balance to their photographs. And though this is the second rule I'm going to talk about, in many ways I think the rule of thirds is the single most important rule of photography that you can learn and apply.

Here's what you should do: in your mind, draw two horizontal and two vertical lines through your viewfinder so that you have divided it into thirds. In other words, your image should be broken into nine zones with four interior corners where the lines intersect. (See Figure 3-4 for an example of this technique.) It is these corners that constitute the "sweet spots" in your picture. If you place something—typically the focal point—in any of these intersections, you'll typically end up with an interesting composition.

This really, really is the golden rule of photography. Thumb through a magazine. Open a photography book. Watch television. No matter where you look, you will find that professional

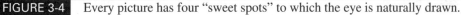

FIGURE 3-4   Every picture has four "sweet spots" to which the eye is naturally drawn.

photographers follow the rule of thirds about 75% of the time. And while the rule of thirds is very easy to do, you may find that it is somewhat counterintuitive. Many people try to put the focal point of their picture dead smack in the middle of the frame. And trust me—there are few things in life more boring than looking at a picture in which the subject is always right in the middle. Compare the two images in Figure 3-5. I think you'll agree that the one on the right, in which the subject is not in the center, is the better photograph.

Fill the Frame

Don't forget to get the most mileage you can out of the frame in which you're working. What the heck does that mean? Essentially, all I am saying is that you should minimize the amount of dead space in a photograph. Once you decide what the focal point of your image is (remember the first rule!), there's no reason to relegate it to a small portion of the picture. Get close. Zoom in. Walk over to it. Whatever you need to do, do it in order to keep your focal point from being a small

FIGURE 3-5   As a general rule, avoid putting your focal point in the center of the photograph.

part of the overall image. Take a look at Figure 3-6, for instance. When I visited London and took pictures of the changing of the guard, I found that the common wide-angle shots of the event resulted in rather unimpressive photographs. I decided that the real star of the show was the guard's face, so I zoomed in for a very tight shot. Certainly, all of your photographs don't need to be this close. Getting a tight shot of your subject is not always a natural or intuitive thing to do; so you should go out of your way to try this technique whenever you think of it.

The "fill the frame" rule certainly applies in the world of 35mm photography, but it is absolutely essential in digital photography. That's because in 35mm photography, it's not difficult to crop and enlarge an image and still retain a reasonable amount of image quality, as long as you do not overly enlarge the final image. In digital photography, however, we're dealing with pixels, not grains of silver halide. And it seems like there are rarely enough pixels to go around.

If you are using a 3.34-megapixel digital camera, for instance, the best you can hope to do is print your photograph at 11x17 inches before the pixels start to become obvious. (See Chapter 15 for details on printing.) That's probably enough resolution for most practical applications, but consider what happens if you need to crop your image because the subject was just too small the way the photograph was originally taken. If you crop out half of the pixels in the photo, you'll be lucky to get a good-looking 8x10-inch photograph with the resulting crop. If your digital camera captures smaller images—like 2 megapixel or even 1 megapixel—then you can imagine how critical it is to compose the picture properly the first time. There really aren't any pixels to spare.

FIGURE 3-6 This shot is almost uncomfortably close, and that's why it works so well.

Move the Horizon

This rule is closely related to the rule of thirds. If you follow the rule of thirds to the letter, you probably won't make this mistake anyway, but it is important enough to mention explicitly.

No doubt you have seen photographs in which the photographer chose to place the horizon right in the middle of the photograph. Actually, the photographer probably did not make a conscious decision to do this—if he or she had, then the horizon probably would have ended up somewhere else.

Running the horizon right through the middle of a photograph is akin to putting the subject smack dab in the middle. It's boring because it violates the rule of thirds. Instead, try putting the horizon along a rule-of-thirds line. As you can well imagine, that actually gives you two choices for where to put the horizon in any given picture. You can put the horizon in the top third or the bottom third of your composition. How do you decide which? It's easy: if you want to emphasize the distant landscape and sky, put the horizon on the bottom third line. If you are taking a seascape where you want to emphasize the foreground, such as in Figure 3-7, the horizon belongs in the upper third of the picture. Of course, these are guidelines. Digital film is cheap—it's basically free. Experiment.

FIGURE 3-7   The horizon usually works best above or below the center of the picture.

Use Lines, Symmetry, and Patterns

Photographs are two-dimensional representations of three-dimensional scenes. The question, then, is how to best lead viewers through a picture so they get a sense of the real depth that the image is trying to depict.

Keep the Horizon Straight

This may seem obvious, but how many times have you seen a photo in which the horizon was a little cockeyed? Vertically oriented pictures can get by with a slightly off-kilter horizon, but if you take a horizontally oriented image and the horizon is not straight, it affects the feel of the photograph. Try to be as careful as possible while photographing an expansive horizon. But if you goof, remember that it's a digital photo. You can always correct for an angled horizon on the computer (see Chapter 12).

The answer to that question is simpler than you might think. When you compose an image in the viewfinder, look for natural or artificial lines that might lead the viewer's eyes through the photo. These lines can create a sense of depth and perspective that is often lost in the two-dimensional photograph. Lines can be formed in almost any situation: you might see a row of trees, the shape of a skyscraper from the ground, or the route of the backyard fence. Personally, I enjoy using the natural flow of a stream or road to lead the eye from one end of the picture to the other. Figure 3-8 is one example of this technique.

While lines like these can fit in with any kind of lens or composition, you may find that this works best when seen through wide-angle lenses. That's because telephoto lenses compress your scene and make it harder to see long, sweeping lines.

Another trick of the trade is to look for repetition and patterns, and incorporate those into your image. Patterns, like those that you see in nature or man-made objects, can create interesting effects. Like lines, they can add a sense of depth to your images. Try combining these patterns with a sense of symmetry. When you employ symmetry, you are balancing both sides of the photograph. That can also help lead the eye through your image.

FIGURE 3-8   A long, straight road is a powerful tool for creating implied motion in a photograph.

Every Picture Tells a Story

Throughout this chapter, and in fact throughout the book, you'll notice references to "leading the viewer through a picture." What do I mean by that? Well, when you've done your job as a photographer, you've created an image with depth, motion, and some sort of story. When you look at a good photograph or painting, your eyes naturally start in one place and move to another. That's in sharp contrast to a typical snapshot that has no particular story to tell; the focal point is haphazardly placed, and it's cluttered enough that there's no obvious path for the eye to take. Good artists can use techniques like lines, symmetry, patterns, and multiple focal points to lead the viewer in a specific way through an image. If you can create an image like that, consider it a success.

Use Foreground to Balance the Background

If you're trying to photograph a distant subject—a landscape or cityscape, for example—a common trick is to place something of interest in the foreground to provide a sense of balance. When done well, the viewer's eyes are drawn immediately to the foreground object, and then they'll wander to the background. This is a very effective technique for adding a sense of depth and perspective to a photograph, as well as giving the foreground a sense of scale. Figure 3-9, for instance, demonstrates this technique.

Know When to Break the Rules

Now that I've spent the last few pages telling you what the rules of composition actually are, we can talk a little about how to ignore them.

Don't get me wrong—I love the rules of composition and I think you should follow them. After you become comfortable with concepts like the rule of thirds and filling the frame with the focal point, however, you'll find that you can take even better pictures by bending or breaking

FIGURE 3-9   The fence post in the foreground of this picture is the anchor that gives the image a sense of perspective.

those same rules. This is an area of photography that is best experimented with and learned on your own, but here are a few pointers to help you get started:

- **Change your perspective**. Technically, we're not breaking any rules of composition here, but this is something that few people think about, yet it can have a profound impact on the quality of your photos. Simply put, experiment with different ways to see the same scene. Try taking your picture by holding the camera horizontally, and then see how you might frame the picture by turning the camera vertically. Take a look at the picture in Figure 3-10. I originally took this picture as you see it on the left. Afterwards, I found that I liked the picture better when I cropped it for a horizontal orientation. Also, don't forget that you can get low to the ground or stand up on a chair or table to get a higher perspective on the same scene. You have a lot of options: try them.

- **Ignore symmetry**. Sure, symmetry is great. But just as often as symmetry works well in a photograph, I have found you can get an even better image if you intentionally skew the photo to strip out the symmetry. When the viewer expects symmetry and doesn't get it, you have introduced tension and drama into an image. And that's not bad, especially if all you've done is photograph some road, train track, or river.

- **Surprise the viewer**. If you've seen one landscape, you've seen them all. That's not really true, but it can sometimes seem that way. Go for the unusual by framing your picture in a totally unexpected way. One of my favorite tricks is shooting landscapes through the side view mirror of a car—you can see it in Figure 3-11.

FIGURE 3-10   Experiment with taking your pictures from many different angles, orientations, and perspectives.

FIGURE 3-11   Successful pictures are often a matter of surprising the viewer.

- **Use several focal points**. While most pictures rely on just one or two focal points, sometimes you need even more, especially when you're shooting a picture like a family portrait. If you're taking a picture with several people in it, you can often overcome a cluttered look by arranging the subjects into a geometric pattern. If the subjects' heads form a triangle shape, for instance, you have introduced order into the photo despite the fact that there are a lot of people in it.

Using Depth of Field

The last important frontier that you need to understand for proper composition is called *depth of field*. Depth of field refers to the region of proper focus that is available to you in any photographic image. When you focus your camera, you don't get a paper-thin region of proper focus in an image; instead, there's some distance in front and behind your subject that will also be in focus. This entire region of sharp focus is called the depth of field, or sometimes the depth of focus.

What determines depth of field? There are actually three factors that contribute to the depth of field that is available to you for any picture you plan to take. Let's look at these factors one at a time, and then combine them.

- ■ **Aperture** The aperture of your lens is the first major factor that influences depth of field. We talked about aperture back in Chapter 2—it's the size of the lens opening that determines how much light reaches your camera's CCD. Aperture is measured in f/stops, where lower f/numbers represent bigger openings and higher f/numbers are smaller openings. In addition, the smaller the aperture's actual opening (or, in other words, the higher the f/number), the greater the depth of field will be. As you can see here, the aperture of your lens directly influences how deep the depth of field is in any given picture:

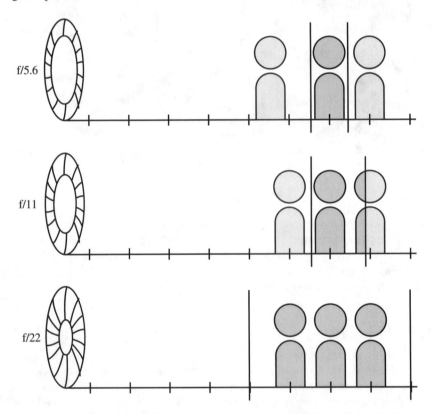

- ■ **Focal length** As we will discuss in the upcoming section "Getting the Most Out of Your Zoom Lens," focal length is just a measure of your lens's ability to magnify a scene. And while most people focus on a lens's magnification, depth of field plays an important role here as well. In simple terms, the more you magnify your subject, the less depth of field you have available. When shooting with a normal or wide-angle lens, you have a lot of depth of field. If you zoom out to a telephoto magnification, your depth of field drops dramatically. Likewise, macro photography (also known as close-up photography) has very little depth of field as well, since you are greatly magnifying a small object. See Chapter 5 for details on macro photography. This illustration graphically demonstrates the effect of focal length on depth of field:

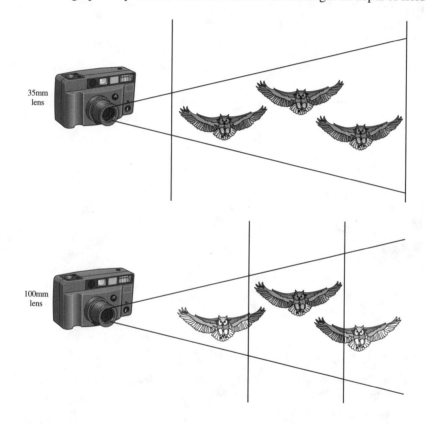

■ **Subject distance**   Last but not least, your distance from the subject determines how much depth of field you can get in your scene. If you photograph a subject that is far away, the depth of field will be much greater than it is for a subject that is close to the camera. In practical terms, that means the region of sharp focus for a macro shot—where the subject is only a few inches from the camera—is extremely narrow, and you need to focus very, very precisely. If you're photographing something very far away—like a distant horizon—a vast region in front of and behind the image will be in sharp focus. Here is what this looks like graphically:

Applying Depth of Field to Your Pictures

As you can imagine, these three factors—aperture, depth of field, and subject distance—work together in any shooting situation.

Specifically, suppose you try to take a picture with an aperture of f/5.6. At a given distance from your subject, and at a given focal length, that f/stop will yield a certain depth of field. But what happens if you change the other two factors? If you get closer to the subject, such as if you walk toward it, or if you increase the focal length by zooming in, the depth of field decreases.

3

So what is the point of all this? Why do you care about depth of field at all? The answer is that depth of field is an extremely important element in the overall composition of your photographs. Using depth of field, you can isolate your subject by making sure it is the only sharply focused person or object in the frame. Alternately, you can increase depth of field to make the entire image—from foreground to background—as sharp as possible. Figure 3-12 shows the effect of depth of field on a simple portrait; on the left, the child in the background is in sharp focus thanks to a deep depth of field. On the right, nothing has changed except the f/stop. By decreasing the f/number (and thus increasing the size of the lens opening), the background child is now blurry and indistinct. Side by side, I think these two pictures would make a great album cover for some psychedelic band. But I digress.

Getting the Most Out of Your Zoom Lens

As we discussed in Chapters 1 and 2, your digital camera probably comes with a zoom lens that allows you to vary the focal length from a wide-angle or normal perspective all the way through some moderate telephoto length.

FIGURE 3-12   Varying the depth of field with the camera aperture

Maximizing Depth of Field

There are three ways to maximize the depth of field in your image:

- Use a lens with a short focal length, such as the normal or wide-angle setting on your camera's zoom.

- Focus on a distant subject. If you're trying to get both a nearby tree and a more distant house in focus simultaneously, for instance, focusing on the house, rather than the tree, is more likely to deliver both subjects in focus.

- Use the smallest aperture you can, such as f/11or f/16.

Not surprisingly, you can minimize the depth of field in a picture by doing exactly the opposite of these things.

As you probably recall, focal length is just a measure of the magnification that the lens provides. A larger focal length produces greater magnification; hence long focal length lenses are great for capturing fast action or enlarging objects that are moderately far away. You can see the effect of a zoom lens on magnification in Figure 3-13.

A key fact to remember, however, is that the focal length of the given lens also affects the camera's angle of view. Because a telephoto lens magnifies distant objects, it has a very narrow angle of view. As you reduce the magnification and zoom out toward smaller focal lengths, the angle of view likewise increases. You can see this graphically in Figure 3-14.

At the extreme end of the scale—specifically, wide-angle lenses—the image is actually shrunk with respect to what the human eye can see. The angle of view becomes extreme, sometimes even greater than 180 degrees. This kind of wide-angle lens is known as a *fish-eye lens* due to the peculiar effect of the angle of view.

The focal length of your lens has one other important characteristic. Depending upon whether you have your lens set to wide angle, normal, or telephoto, you'll get a very different depth of field. As you saw previously in this chapter, a telephoto setting yields minimal depth of field, while a wide-angle setting generates a lot of focusing depth.

The telephoto end of your zoom lens is great for capturing distant subjects, but the additional magnification can create blurry pictures. Especially if you are photographing in low light, where your camera might choose a slow shutter speed, I highly recommend that you take telephoto images with a tripod.

FIGURE 3-13 These three views, all taken from the same position, show the effect of a zoom lens on the magnification of the subject.

Using Your Camera's Exposure Modes

Almost every digital camera on the market makes it easy to take quick-and-dirty snapshots using an automatic exposure mode. Automatic exposure is great much of the time, but I hope that you

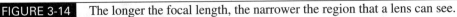

FIGURE 3-14 The longer the focal length, the narrower the region that a lens can see.

will sometimes want to get a little more creative. And when that happens, you may need to adjust the exposure of your photographs as we talked about both in this chapter and in Chapter 2.

Not all cameras provide manual exposure settings; if yours does not, then you might want to think about upgrading at some point in the future to a more full-featured camera. In my experience, most cameras that cost about $500 have at least some manual exposure adjustments. When you reach $1000, these cameras are about as full featured as they come, with all of the amenities you'd expect from a 35mm SLR camera. The Nikon CoolPix 990, for instance, is an excellent example

3

Taking a Zoomed Picture

Not all special effects need to be done inside a computer. The *zoomed* picture is a good example of a special effect that you can do "in the lens" of your camera without doing any processing on the computer whatsoever. Unfortunately, there are very few digital cameras that will let you achieve this effect. To take it, you need a digital camera that allows you to change the zoom setting during the exposure; generally, only professional SLR-style digital cameras are capable of this feat.

If you do have a camera like the Olympus Camedia E-10, however, here's how to do it. Start by choosing a scene that you want to zoom through. You'll get the best results with a brightly colored subject and a simple background that won't be too busy. Mount your camera on a tripod to minimize camera shake. If you have very steady hands, you might want to try holding the camera yourself.

Set your shutter speed for about 1/4 second. You'll need that much time to slide the zoom lens during exposure. Then, just as you press the shutter release, start zooming with a firm, steady, and consistent motion. Just as in golf, be sure that you follow through the zoom motion even after the shutter releases. That way, you won't stop moving the zoom in the middle of the exposure. You may need to practice this a few times to get the shot right; remember, electronic film is free.

of a camera that has automatic exposure modes as well as manual, priority, and program settings. Here's what each of these settings does, and when you would want to use them:

- **Automatic**   In this mode, both shutter speed and aperture settings are selected by the camera to match the current lighting. Usually, automatic modes try to select the fastest shutter speed possible in order to minimize camera shake when you take a picture. There's generally nothing you can do to change the settings that the camera chooses when set to fully automatic, except for adjusting the exposure compensation (EV) dial to over- or underexpose the scene.

- **Program**   The program mode (usually indicated by the letter *P* on your camera's dial or LCD display) is similar to an automatic mode. Although the camera selects both the aperture and shutter, you can generally modify the camera's selection by turning a dial or pressing a button. The effect: you can increase or decrease the shutter speed, and the camera will adjust the aperture to match. This is a good compromise between fully automatic operation and manual selection. Use this mode if you don't want to worry about devising your own exposure values, but still want some say over the shutter speed or aperture.

- **Shutter priority**   This setting is usually indicated by the letter *S* on your camera's mode dial or LCD display. Using this mode, you can dial in whatever shutter speed you like, and the camera accommodates by setting the appropriate aperture to match. This mode is ideal for locking in a speed fast enough to freeze action scenes, or slow enough to intentionally blur motion.

- **Aperture priority**   This setting is usually indicated by the letter *A* on your mode dial or LCD display. Using this mode, you can dial in the aperture setting you like, and the camera accommodates by setting the appropriate shutter speed. Use this mode if you are trying to achieve a particular depth of field and you don't care about the shutter speed.

- **Manual**   The manual mode (typically indicated with an *M*) is like an old-style noncomputerized camera. In manual mode, you select the aperture and shutter speed on your own, sometimes with the help of the camera's recommendation. This mode is best used for long exposures or other special situations when the camera's meter is not reliable.

Choosing Exposure Modes and Lenses in Special Situations

Now that you know what your camera's various exposure modes are for, you can think about using them when you encounter unique photographic situations. Every situation is a little bit different, but here are a few general guidelines that can get you started.

Portrait Photography

Taking pictures of people can be fun but intimidating. It's hard to get a natural pose from people when they know they are being photographed. The best way to capture good portraits is to work

What Is a Shift Program?

Some cameras—like the Nikon CoolPix 990—have a "shift program" mode. Your camera has this if you set it to program and then see an asterisk appear next to the *P* in the LCD display when you turn the camera's settings dial.

Shift program mode lets you shift the shutter speed up or down while in program mode. The camera automatically adjusts the aperture setting, so you can tweak the exposure without sacrificing the camera's ability to ensure a properly exposed picture.

with your subjects so they are a little more at ease. If you're trying to capture spontaneous, candid moments, then back off and try to blend in with the background. If you're trying to capture a fairly formal-looking portrait, you have a little more work cut out for you. It's up to you as the photographer to put your subjects at ease. Talk to your subjects and get them to respond. If you can get them to loosen up, they'll exhibit more natural responses and look better on film. Take pictures periodically as you pose your subjects to get them used to the shutter going off, even if it isn't a picture you intend to keep.

The best way to capture portraits is typically with the medium telephoto lens: in the 35mm world, that would be about 100mm. For a typical digital camera, that's near the maximum magnification for your zoom lens. I also suggest that you work in aperture priority mode if that is possible for your camera. Aperture priority will allow you to change the depth of field quickly and easily as you frame your images. Specifically, good portraits have very shallow depth of field. You want to draw attention to the subject of your picture, and leave the background an indistinct blur. Figure 3-15, for instance, demonstrates shallow depth of field in a fairly candid portrait.

You can't see the effect of aperture on depth of field in the optical viewfinder, but the LCD display can show you the depth of field. To see, press the shutter release halfway down. That locks in the focus and triggers the aperture to close to the proper position for the impending picture. It's now—with the shutter halfway depressed—that you can see the depth of field in your picture.

Action Photography

Action photography is often considered the most exciting kind of photography, but it's also the most demanding for both your technique and your equipment. As in all kinds of photography, you can no doubt take some great pictures with anything from a wide-angle lens all the way up to the photographic equivalent of the Hubble telescope. And wide-angle lenses do, in fact, have a role in action photography. But the essence of many action shots is a highly magnified immediacy—something you can only get with the telephoto lens.

The shutter priority setting on your digital camera was born for action photography. To freeze action, you'll need to use a fairly fast shutter speed. Luckily, this higher shutter speed

FIGURE 3-15 Portraits tend to work best with moderate telephoto magnification and low f/numbers.

works to your advantage by opening up the aperture and diminishing the depth of field; this focuses the viewer's attention specifically on your subject. On the downside, of course, focusing is more critical since the depth of field is more shallow.

In general, I recommend that you use the fastest shutter speed available to capture action. On the other hand, you can use a technique called *panning* to capture the subject in good, sharp focus and keep the background as a motion blur. See Figure 3-16 for an example of panning that I used to freeze a child's wild ride at a Renaissance Festival. This is convenient both when you want to make a somewhat artistic statement about the subject's motion and when you know the camera can't muster up a fast enough shutter speed to freeze the motion the ordinary way.

Panning involves some effort on your part. To create a good pan, you need to twist your body in synch with the motion of the subject as you press the shutter release. Here's how:

1. Position yourself where you can twist your body to follow the motion of the moving subject without having the camera's line of sight blocked by something else.

2. Set the camera's shutter speed for about 1/60. Feel free to experiment with this, but if you set the shutter speed too slow, you can't capture the subject effectively—it blurs. And if the shutter is too fast, you won't get the pretty blur in the background.

3. Twist your body with the motion of the subject and track it through the camera's
viewfinder or on the LCD display. Press the shutter release and continue tracking the
subject until after you hear the shutter close again. Just like in baseball or golf, ensure
that you follow through the motion even after the shutter releases. That way, you don't
stop panning in the middle of the exposure. You may need to practice this a few times to
get the shot right, but electronic film is free.

3

*The farther away the background is, the less motion blur effect you'll get. For best
results, get close to the object and its background. If the background is too far away,
the blur will be minimal and it'll just look out of focus.*

Nature and Landscapes

Unlike action photography and portraiture that rely on telephoto lenses to compress the action
into an intimate experience, landscapes typically work best with wide-angle lenses that allow
you to include huge, expansive swaths of land, air, and sea in a single frame. Zoom out for best

FIGURE 3-16   Panning freezes the subject while blurring the background.

results most of the time, and adjust the camera's exposure in aperture priority mode (if possible) to get deep or shallow depth of field, depending upon what works best for the picture in question.

There are a few special kinds of nature shots that warrant special mention.

Photographing a Waterfall or Running Stream   There are two ways to capture running water in a photograph: with a fast, freeze-framing shot or with a longer exposure that blurs the water into a continuous stream effect. Both effects can look good, but I have a fondness for the latter. The effect looks great, and it's very easy to do: you simply need to take a long exposure of the water. Here's how:

■ You need to ensure that your camera will give you a long exposure, on the order of a half second. You can get this by shooting in automatic mode in the early morning or late afternoon, or using a manual mode if your camera allows.

■ Set your camera on a tripod (the long exposure requires a steady support).

■ Compose the image and take the shot.

 How to ...   Capture the Moment

Most digital cameras have a two-step shutter release; only very inexpensive fixed-focus cameras do not. Knowing how to use this feature is key to taking great pictures.

When you put a little pressure on the shutter release button, the camera springs into action: it locks in both the focus and the exposure setting. If you continue to hold down the shutter button, the focus and exposure won't change; you can then recompose the picture and, when it meets your approval, press the shutter release all the way to actually take the picture.

There are a lot of reasons why you might want to use the focus/exposure lock step without pressing the button all the way down:

■ Focus lock takes a fraction of a second. If you're taking an action shot or some other photo in which you want to precisely control the instant of exposure, lock the exposure and focus first; then wait with your finger on the shutter until you are absolutely ready to take the picture. Then, all it takes is a hair more pressure to capture the scene more or less instantly.

■ If you want to use the camera's spot meter, it's usually found in the dead center of the frame. To lock in an exposure value based on some other part of the image, point your camera accordingly and press the shutter release halfway down. Then recompose the picture and snap the shutter. This is a handy technique, even with other exposure modes. To get a rich, blue sky, for instance, it might help to tip the camera up and lock the exposure in based on what's above the horizon. Then tip the camera back down and take the picture.

■ If you want something that's off to the side of your picture to be in sharp focus—and this commonly is the case if you follow the rule of thirds—then point the camera at your off-center subject and lock the focus. Then recompose the shot to put the subject off to the side, and snap the picture.

3

Shooting Wildlife   Wildlife photography is like action photography; it typically takes a telephoto lens, fast shutter speed, and a tripod. Try to fill the frame as much as possible. Figure 3-17, for instance, shows a pair of wolves frolicking that would have been impossible to shoot without a fast shutter and a lens with a long reach.

FIGURE 3-17   Wildlife photography is similar to action photography.

Chapter 4 Flash and Lighting

How to...

- Use your flash for primary lighting
- Fill in shadows with your flash
- Keep from underexposing close-ups
- Use the various flash settings on your camera
- Optimize lighting outdoors
- Optimize lighting indoors
- Avoid red eye in low-light photos
- Balance your scenes based on the kind of lighting around you
- Use a reflector to fill in shadows
- Take interesting photos at night

Photography is all about light. In previous chapters, I have talked about how to work with the existing light in a scene to control aspects of your photograph, like depth of field. Sometimes, using the light that you already have isn't quite enough, however. That's why photographers spend so much time with flash units, strobes, reflector units, and other gadgets that help to enhance or supplement natural light.

In this chapter, we'll talk a fair bit about using the electronic flash. Almost every digital camera made today—with the exception of very inexpensive VGA-resolution cameras—comes with a built-in flash unit. The flash is a way to bring extra light with you and brighten many kinds of pictures. On the other hand, I have found that most people don't really know how to take advantage of the flash that is built into their camera, so in this chapter I discuss techniques like fill flash, red eye reduction, and bounce flash.

Lighting isn't just about using a flash, either. You can use a reflector to spread light around for a more pleasing effect, and play with the white balance built into your camera for better lighting control as well. And let's not forget about night photography. It's one of my favorite subjects, and in the next few pages I will explain how you can try your hand at this as well. Taking pictures at night can yield some of the most artistic and beautiful images you'll ever see.

The Basics of Flash Photography

These days, most digital cameras have an electronic flash unit built right into the camera body. The flash is designed to fire for a very short period of time and illuminate your scene in one of two ways:

- Act as the main source of light indoors or in the dark
- Serve as a secondary source of light to fill in shadows when you're shooting in bright light, such as outdoors

In general, your flash will probably know when to fire. When your camera is set to the fully automatic exposure mode, the flash will probably come on as needed and not fire when it is not needed. Of course, you can probably figure out when you need a flash more effectively than your camera can. There will be situations when you may want your flash to fire when it would probably stay off, and vice versa. That's why your camera has several flash modes to choose from. We'll talk about those later in the chapter.

Stay Within the Range of Your Flash

How far will the light from your flash travel? That's something you need to know if you expect to get the most out of your flash. The flash built into most digital cameras is not extremely powerful; at best, you can expect to get a range of about 20 feet. To find the range of your camera's flash, refer to the owner's manual that came with your camera. You can almost always find the flash range listed in the specifications section of the manual. If you cannot find the range of your flash listed there, assume it is no more than about 15 feet.

The range of your flash also depends upon two other factors: the current ISO (light sensitivity) setting on your camera and the focal length setting of the zoom lens. The first factor—ISO—is pretty obvious. The more sensitive the CCD is made to light, the more effective the flash will be. To understand the relationship between focal length and flash range, though, take a look at Figure 4-1. It is an unfortunate side effect of zoom lens technology that when you increase the focal length to telephoto, you typically process less light than when you are using a wide angle or normal focal lengths. Since there's less light getting through the lens barrel to the CCD at telephoto magnifications, the flash has less range.

If you're used to the great range you would get from an external flash unit mounted on top of a 35mm SLR camera, you might be disappointed by the range from a digital camera flash. It stands to reason, though, that the small flash built into a digital camera could not have the same power as the large flash head—with lots of AA batteries—mounted on an SLR.

That means you'll have to be aware of how far you're trying to get the flash to throw light, especially at night or in very dark conditions. If your subject is very far away, such as 25 feet or more, it is unlikely that the built-in flash will have any effect at all on your photograph. See Figure 4-2. Here, you can see that the flash is less effective at increased distances from the subject. In fact, some digital cameras disable the flash automatically when they sense that the lens is focused on infinity. You might want to check your camera manual or experiment to see if that applies to you.

Getting Too Close

Believe it or not, it's possible to get too close to your subject as well. Many digital camera flash units overexpose the subject when you are within a few feet. Since you know about the light-reducing properties of a telephoto lens, you might expect that you can get closer when you zoom in than if you are zoomed out. And you'd be right; with a typical camera, you cannot shoot any closer than about 3 feet when set on normal zoom, but you can shoot to within a single foot if you are zoomed in to telephoto.

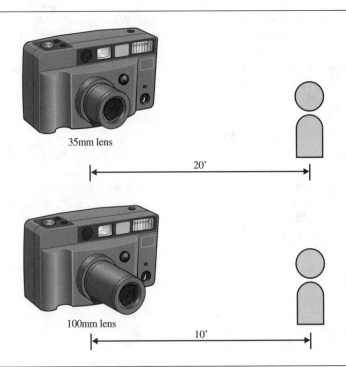

FIGURE 4-1   A telephoto lens, because it processes less light, reduces the range of your flash.

FIGURE 4-2   These snapshots demonstrate the falloff in light intensity as you back away from your subject.

FIGURE 4-3   Your flash may overexpose the scene if you get too close.

As you can see from Figure 4-3, close-up photos are easy to overexpose if you leave the flash turned on. There are a few ways to work around this problem, depending upon what your flash unit is capable of doing:

- Turn the flash off completely and shoot with natural light.
- Bounce the flash off a plain white reflector, such as the ceiling or a reflector card. You'll probably need an external flash unit to bounce, though.
- Reduce the flash's power setting to 50% or 25%.
- Cover the flash with a tissue to reduce its intensity.

TIP   *For many digital cameras, there's an optimum range for your flash photographs. Try to stay between about 5 and 14 feet from your subject. Avoid using the flash in situations where the subject is more than about 15 feet away or closer than 3 feet.*

Master Your Flash Modes

In this digital age, "on" and "off" are just too easy. Instead, your camera's flash has three or more modes, each intended for a specific photographic situation. Here's the rundown of your options. Your camera may not include all of these features, so you might want to check out your camera manual before you get your heart set on trying all of them out. Your camera should have some, if not all, of these modes:

■ **Off**   This one is easy. When you set your camera to this mode, no matter how strongly your camera believes that you need extra light, the flash will not fire. This is handy for situations where you are not allowed to fire a flash, such as in a church or a museum, or when you're too close to the subject and think you might overexpose it. You may also want to turn off the flash in many night photography situations. We'll talk about that later in the chapter.

Auto

■ **Auto**   This is the standard mode that you'll probably want to leave your flash in most of the time. When set to auto, the flash determines whether it needs to fire based on the amount of light in the scene. This is a good mode to use when you don't want to think about whether the flash needs to fire. For typical snapshot photography, just set your flash to auto.

■ **Forced**   This mode goes by many different names depending upon the camera you are using. Sometimes called "forced flash," "fill flash," or just "on," forced flash is probably the most appropriate name. When you set your camera's flash to this mode, it will fire regardless of how much light is available. Why would you want to use this mode? It's most useful as a fill flash: when you're shooting outdoors in natural light, the fill flash can erase shadows that would appear based on the way the sun hits your subject. Fill flash, or forced flash, is great for portraits.

■ **Red eye**   Red eye reduction mode has become extremely popular in all sorts of cameras, both digital and analog. By preflashing the camera flash several times quickly right before the picture is taken, the red eye reduction mode forces your subject's pupils to close down to a smaller size, thus decreasing the chances that they will reflect the light of the flash. When you use this mode, remember that it will take a fraction of a second longer for the picture to be taken. If you're photographing people in a dark room, however, it is probably worth the extra time. You do not need to use red eye reduction outdoors or in bright light.

Low

■ **Low power**   Some digital cameras let you control the power output of the flash. You might be able to reduce its intensity by 50% or more. You can use this mode when you are using the flash to fill in shadows or when you are taking a close-up and a full flash burst would overexpose your subject.

Slow

■ **Slow**   In the world of 35mm photography, this slow setting is sometimes referred to as a *rear curtain flash*. Of course, that name may not help you understand what the slow setting does. When you set the camera to slow flash, it fires the flash at the tail end of the exposure. It's used most often at night, when the exposure is long (such as a second or more). What does it do? Suppose you were trying to take a picture of a car driving down the street. With an ordinary flash exposure, the flash fires right away, thus freezing the car at the start of the frame. In a long exposure, you will then see headlights cut through the car and out of the frame. The slow mode, however, saves the flash for the end. In a picture taken with this mode, you will see headlights that travel through the frame and then meet up with the rear of a flash-frozen car. The car is leaving the picture at the end of the exposure, just like it should. As you can see, you won't use this mode all the time, but it is indispensable when you need to get a certain kind of long-exposure photograph.

Improve Your Outdoor Photographs

In my experience, people are more disappointed with their outdoor photography than any other kind of images. They complain about the washed-out sky—it was very blue when they took the picture—as well as ugly shadows on people's faces, bad exposure, and highly contrasting, harsh shadows that go through their pictures.

Why do all these problems occur? At the most basic level, it's because your digital camera works very differently from the way your eyes do. When you look around outside, your pupils—the apertures of your eyes—change diameter constantly to adjust for varying light conditions throughout the scene. When you look toward the sky, your pupils close so you see rich, blue colors. Look under a tree, and your pupils immediately open to help you see in the deep shadows that are down there. And then there's the fact that your eyes have a much wider range of exposure values than a camera does. When you press the shutter release on your camera, it has to choose a single exposure level and try to depict the entire scene with that one reading—regardless of how dramatically the light changes throughout the picture. As I mentioned in Chapter 3, it is a miracle that we can get good pictures at all. That said, there are many strategies we can employ to get great pictures outdoors.

Beware the Sun

When you take pictures outdoors, always check your watch. By that I mean that there are better and worse times during the day to take pictures. Perhaps the worst time of all is midday, when the sun is directly overhead. The noon sun creates extremely harsh shadows and casts unflattering light for almost any kind of photographic project. People look their worst when you photograph them between about 10 in the morning and 2 in the afternoon, when the extremely bright light (particularly in the summertime) can tend to overwhelm a digital camera.

The alternative? Shoot early or late in the day. Photographers traditionally like the warm colors created by the sun in the late afternoon, but the morning is almost as good. If you are traveling on vacation, for instance, and want to get really great pictures, plan your photo exploits for the early morning hours and then again for late in the day. Heck, it's too hot in the middle of the day to pay too much attention to photography anyway.

If you make a conscious effort to take your best pictures before or after the high noon sun, you're halfway there. You also need to think about the position of the sun in the sky.

In the old days, new photographers were taught to take pictures with the sun to their back. The reason was simple: the sun would best illuminate the subject. Unfortunately, if you were photographing people, the sun would blast that light in the face, causing them to squint. That made for some mighty ugly pictures. A much better solution is to position the sun over your left or right shoulder. But no matter where you put the sun, don't shoot into it unless you are intentionally trying to photograph a sunset or a silhouette.

Shooting Silhouettes

It's easy to photograph a silhouette—in fact, new photographers do it all the time. They just don't do it on purpose.

The easiest way to photograph a silhouette is simply to position yourself so that the subject you would like to silhouette is arranged against a bright background, such as the sky. Point the camera directly into the sky and slightly depress your camera's shutter release— that locks in the exposure based on the bright sky. Then recompose your picture and shoot. What you'll probably get is a grossly underexposed subject, since the exposure was based on the brighter sky. If your subject isn't quite silhouetted, you can underexpose the image even more using the EV controls on your camera.

Add Fill Flash

While most people think of their camera's flash as something to use at night or in the dark, it's also a great way to improve the look of your photographs in the daytime. Set your camera's flash to its forced flash mode, and use it to shoot portraits and other outdoor photographs. You'll find that the flash fills in shadows nicely, dramatically improving the quality of your images. You'll be surprised, in fact, at how much fill flash can do to improve photos that you thought were pretty good to begin with. Check out Figure 4-4, for instance. Here you can see two portraits—one with a fill flash, and one without. Remember, you'll need to be fairly close for this to work. Stay within 10 to 15 feet of your subject.

FIGURE 4-4   A little fill flash can go a long way.

Reflect Some Light

A second source of light is just the ticket to eliminate shadows, reduce contrast, and even out the lighting in your pictures. Sometimes you can do that with fill flash, and sometimes a small reflector will do the job.

A reflector is often better than a flash, because the light from a reflector is softer, and that typically makes better pictures. In other words, it's always better to use natural light—and that includes reflecting it—than to use an electronic flash.

There are two ways to get into reflectors: the cheap way and the expensive way. Believe it or not, you don't need an expensive reflector from your local photo shop in order to move light around—you can have a lot of success using a glossy white sheet of poster board. Purchase a sheet of poster board from your local art supply store for a dollar or two to try it out. The problem with poster board, of course, is that it is often difficult to carry around. For a more compact reflector solution, pick up a photo reflector at your local camera store. Personally, I really like PhotoFlex Litediscs. These clever little reflectors fold up so small that you can almost put them in your pocket. Take them out of the bag, however, and they pop open to a variety of handy sizes. I use a Litedisc that measures about 24 inches in diameter (see it in Figure 4-5), and I find that's a great size for most of the things that I want to photograph.

When you're ready to take a picture with your reflector, you'll probably need some help. It's fiendishly difficult to hold a reflector and take a picture at the same time. So instead of trying some feat of photographic gymnastics, ask an assistant to hold the reflector such that light reflects

FIGURE 4-5   Instead of using the flash, ask someone to hold a reflector near your subject. By holding it level with the ground, you can reflect light up into the subject's face.

from the sky onto your subject. Try to hold the reflector to minimize shadows or illuminate the dark side of your subject.

Reflectors serve a second important purpose as well. When you're out in the field trying to take a picture, the wind can sometimes get in the way. You'll notice this most often when you're trying to take a close-up of a light, bendable subject like a flower. As I talk about in Chapter 5, just a little breeze can create an out-of-focus and blurry macrophoto. The solution? Compose your picture so that you can use the reflector not only to add light to the scene, but also to serve as a wind break. That's right, reflectors can block the breeze and give you a more stable picture. See Figure 4-6 for a look at how you can use a reflector this way.

TIP   *A common way to use a reflector is to hold it roughly parallel to the ground, just under a person's face. That throws light upward, into the shadowy areas of the face, giving you softer, more even illumination.*

4

FIGURE 4-6 Reflectors can block the wind as well as reflect light.

Bounce Your Light

If your digital camera has a hot shoe or an input for a flash synch cable, you can attach external flash units for additional light and control over your images. I love using flash units designed for 35mm SLRs because the flash head tilts. That means you can tilt the flash so that it reflects light off the ceiling or a wall, thus diffusing the light and creating a softer effect. Be sure that you're not reflecting light off colored walls, though, or you might paint your subject some horrible shade of yellow.

Improve Your Indoor Photographs

Indoors, we are often much less concerned about harsh sunlight than we are about having enough light and light of the proper color. The evil red eye is also the nemesis of many indoor photographs. For common snapshots, there's probably nothing wrong with simply using your flash and leaving the camera in its fully automatic mode. But if you want to get really good at indoor photos, there are a few things you can do to shift the odds in your favor.

Use Window Light

The best light is natural light. Whenever possible, position your subject near a window so that you can take advantage of the natural light pouring into your house. If you want to try the window technique, here are a few tips:

- Avoid using windows where the light streams in directly and thus creates harsh shadows. Instead, pick a window in which you get more diffused, indirect light.

- Position yourself with your back to the window and turn your subject so she faces mostly head-on into the window, with some light spilling over to the side of her face.

- If necessary fill in the side of the subject's face with a reflector to eliminate shadows. You can also use your camera's flash as a fill flash.

Avoid the Red Eye

As I mentioned earlier in the chapter, the dreaded red eye is the effect that happens when the flash reflects off your subject's pupils. You can get this effect with any living subject—though it looks particularly creepy when you photograph dogs. Red eye happens most frequently indoors, because everyone's pupils are wide open, to see better in dim indoor light.

Once you understand what causes red eye, it's easy to prevent. Here are the most common ways of avoiding red eye:

- **Use the red eye reduction mode on your digital camera.**   This is the easiest solution most of the time. When you turn on the red eye reduction mode, your camera triggers the flash several times rapidly right before the picture is taken. When you use this mode, remember the delay that happens between the time that you press the shutter release and when the picture is actually taken.

- **Use an external flash off-camera.**   If you have a digital camera with a hot shoe for an external flash, or one that includes a flash synch cable port, you can connect external flash units. The Nikon CoolPix 990, for instance, lets you connect as many as five separate flash units to the camera. The cool thing about using a separate flash is that you can hold it away from the camera. The farther you get the flash away from the camera lens (to the left or right of the camera), the less susceptible your picture will be to red eye, since the light won't reflect directly back to the camera.

■ **Photograph people outdoors, or near windows.** If you can arrange your subjects near a bright source of natural light, you can avoid the red eye problem entirely, since their pupils will already be closed due to the strong light source.

Correct the Color Balance

The color of artificial light is dramatically different from natural outdoor light. In fact, every kind of artificial light has its own unique properties. And that means that different kinds of artificial light have subtly different colors.

It is because of these variations in color that many indoor photographs simply don't look natural. Your camera has a way to adjust for these different light sources. Called *white balance*, it will help you to make sure that you get natural colors in your pictures regardless of what kind of artificial light you use. If you find that the automatic white balance setting in your camera gives you unpredictable results, then be sure to read the next section, and manually adjust your camera's white balance before every indoor photographic session.

Correcting Images with White Balance

As mentioned above, many digital cameras come with a control for something called white balance. White balance is important because different light sources have different *color temperatures*, meaning that a scene will appear to have a slightly different color tone depending upon how it is illuminated.

You have probably noticed this yourself without really even paying attention. You may have seen, for instance, that ordinary light bulbs appear more yellow than the light that streams in from outdoors. And other sources—like candlelight and fluorescent lighting—are certainly a very different color than sunlight.

Photographers and scientists have gone to the trouble of cataloging the different color temperatures exhibited by various light sources. Higher temperatures appear warm, or slightly reddish, while cooler light sources tend to add a blue tone to your pictures. It's not at all unlike the way a flame has different colors at its outside and center. Why? Because those different parts of the flame are different temperatures.

As a point of comparison, this chart shows the color temperatures of several common light sources:

Source	Color Temperature (Degrees Kelvin)
Candlelight	2000
Sunset	3000
Tungsten light	3200
Fluorescent light	5000
Daylight	5500
Camera flash	5600

If your camera is balanced for one kind of light source (daylight, for instance) and you photograph a scene that has been illuminated by a very different temperature of light (such as tungsten), the resulting image won't reflect the true colors in the scene. What should be white will turn out looking somewhat reddish. Ordinarily, we don't notice this ourselves because, as I've said before, the human brain is very good at interpreting what the eyes see. Our brain adjusts for different color temperatures so that white almost always looks white, no matter what color light we're seeing it in. Of course, cameras aren't quite that smart. And that's why we need a white balance adjustment.

The white balance setting on your camera allows you to specify exactly what the color temperature of the scene is. In most cases, your camera can automatically adjust to conditions. If need be, however, you can do it yourself. You'll know that you need to adjust the white balance if your pictures routinely come out shifted to the blue or red end of the spectrum. If your whites are not white—in other words, your camera doesn't do a good job of correcting the white balance— then you need to do it yourself.

TIP   *If you get in the habit of manually adjusting the white balance, remember to reset the white balance to auto when you are done with each shoot. Otherwise, you might forget that your camera is balanced for fluorescent light when you shoot outdoors, and you'll get very funky results.*

Adjusting White Balance Presets

Most digital cameras let you choose from a small collection of white balance presets. In addition to automatic white balance selection, your camera probably includes white balance settings for conditions like incandescent lights, fluorescent lights, an external flash unit, and cloudy or overcast days.

Choosing a White Balance Preset

Changing your white balance setting varies from camera to camera, but the process is typically fairly simple. For the specifics on your camera model, check your camera's user guide. In general though, this is the process:

- Turn your camera on and set it to its normal record mode. If your camera has a separate record mode specifically for manual photography, you'll probably need this one instead.
- Press the menu button on your camera so that you see a set of menus in the LCD display.
- Find the option for white balance.
- Scroll through the white balance options until you find the lighting conditions that best represent your scene.
- Press menu again to turn off the menus. You can now take your picture.

Measuring White Balance Yourself

Sometimes these white balance presets just don't get the job done. If you are in a tricky lighting situation, such as a room that has both incandescent light and candlelight, you may need to set the white balance manually based on the actual lighting conditions in the room. This may sound complicated, but it's really not that hard. Before you start, you'll simply need one additional item: a white surface that the camera can use to set the white balance. Typically, you can get by with a small square of white poster board or typing paper. For better and more consistent results, though, I recommend that you purchase an 18% gray card from your local photo shop. Professional photographers use these small gray cards to judge exposure all the time, since the exposure meters in most cameras are optimized to treat 18% gray as white. You can get a gray card for just a few dollars, and you'll be surprised at how handy it is for setting white balance.

So, here is how to set the white balance yourself:

4

1. Ask your subject or an assistant to hold the gray card with the gray side facing you. Make sure the card is where you're actually going to take the picture, so you are measuring the actual light as it will be in your scene.

2. Turn on your camera and set it to the record mode.

3. Activate the menu system on your LCD display.

4. Find the white balance controls in the menu system.

5. Scroll through the white balance until you find the option to record it yourself. Select this option.

6. You should now see something on the LCD display directing you to photograph a white object. Compose your scene so that the gray card—or whatever you are using to set the white balance—fills the frame.

7. Take the picture and exit the menu system.

The camera will now expose any pictures you take using this new white balance value. Be sure to reset the white balance back to automatic when you're done taking these pictures; otherwise,

Experiment with White Balance

Don't think that white balance is only used to get perfectly white whites in your pictures. Certainly, that is the reason most people use this mode. On the other hand, photography is an art, not a science. By changing the white balance values of your camera, you can get some creative results that you might like better than if the white balance were set properly. As one example, I sometimes like the warmer colors I can get by misadjusting the white balance when shooting portraits. By making my subject's face a bit redder, I think the photo looks richer and more lifelike. Try it yourself and remember that photography is all about trying new things.

you may try taking pictures a day or two later in very different lighting conditions and get bizarre results because the white balance is completely askew.

NOTE   *Many cameras set white balance in the way described above, but your camera may do it slightly differently. Refer to your camera's user manual for exact details.*

Trying Your Hand at Night Photography

Taking pictures at night is a rewarding, exciting activity; unfortunately, digital cameras don't always make it easy to do. On the plus side, taking pictures with a digital camera is essentially free, since you're not buying film. So you can experiment to your heart's content without wasting any film.

Not every camera is cut out for night photography. Low-light photography requires long exposure times; if your digital camera is not capable of shutter speeds of 1 second or more, you will probably have some trouble getting decent night shots. In fact, your camera should have a manual exposure mode so you can dial in the shutter speed by hand. Automatic exposure settings aren't likely to give you anything even remotely interesting. If you're shopping for a camera and are specifically interested in night shots, try to get a camera with a bulb setting—that's photography lingo for a shutter that stays open an indefinite period of time, usually for as long as you hold the shutter release down.

Taking Your First Night Shots

So, you're ready to take your first pictures at night. I recommend that you choose an interesting locale to begin with. Go downtown, where there are lots of neon store lights and cars with headlights on. Alternately, try a local carnival or fairground. The idea is to find a location that has lots of interesting lights and motion.

To take your first night pictures, do this:

1. Mount your camera on a tripod. Your exposure times will be a half second or longer; there is absolutely no way you can hold the camera for that amount of time without introducing an incredible amount of blur.

2. Switch your camera to its manual exposure mode, if it has one. Set the aperture to a medium setting, such as f/5.6. Set the shutter speed to 1/2.

3. Point the camera at something interesting. If this is the first time you are trying night photography, I suggest you go to a fairly busy intersection downtown, and frame the street and a store or two in your viewfinder, kind of like the picture in Figure 4-7.

4. When a car is about to enter your viewfinder, take the picture. You should be able to get fairly instant feedback on how your picture came out by looking at it in the camera's LCD display. No matter how good or bad the picture came out, do not delete it.

5. Now double the shutter speed. Try an exposure of 1 second, and shoot the same scene again.

6. Take more pictures, varying the shutter speed so you can get a feel for what kind of results your camera gives at night at various shutter speeds. You will very likely find that your camera won't expose a picture for more than a few seconds; many cameras limit the shutter speed to 5 or 10 seconds. That's OK—just work your way up until you hit your camera's maximum shutter speed.

7. If your camera automatically records exposure information for each picture, great. If not, write down all of your exposure information so you'll remember what you did later and learn from your efforts.

FIGURE 4-7   Light trails at night can make for some very exciting pictures.

TIP *If your camera does not let you manually choose the shutter speed and aperture, try using its EV adjustment to overexpose your picture by one, two, or even three stops. For example: first set your camera to EV -3, and then focus the camera on the darkest part of the scene. Then shoot.*

When you're all done, you can compare your pictures side-by-side and see the effect of increasing exposure time. As you can see from Figure 4-8, there is no such thing as the one perfect exposure in a night photograph. Increasing the exposure means longer light trails and brighter points of light. Eventually, too much exposure time will lead to obviously overexposed images. But for the most part, the exposure you choose is a matter of personal taste.

TIP *Don't trust your camera's exposure meter at night. You might want to start with whatever your camera's meter suggests, but you can almost always get more interesting pictures by doubling or tripling the shutter speed that's suggested by the camera.*

CCDs and Noise

Night photography is a little trickier with a digital camera than with a 35mm SLR. Don't get me wrong—film has its own problems. *Reciprocity failure*, for instance, is a phenomenon that affects 35mm film. What it means is that film reacts somewhat unpredictably during very long exposures, such as at night. Film is designed to be exposed to light for a fraction of a second; if you leave the shutter open for 10 seconds, the reliable relationship between the aperture size and shutter speed begins to fail. That makes night photography for 35mm photographers something of a guessing game.

For digital photography, we have a completely different problem to contend with. When you expose a CCD to light, it gets hot. This heat manifests itself in the form of noise in your final

FIGURE 4-8   Longer exposure times lead to longer light trails and brighter points of light.

picture. After all, the light and heat are forms of energy, and the heat energy collecting on the CCD has a negative effect on the picture. For short exposures, this is rarely, if ever, an issue. You might see some noise in your picture if you set the camera's ISO value to a very high number when you're shooting in bright light, but usually, the shutter speed is so short that there is little time for the CCD to generate noise in the final image. When you are measuring the exposure in seconds, however, noise can build up quickly. Take a look at Figure 4-9. Here you can see how digital noise affects a picture as the shutter speed is more than a few seconds long.

Some cameras, like the Olympus Camedia E-10, are designed to minimize this long-exposure noise. The CCD is built directly onto a heat sink to carry excess energy away during long exposures. Most digital cameras don't have that feature, however, and as a result you'll simply have to live with that noise. There are two ways to minimize this effect: keep the shutter speed as short as possible to get the effect you're looking for, or run a noise reduction or despeckle filter on your picture in an image editor after you transfer it to the computer.

4

FIGURE 4-9   CCDs are generally not optimized to take long exposures at night.

Cool Things to Photograph at Night

There are all kinds of things to photograph when the sun goes down, and each one requires a somewhat different technique. Here are some suggestions to get you started:

- **The moon** When shooting the moon, remember that it is a very bright object. If you can get enough magnification out of your lens so that the moon fills up at least half of the frame, you'll need to shoot a fairly fast shutter speed or even set the EV value to underexpose the frame. And be sure to use a tripod.

- **Sunset** The sky is full of rich, gorgeous colors around sunset. Base your exposure on the sky itself, not your subject or anything on the ground. And take a few extra pictures, bracketing your exposure to make sure you get the shot.

- **Dusk** I have found that photographing lighted buildings and headlight trails works particularly well when you can get the rich blue colors of dusk in the sky at the same time.

Chapter 5 Taking Close-Ups

How to...

- ◼ Set your camera to its close-focus mode
- ◼ Close-focus a manual-focus camera
- ◼ Ensure proper focus when shooting very close-up
- ◼ Use the correction marks in the optical viewfinder
- ◼ Use optional close-focus lenses
- ◼ Interpret diopter numbers
- ◼ Configure a tripod for semisteady macro shots
- ◼ Blur the background
- ◼ Maximize your depth of field for sharper pictures
- ◼ Eliminate reflections from glass display cases

Close-up photography, also known as *macro photography*, is one of the most exciting areas for experimenting with your digital camera. It's a whole different world down there when you get within a few inches of your subject; we're used to seeing things from five or six feet off the ground. But when you're within an inch or so of your subject, and it is magnified to several times its normal size, photography suddenly seems like magic.

You might think I'm exaggerating, but macro photography really is a lot of fun. And just because you have a digital camera—not a multi-thousand-dollar large-format camera—don't think that you can't play along. Certainly, having a digital camera means that you may have to shoot your close-ups in a different way than traditional photographers do. But that is true of any kind of camera. Each format has its own unique characteristics, and here in the land of digital photography we will talk about how to get the most out of your digital camera when you are taking pictures in the Lilliputian world.

Capturing the Microscopic World

First of all, let's talk about some terminology. When we discuss close-up photography, what we really mean is macro photography. We're not talking about close-ups in the portraiture sense—there are no "I'm ready for my close-up, Mr. DeMille" situations in this chapter. I hope I didn't disappoint you.

Instead, close-up photography is all about photographing the world around us such that we capture small objects, highly magnified. That usually means getting pretty close to the subject—like within a few inches, as in this shot:

Using 35mm SLR equipment or even larger gear, like medium- and large-format cameras, we can get incredibly magnified views of small subjects. We could magnify the eyes of a fly to fill up an 8x10-inch print. In digital photography, we typically can't get quite as close as that, though we can take impressive close-ups nonetheless. If you would be happy with getting the fly itself blown up to 8x10 inches, then keep reading.

Coaxing a Digital Camera to Take Close-Ups

Virtually every digital camera on the market has a close-focus mode. How that mode works, though, depends upon whether your camera has a fixed-focus or autofocus lens.

Autofocus Cameras

In cameras with autofocus lenses (and that represents about 95 percent of the cameras on the market today), you enter close-focus mode (also called *macro* mode) by pressing a button on the camera body. A tulip typically represents close-focus; you should see a button somewhere on your camera with such a symbol. You can see the close-focus button control on the Nikon CoolPix 990 in Figure 5-1. Often, as in the 990, the camera buttons perform more than one function. You may need to press the button several times before the macro mode is actually

FIGURE 5-1   Switch your camera into close-focus mode by pressing the tulip.

enabled, usually indicated by a tulip somewhere on the camera's LCD display. That tulip is a reminder that you are in close-focus mode, and you will get good results when shooting within only a few inches of the camera.

Fixed-Focus Cameras

Though they are increasingly rare, fixed-focus cameras still exist. If you have one of these relics, I suggest you upgrade to an autofocus camera as soon as possible. Nonetheless, even these models usually include a close-focus mode, though it's harder to use. You may need to slide a manual-focusing dial or lever to get your picture in the proper focus (as in the Canon PowerShot pictured in Figure 5-2), or you might need to position your camera a specific distance from the subject. Several Kodak models feature a fixed-focus distance when shooting macros—around 8 inches. As you might surmise, it's not easy to capture good, sharp photos when you have such a rigid focusing distance.

FIGURE 5-2 If your camera has a fixed-focus lens, it may include a manual focus control for close-ups.

How to ... Ensure Good Focus in Close-up Mode

Close-focus photography is a bit temperamental. For starters, the acceptable focusing distance for macro lenses is much shorter than in the normal photo world. You should check your camera manual to discover what the minimum and maximum focus distances are for your camera's lens. Typically, you might be able to get as close as 5 inches or as far away as 3 feet. These numbers vary, though.

Here's what you should do when you're trying to take a close-up photo:

1. Verify the close-focusing range of your camera.

2. Press the macro button on your camera to enter the close-focus mode.

3. Position your camera in front of the subject somewhere inside the range.

4. Press the shutter release down halfway to lock in exposure and focus. Look for the camera's visual focus indicator. Most cameras use a light near the viewfinder to indicate that the image is in focus.

5. If you're having trouble getting the image in focus, point the camera at an edge or some sharply defined region of the subject (without changing the distance to the subject). This may help the camera lock onto the subject.

6. When you're ready, take the picture by pressing the rest of the way down on the shutter release.

That's it in a nutshell. The point is that you need to be very sensitive to focus when shooting close-ups, and you may need to slightly reorient the camera to get a good, solid focus lock. Also, when you do get a lock, make sure that you're actually focused on the right subject. The depth of field is quite shallow at this close distance to your subject, and it's easy to get an out-of-focus image.

Close-up Enemy No. 1: Parallax

Most digital cameras are rangefinders, as I mentioned back in Chapter 1. Rangefinders are cameras that don't show you the actual scene in the optical viewfinder. Instead, using the viewfinder is like looking through one window in your house, while someone else looks through a nearby window. You both see essentially the same scene, though they are not identical. If the two if you look to the horizon, for instance, the two scenes are virtually indistinguishable. If you're both looking at a person walking toward the house, though, as the person gets closer and closer, your two views become increasingly different.

And that is what it is like when you look through the optical viewfinder and the camera uses the nearby lens to take the photograph. SLR-style cameras don't have this problem, because the optical viewfinder actually looks through the lens right up until the moment of exposure.

The problem, as you have probably guessed, manifests itself when you try to take a close-up with a rangefinder digital camera. Since your subject is only a few inches away, the difference in view between the viewfinder and the lens means that you're not even looking at what the lens is about to take a picture of. That's why most digital cameras have indicators in the optical viewfinder. Called *close-focus*, *parallax*, or *correction marks*, these lines show you how to line up the photograph when you are shooting a close-up. See Figure 5-3, for instance. Here, you can see the effect of parallax on a photo. The image on the left represents what I saw in the viewfinder; the image on the right represents what the lens actually photographed.

Framing a Close-Up

So, now you understand the principle behind parallax and close-up photography. Let's apply this so you can see how to take a close-up photo.

Look through your rangefinder camera's optical viewfinder. Hopefully, you can see some correction marks. If the lens is located to the right of the optical viewfinder (as it is in most cameras), you should see correction marks on the left side of the viewfinder. Why is that? Well, these marks represent the left edge of the photo when shooting at close distances. Since the lens is off to the right of the viewfinder, you will need to point the camera slightly to the left in order to take the picture you desire. In actual operation, just recompose the scene so the correction marks help frame the left edge of your picture.

You might have correction marks at the top or bottom of the viewfinder as well. If the lens is below the optical viewfinder (as it often is), correction marks at the top of the frame show you how to reorient the camera slightly higher than you would otherwise.

If all this is just a little confusing, take a look at Figure 5-4. Here, you can see how I have oriented my camera to use the correction marks at close distance.

FIGURE 5-3   You can't trust your viewfinder when taking close-ups, since it sees a slightly different scene than the lens does.

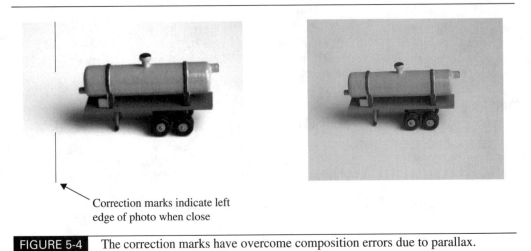

Correction marks indicate left
edge of photo when close

FIGURE 5-4   The correction marks have overcome composition errors due to parallax.

Correction marks are a guide to help you frame macro photographs. But there are some very important things to remember about correction marks:

- **Correction marks are only approximate.**   They help you adjust for parallax error, but they are not perfect. This should be obvious when you realize that parallax varies depending upon your distance from the subject.

- **Correction marks work only at close range.**   Parallax, by definition, diminishes with distance from the subject. At ordinary distances you don't need to worry about the marks at all. In fact, if you use them when shooting a subject that is 10 feet away, they will simply introduce composition error in exactly the opposite direction. Remember though, that they are important when using your macro mode.

- **You can avoid using correction marks entirely.**   Instead of relying on the optical viewfinder when shooting close-ups, use the camera's LCD display instead. The LCD display shows you exactly what the lens sees, and therefore there's no parallax at all when using it.

Using Add-on Lenses

The macro mode built into your digital camera is certainly a nice start for taking close-up pictures, and you can get some pretty good results with it. But if you yearn for greater magnification than your camera is capable of providing, there is an answer: add-on lenses.

Many cameras are designed to accommodate additional lenses and filters. Of course, SLR-style digital cameras with interchangeable lenses spring directly to mind. Cameras like the Nikon D1 accept all of the traditional 35mm lenses in the Nikon family. Many of these lenses—such as the Nikon lens shown here—have macro modes that allow you to get excellent magnification.

But what if you're not using a camera like that?

Actually, many digital cameras accept add-on lenses as well. These are lenses that snap or screw on to the front of your camera's built-in lens. As you can see in Figure 5-5, the Kodak DC 4800 is a fairly common rangefinder digicam, but it accepts a wide variety of additional lenses thanks to a snap-on lens adapter.

FIGURE 5-5   Many cameras, including Kodak and Epson models, are compatible with snap-on lenses that provide telephoto, wide-angle, and macro capabilities.

You can look online for data on lenses for your camera. First, check out the camera manufacturer's Web site for compatible accessories, including lenses. Also visit Tiffen (www.tiffen.com) and Raynox (www.digitaletc.com). Tiffen is the largest manufacturer of add-on lenses for digital cameras, and they're likely to have something for your camera; while Raynox has a variety of macro lenses as well.

The most common close-up lenses for digital cameras look like the ones shown in Figure 5-6. They are usually made from a single element of glass and are threaded to screw onto the front of the camera lens, an adapter, or even each other.

Understanding Macro Lens Lingo

With rare exceptions, close-up lenses are not described in terms of focal length, like other lenses. That's because they're essentially just magnifying glasses that go in front of the camera's normal lens. Instead, close-focus lenses are described using the term diopter.

A *diopter* is an indirect measure of focal length. It tells you both how close you can get to the subject and what relative magnification the lens provides. Close-up lenses typically come in a variety of strengths, from +1 to +10.

FIGURE 5-6   A typical set of close-up lenses

That's right—you can actually combine close-up lenses by threading them together. Adding a +10 lens to a +7 lens yields an impressive +17 magnification. For that reason, I suggest getting close-up lenses as a set instead of one at a time. That way, you can combine them however you see fit to get the magnification you need for a given picture. Check out Figure 5-7. This picture shows the effect of three different magnifications: the camera's built-in macro capability, +10, and +17. The images were taken with the Kodak DC 4800.

> *When combining close-up lenses, put the highest magnification on first, closest to the camera lens. That way, you can remove them in smaller increments to achieve just the right magnification.*

Close-up Techniques

As we've already talked about, taking close-up pictures is a very different experience from taking images at ordinary focal lengths. Though it's not particularly difficult to get really good macro photos, it does take a little more care and a slightly different approach.

FIGURE 5-7   These images were taken from the same distance, but with different combinations of close-up lenses.

First of all, you'll find that your subjects are slightly different in macro photography. Obviously, you won't be taking a lot of people pictures from 2 inches away. There are numerous choices, however. I suggest that you start by taking pictures of things that don't move. For example:

Once you have coins and stamps pretty well in hand, you can move on to photographing insects, flowers, and other mobile or semimobile subjects.

In fact, lots of subjects look radically different at close range and magnified than they appear from a human perspective. Some subjects can even take on an almost fractal appearance—that is, their underlying structure can seem to have a nearly infinite amount of complexity, as you can see from these ice crystals on a tree branch, captured on a chilly April morning:

That's why I think macro photos make for some very exciting images. Here are a few subjects you might want to consider trying your hand at:

- Hobby subjects like stamps, coins, and models
- Wildlife like plants, flowers, leaves, insects, and butterflies
- Found objects like rubber bands, paperclips, and fabric
- Snow, ice, and water

A Steady Base

Without a doubt, you should invest in a tripod if you plan to take many close-up photographs. Although you can get away with holding the camera in your hands most of the time, the extreme magnification provided by close-up lenses tends to make even the most subtle shake ruin your picture. In close-up photography, I highly recommend planting your camera securely on the floor, or ground, with a tripod.

You do not need to purchase a large or particularly heavy tripod. Some of the very large tripods that feature separate, expensive head units are designed for the rigors of 35mm photography, where the camera itself can weigh over 10 pounds. Most digital cameras only weigh a pound or two, so lightweight tripods are usually sufficient.

When you set your camera up on the tripod, you can even leave the head unit somewhat loose. That helps you move the camera around and position it with minimal fuss. This is really up to you—try leaving the head a little loose, and if you can consistently get sharp images, work this way. If you find that your images are always a bit blurry, and you think that it's because you're leaving the head unit loose, then tighten everything up before you take your picture.

Here's a perfect example: In Figure 5-8, you see a bee that I photographed hovering around a columbine. If I had tightened down every knob and lever on my tripod, there's no way I could have caught the little guy as it flitted around somewhat randomly. Instead, the tripod gave me the support I needed, and I left the head unit loose so I could move the camera around to catch the bee at just the right moment.

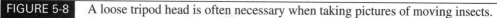

FIGURE 5-8   A loose tripod head is often necessary when taking pictures of moving insects.

Keep the Subject Sharp

Way back in Chapter 3, I spent a lot of time talking about depth of field. If there were ever a time when depth of field was important, this is it. The reason? At high magnification in very short focusing distances, depth of field becomes vanishingly small. In fact, it's not unusual to find that the total depth of field in a close-up photograph is only about half an inch. In Figure 5-9, for instance, you can see that only part of the flower is in sharp focus, while most of the image is blurred. Even parts of the flower are out of sharp focus.

That said, the focusing range of your camera is always at a premium in close-up photography. Even if you want your background to be out of focus, you often want the most depth of field you can possibly get your hands on, since the background will almost certainly be out of focus anyway.

FIGURE 5-9   It's easy to blur the background in a close-up; the hard part is getting everything that you want to be sharply focused in focus.

Here are a few things you should keep in mind to help you control the depth of field in your photograph:

- **Distance**   Remember that the closer you get to your subject, the less depth of field you will have available. So to regain depth of field, back away from your subject. To do that, you may have to remove a close-up lens from the front of your camera if you're using one or more add-on lenses.
- **Aperture**   Another way to increase depth of field is to close the aperture as much as possible. You may need to enter your camera's manual exposure mode to control this.
- **Light**   The more light available, the more you can close the aperture. You can use the camera's built-in flash, use an external flash if your camera allows it, or just shoot in situations where there is a lot of natural light.

Be careful when you compose your picture so that the subject is parallel to the lens, not perpendicular. If your subject has depth with respect to the axis of your lens, part of it will be in focus and part of it will not be.

Mind the Background

The background is an important part of your photograph. In general, you probably want your background to be fairly indistinct. As luck would have it, that is not too hard to do in a close-up photograph. After all, there's precious little depth of field to begin with, so the background will probably be blurry. Here are a few tips for tweaking the background of your photograph:

- **Turn it black.**   If you use your flash, you'll throw so much light onto the primary subject, that the background—especially if it is more than a few inches away from the subject—will be black. This is a good effect in certain situations, but it doesn't look particularly natural. That's why many professional macro photographers avoid using flash units when shooting flowers in the field.

- **Use a plain background.** You can insert a prepared background—a piece of poster board, for example—between the main subject and a distracting background. If the poster board is far enough away, it'll be out of focus and give you a plain, diffused look.

- **Blur it out of existence.** As I have already mentioned, depth of field is perhaps your most powerful tool when taking close-ups. You can check how much depth of field you currently have by half-depressing the shutter release. The camera's LCD display will show you the image with the aperture closed to the appropriate level, and that will give you your final depth of field. If you need more or less depth of field, let go of the shutter release and tweak the camera settings. Just check your depth of field over and over in the camera's display until you are happy with the result. I took the image shown in Figure 5-10 with a very wide aperture to blur the background while keeping the monk's head flower quite sharp.

FIGURE 5-10 This image was taken with a very wide aperture.

Beware of the Flash

You might start to get the impression that I am not a big fan of the electronic flash unit built into many digital cameras. Flashes that have limited range can make your pictures look artificial, and sometimes create harsh shadows. Nonetheless, flash units are admittedly an essential tool, and I don't hesitate to use them when needed.

On the other hand, you should be aware of two key limitations that may be inherent in your camera's flash unit when used in close-up photography:

- **Overexposure**   Unfortunately, some digital camera flash units are not designed for very close range. When you're taking a close-up (and you're within, say, a few inches of your subject), some camera flash units badly overexpose the subject. These flash units expect the subject to be several feet away and don't react well when the subject is much closer. You can find out if your camera suffers from this problem yourself very easily. Just take a test picture or two and evaluate the results. Of course, there are workarounds to this problem. You can try underexposing the picture using the EV controls on your camera, or try a low-tech solution: lay a piece of thin tissue in front of the flash to diffuse the light.

- **Blockage**   Some flash units are positioned so that the lens itself blocks some of the light when the subject is too close to the camera. In my book, this is a camera design deficiency, plain and simple. Nonetheless, if your camera is affected by this particular glitch, it's easy to see for yourself. As in Figure 5-10, there will be a huge shadow in part of the picture where the lens got in the way of the flash. Ordinarily, your camera may not suffer from this problem, but may become prone to light blockage if you add snap-on lenses.

Shooting Through Glass

Sometimes you might want to take a close-up of something that is under a sheet of glass—jewelry in a display case, for example. There's a common problem with this kind of subject, though: light from the sun or overhead lamps can reflect off the glass and cause unwanted glare in your picture. Not only is glare like this ugly, it can actually make it difficult to see what it is you were trying to photograph under the glass. The solution? Use a polarizing filter. A polarizer does a few nifty things for your photograph, but the most important one is that it eliminates reflections caused by glass and water by blocking polarized light.

FIGURE 5-11   You'll have to turn off the flash when taking close-ups with this camera since the lens blocks some of the light.

Polarizing filters are sold in many sizes and for many digital cameras. It's not a bad idea to carry one in your camera bag for those occasions when it might come in handy. Polarizers are usually two-piece devices that rotate on the end of your camera—you turn the outer layer until the reflections are minimized.

That may sound complicated, but it's actually pretty easy. The LCD display on your camera gives you immediate feedback on the effect of the filter. If you can see a reflection in the display, continue turning the polarizer until the reflection is gone (or at least minimized). Keep in mind that a polarizer is most effective when you photograph at a 34-degree angle from the reflective surface, as demonstrated in this illustration:

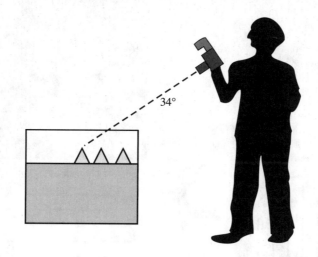

If you use your polarizer properly, you can reduce glare significantly—sometimes completely. In Figure 5-12, for instance, you can see the effect of a polarizing filter. The image on the left is uncorrected; it's what you would get without a polarizer. The image on the right has had its reflections stripped away using a polarizing filter.

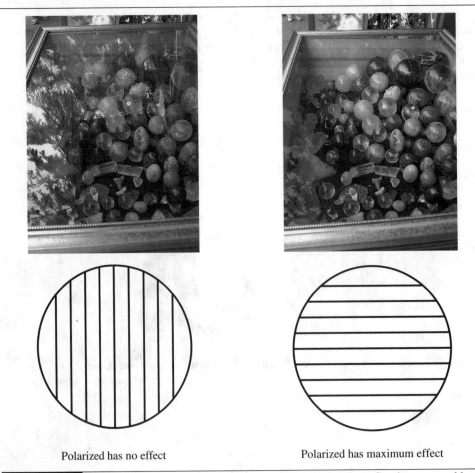

Polarized has no effect   Polarized has maximum effect

FIGURE 5-12 By turning a polarizing filter, you can minimize the reflections caused by light and glass.

Chapter 6

Pushing Your Camera to Its Limits

How to...

- Take pictures in special color modes like black and white or sepia
- Determine when to use special color modes on the camera or wait and process images on the PC
- Shoot a series of panoramic photos
- Add wide-angle and telephoto lenses to your camera
- Avoid vignetting when using add-on lenses
- Correct for distortion caused by wide-angle lenses
- Interpret lens magnification numbers
- Take a series of time-lapse photos
- Turn time-lapse photos into a movie
- Extend the life of your camera's batteries

These days, cameras are no longer just cameras. Take a look at the most common cameras in the local computer or camera shop, and you'll find that many models are designed to record movies, take panoramic photographs, record sound, and do a host of other things as well. It seems that camera manufacturers must think that if you like a camera, you'll like a camera that washes dishes and plays music even better.

Most of this book concentrates on how to use your camera to take good pictures. A lot of the extra features that you find on cameras are, in my opinion, usually just gimmicks. On the other hand, every once in a while you may find a useful, creative application for one of the gizmos built into your camera. And that's where this chapter comes in: look here for information about all those other things your camera can do.

And that's not all. This chapter is about pushing your camera to its limits. That means we'll talk about how to do unusual things with your camera, like use it to perform time-lapse photography. Your camera is no good without batteries, so we'll talk about how to get the most battery life out of your camera as well.

Get Creative

Your camera may come with photo modes besides the ones that we have already discussed, especially if it's a high-end model. The most common features you'll encounter in digital cameras are additional color modes. By setting your camera to the appropriate mode, you might be able to take pictures in black and white or with a sepia tone.

TIP *If your camera does not come with one of these special effects modes, you can always convert your images to black and white or sepia on a computer after you've taken them. Refer to Chapter 13 for information on how to do that.*

Using the black-and-white or sepia mode on your camera allows you to capture images that have a somewhat old-fashioned look. Very old photographs, of course, have a brownish tint that is called sepia.

You might also want to use the black-and-white mode if your final output is going to be in print, like a newsletter. Black-and-white images take up less space on a memory card, so you can typically take more black-and-white images than color images. So if your pictures need to be black and white in the end anyway, you might as well take them in black and white to begin with.

The downside? If you might want some of those images in color for a different application, it's simply not possible to put the color back in later. If you're not sure how your images might be used, I recommend that you start with ordinary color and save them to your computer's hard disk in that format. Later, you can convert the images to black and white in an image processing program if necessary. See Chapter 13 for information on how to do that.

In summary, here are the pros and cons of using the special effect modes on your camera:

Pros	Cons
• Images typically take up less space. • You get a specific effect immediately without the need to process it on a computer.	• If you later need the original color image, you won't have it. • If you forget to switch out of the selected mode, you may find a whole memory card full of sepia-toned images.

The Old-Fashioned Look

If you want an authentic-looking old-time photograph, you can't go wrong with your camera's sepia mode. People instantly recognize the brownish hue of the sepia-toned image as something that is quite old—or at least supposed to look that way. But in addition to just using a little sepia color, there are other things you can do to ensure that the image looks more authentic. Try these tips:

■ Pay attention to costumes and props. If your goal is to take a picture that is set in a specific period, it will look more authentic with the right garb, regardless of whether it is colored sepia or not.

■ Use natural light. Avoid using an electronic flash, which can get in the way of the picture's look.

■ After you take the picture, fine-tune it with an image processing program. In Chapter 13, you'll see how you can make the picture look aged, such as with simulated paper tears.

Make a Panorama

Panoramic photographs have been around for a long time. Before digital photography came along, there were two ways to make a panorama. Special cameras—loaded with special extra-wide film—were capable of taking photos that were much wider than they were tall. In fact, Advanced

Photo System (APS) cameras still do this with contemporary film. Unfortunately, APS cameras cannot make very wide panoramas; actually, all you get with a panoramic shot using APS film is a picture in which the image has been cropped to make the film seem wide. In other words, APS cameras simply throw away information to give you the impression that you have taken a panoramic photograph. Here's an illustration that demonstrates the various ways in which an APS negative can be printed:

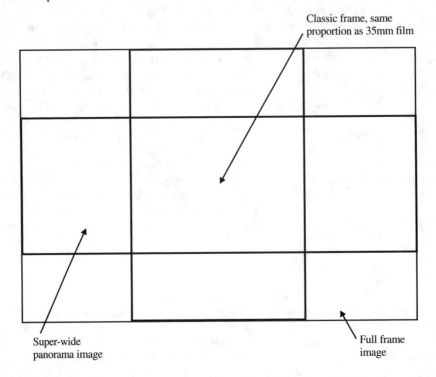

Classic frame, same proportion as 35mm film

Super-wide panorama image

Full frame image

The other way to make a panorama is to take a series of photographs and connect them, sort of like a collage. This collage technique allows you to make very, very wide panoramas. Unfortunately, you can often see the seams between each photograph, since each print is simply layered, one on top of the other.

Digital photography allows us to make panoramas in an entirely new way. Using a still camera, it is a piece of cake to take a high-resolution photograph that spans your entire field of view from left to right, including your peripheral vision—like the one in Figure 6-1. Heck, you can keep going around and take a 360-degree photograph. I can't easily show such a picture on the pages of this book, though, because to squeeze a very long image onto the page, it would become so narrow that you wouldn't be able to see what was in the picture.

Some cameras boast right on the box that they have this capability. Some cameras don't. Either way, you can make a panorama; so don't despair if it appears that your camera does not have a panorama mode. The key ingredient to making a panorama is actually software on your PC. Let's just say that creating a panorama on the PC is actually pretty similar to making a

FIGURE 6-1   Panoramic images allow you to see a scene in much the same way that your eyes see the world.

collage of prints. The software simply takes a series of photographs and stitches them together digitally so that the seams are essentially invisible.

Before we get there, though, we need to take the initial batch of pictures. Believe it or not, you can get some very nice panoramic photographs even if you are a bit sloppy when you take the original images. For best results, however, you should be as careful as possible when you take your pictures. Just like the old computer axiom "garbage in, garbage out," the better your original images are, the better the final panorama will be.

Getting the Right Overlap

Perhaps the single most important step in making a panorama is getting the correct overlap. The software on your PC will need to know how to combine each image in order to make the finished panorama. To do this, we try to get about 25% of the scene to overlap between each pair of pictures. Take a look at the illustration below, for instance. If you make sure that some of the scene that you photographed in the first image also appears in the second image, the stitching software on your PC will be able to match them and combine them into one wide picture.

How do you ensure the right amount of overlap? That's where your camera comes in. Some digital cameras have a panorama mode built in that helps you line up each picture using a series of guide marks.

Switch your camera to panorama mode and look in the LCD display. You should see a set of guide marks like the ones shown here. As you take each picture in your panorama, the guide marks help you keep part of the previous shot in the next picture you are about to take.

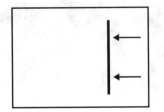

Have the Right Hardware

You can take a series of panoramic photographs by just holding the camera up to your eye. After all, I've done that myself. In England a few years ago, I made a panoramic photo in front of Abbey Road Studios, where the Beatles recorded virtually all of their music. This was something of a religious experience for me, and I was distressed that I didn't have a tripod with me to make the shot perfect. But I made do with what I had—essentially, my body and an Epson digital camera—and the results were fine.

For the best results, though, it pays to travel with the right gear. To take a good panoramic shot, each image should be taken level. Remember that there are two different axes to keep under control. The lens needs to be parallel to the ground, and the horizon needs to stay level in each picture. That's not easy to do when you're holding the camera in your hand.

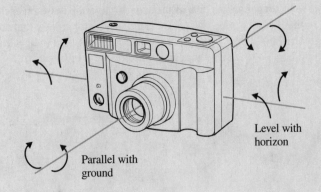

Level with horizon

Parallel with ground

Instead, mount the camera on a lightweight tripod. You can even find a special panorama head for the tripod. This little device makes sure that you rotate the camera the proper amount for each picture in your series. If you don't have a panorama head, simply keep the camera loosened on top of the tripod so you can spin it slightly for each picture.

How to ... **Take a Panoramic Series**

6

Ready?

Now it's time to actually take your panoramic series. Here's what you should do:

- Set up your camera on a tripod in front of the scene that you want to photograph. Make sure that the camera is level with respect to the horizon.

- Turn on your camera and set it to the panorama mode. Frame the rightmost edge of your panorama and take the picture.

- Turn your camera on the tripod slightly to the left so that it is framing the next part of the scene. Make sure, however, that the leftmost 25% of the first image now also appears in the second image. It is this overlap that will allow your computer to line up the image into one seamless panorama.

■ Continue turning the camera and taking additional pictures until you reach the leftmost edge of your panorama. Or if you are taking a 360-degree panorama, continue taking pictures until you reach the first image with a suitable overlap.

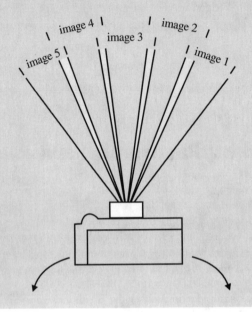

TIP

If your camera does not have a panorama mode, you can still take your panoramic series. Just be sure to include some overlap in each image, using your eyes to estimate distance.

NOTE

Some cameras include a completely different kind of panorama mode—don't be misled. If your camera takes a panorama in a single shot, it's pulling a trick that's more akin to the APS method of changing the film's aspect ratio. Some cameras (like the Epson PhotoPC) simply crop the top and bottom of the image, giving you a narrow image that suggests a panorama, but in reality it is no wider than a image taken with a standard megapixel camera. I suggest avoiding this mode, since you can always crop a standard picture to this aspect ratio on your own later in an image processing program.

Adding Lenses for Different Perspectives

As you've already seen in Chapter 5, you can attach additional lenses to many digital cameras to enhance your photographic options. In Chapter 5, for instance, we added close-up lenses to shoot macro photographs.

Your options don't end there. There are add-on lenses that cover the spectrum of photographic possibilities. Even if your camera only comes with a 2X zoom, you can probably enhance that with a set of telephoto, wide-angle, and close-up lenses.

The first thing that you'll need to know is how you will be attaching additional lenses to your camera. Typically, there are three ways of doing this:

- ■ **Threads**   Many digital camera lenses are threaded at the end. If your lens has screw threads, you can probably screw additional lenses directly onto the end. Even so, you may need something called a step-up ring. This is a device that screws onto the end of your lens and provides a different diameter for screwing on the additional lenses. Lens manufacturers typically only make lenses in a few sizes, like 37mm and 43mm. If your camera has a different thread size, you will need the step-up ring. You can get such an animal at the local camera shop or from a filter company like Tiffen (www.tiffen.com). Your camera's manufacturer may sell a step-up ring specifically for your camera as well.

- ■ **Adapters**   Some cameras do not have a threaded lens, but instead allow you to snap additional lenses onto the end of the camera using an adapter. Usually, you'll snap or clip the adapter onto the end of the camera lens and then screw the add-on lenses onto the end of the adapter. Figure 6-2, for instance, shows the Kodak DC 4800 with its lens adapter in place. The camera manufacturer typically makes adapters like these since they are such specialized devices, designed to affix only to specific cameras.

6

FIGURE 6-2   Lens adapters are a common away to add wide-angle and telephoto lenses to your camera.

■ **Jury-rigged**   Unfortunately, not all camera manufacturers include a way to add new lenses. That may sound like the end of the line, but it is possible to affix additional lenses to your camera using homemade adapters, in some cases with an adapter for a different camera, some tubing, or a judicious amount of tape. Sounds like something a fourth grader might do? Well, lots of professionals resort to this method on occasion, so if you try it, you are in good company.

Choosing Lenses

Be sure to visit your camera manufacturer's Web site or your local camera shop to see what kinds of lenses are available for your camera. Even if your camera manufacturer does not sell lenses for your specific model, you can probably get a suitable substitute from a company like Tiffen (www.tiffen.com). Tiffen sells a wide variety of lenses and probably has something that would work for you.

Lenses are typically identified by their X power. In other words, the lens will be marked as something like .5X, 2X, or 3X. This designation tells you what the new focal length will be once the lens is attached to your camera. If it is a 2X lens, for instance, the lens will double the focal length of your camera. Obviously, a 2X lens is a telephoto, and attaching it to a typical digital camera should yield a focal length in the vicinity of 200mm.

If you are looking for a wide-angle lens, shoot for one that has an X power of less than 1. Suppose you purchase a .6X lens. When you attach it to your digital camera, it will reduce the focal length by 40%. Zoomed out at a focal length of 40mm, your camera will actually provide a focal length of 24mm, which is quite wide. If you zoom in to your camera's telephoto position, the add-on lens will still work. Now, your usual 100mm will only be 60mm.

Often, you can purchase add-on lenses in a complete set. Kodak, for instance, sells a convenient collection that includes a 2X telephoto, a .6 wide angle, and a pair of macro lenses (which you can see in Figure 6-3).

Add-on Lens Precautions

While add-on lenses are a powerful tool for expanding your photographic options, you need to take some care in their use. Specifically, some lenses introduce an effect known as vignetting. *Vignetting* is what happens when the lens barrel itself gets into the picture, causing the frame to lose its square shape. Subtle vignetting might simply cause the corners of your pictures to be rounded off, while extreme vignetting (like the example in Figure 6-4) can feature a perfectly round vignette; in this case the edge of the lens itself is included in the photo.

You can avoid unwanted vignetting by keeping an eye on the camera's LCD display. If your add-on lens is prone to vignetting effects, zooming farther into the telephoto range will often eliminate the problem. You can also crop the darkened corners out of your picture or paint over the edges with nearby bits of the picture.

Distortion is another potential effect of adding lenses to your camera. All lenses have some small amount of distortion; after all, no piece of glass or group of optical elements is perfect. But you'll rarely notice any distortion from your camera's principal lens by itself. When you add the

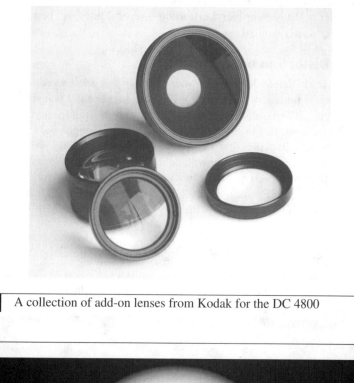

FIGURE 6-3   A collection of add-on lenses from Kodak for the DC 4800

FIGURE 6-4   This image suffers from such a particularly serious case of vignetting, thanks to an add-on telephoto lens, that it looks intentional.

equivalent of a big magnifying glass on the front, though, you can start to see some effects. Most of the time, it'll be either pincushion or barrel distortion—vertical lines will bend in or out of the frame instead of being perfectly straight.

Eliminating Lens Distortion on the PC

Obviously, if you can clearly detect distortion in your photos when using an add-on lens, you should avoid using that lens (unless it's a creative effect you intentionally want to add to your picture). On the other hand, it's possible to remove this sort of distortion from your pictures once they're on the PC. There are utilities available that are designed to straighten such images.

My favorite utility is actually a plug-in filter for Adobe PhotoShop. *Plug-ins* are small programs that extend and enhance PhotoShop with additional capabilities. This one is called LensDoc, and it's sold by Andromeda Software (www.andromeda.com). It works in PhotoShop or any other program that can use PhotoShop plug-ins, like Paint Shop Pro. You can download LensDoc for a free trial. If you have a picture with obvious lens distortion, here's how to use LensDoc to fix the problem:

1. Load the distorted picture into a graphics program, such as Paint Shop Pro.

2. Start LensDoc by choosing it from the Filter menu. In Paint Shop Pro, choose Image | Plug-In Filters | Andromeda | LensDoc. You should then see the LensDoc window:

3. Turn off the three green squares by clicking the second button in Step 2 (the button with three connected green circles).

4.   One at a time, grab the three yellow squares in the image and position them along a line that should be straight, but isn't. Avoid positioning the squares too close to each other.

5.   When you're ready, click the Correct button. Your image should be straightened. See Figure 6-5 for a before-and-after look at lens distortion.

FIGURE 6-5   A wide-angle lens created this highly distorted view on the left, but LensDoc straightened the image quickly and easily.

Essential Add-on Lenses

Granted, this is a matter of opinion, but there are a few add-ons that I highly recommend keeping in your camera bag. I suggest that you carry these lenses if you like to experiment with different perspectives and focal lengths:

- A 2X telephoto.
- A .5 or .6 wide angle.
- A set of close-focus lenses, such as +2, +4, and +10.
- A neutral density filter. This is a translucent piece of glass that fits over the lens. It's designed to reduce the light entering the camera by one or two stops, thus letting you control the "blur" in action shots (such as the one below) or increase the depth of field on a bright day.

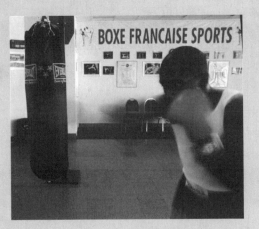

- A polarizer. Discussed in Chapter 5, this add-on filter lets you cut reflections from glass and water.

TIP   *You can increase the accuracy of LensDoc by using the green squares to mark a second line.*

Taking Time-Lapse Photos

If you've ever been impressed by a time-lapse movie of a flower opening or traffic moving on a busy highway, you might want to try it yourself. It's not hard to do, though it's certainly easier if your camera supports time-lapse operations to begin with.

First, a little theory: time-lapse photography is just the process of shooting the same subject over and over with a certain time interval between each shot, so that when you play the images back later in sequence, it's like a movie in which events happen faster than normal time.

If your camera has a time-lapse feature, this is a piece of cake. The control might be on the camera itself (in the menu system) or on your PC. If it's only on your PC, you may need to connect a laptop to the camera to control the time-lapse operation.

If the control is on the camera, though, you don't need any special equipment. You can see a typical time-lapse setting in Figure 6-6. All you need to do is configure the camera's "interval time," which is the interval between photos.

Then, either press the shutter release to take the first picture or choose Start from the camera's menu system—you can see a menu-based time lapse control in the illustration below. (Check your camera manual for details on how to start the time-lapse session.)

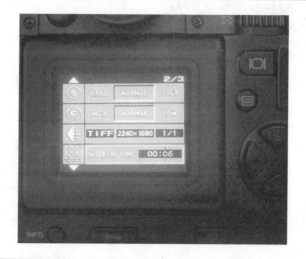

FIGURE 6-6   Configure your camera's time-lapse control to capture a series of time-delayed photos.

If your camera doesn't have a time-lapse control, you can still take a series of photos, but you'll have to shoulder more of the work. Specifically, you'll have to turn the camera on, take a shot, and turn the camera off. Then you need to wait the appropriate time period and repeat the process. When you use automatic time-lapse photography, the camera does all that on its own.

The final results can be worth it, though. Figure 6-7 shows a series of photos that were captured with the time-lapse mode of an Olympus E-10 digital camera.

If you want to try your hand at time-lapse photography, here are a few pointers to keep in mind:

- **Use a tripod.**   This is probably obvious, but I once saw someone try to take a time-lapse series by hand. The effect is ruined if each and every image isn't composed exactly the same way.

- **Choose a subject.**   Most of the time, a time-lapse photo series works best—in other words, it looks its best—when you find a single subject that is going to change over time and make it the focal point of your photos. If too much changes in the frame, the image loses its impact. In simple terms, it looks like a mess.

- **Find the right interval.**   This may take some experimentation, but it can make or break your photos. Choose an interval between shots that best highlights the changes in your subject. If the interval is too long, the subject will change too much between shots, and it'll look disjointed and confusing. If the interval is too short, not enough will happen between frames to make a visual difference.

- **Start fresh.**   Make sure that you have plenty of room on your memory card to take your series. You might want to start with a blank card and reduce the resolution of each image to a manageable 640x480 pixels. If you plan to take a lot of pictures, be sure the camera batteries are fresh (so you don't run out of gas halfway through the series), and perhaps start with a large memory card.

- **Use automatic exposure.**   Most of the time, make sure that the camera is set to automatic exposure. That way, it can react to changing light conditions throughout the day. The exception: if you're taking a series of night shots, configure the camera for the desired manual settings, like f/5.6 for 8 seconds each.

Making Movies

Once your time-lapse series is complete, you might want to turn it into a film. There are several ways to do this:

- **Using video editing software**   If you have a camcorder and make your own home movies, this is a great solution. Just open your favorite video editing program and import all the still time-lapse frames. Arrange them in the filmstrip or timeline so they each play for some small fraction of a second, and then render the movie. Using this technique, you

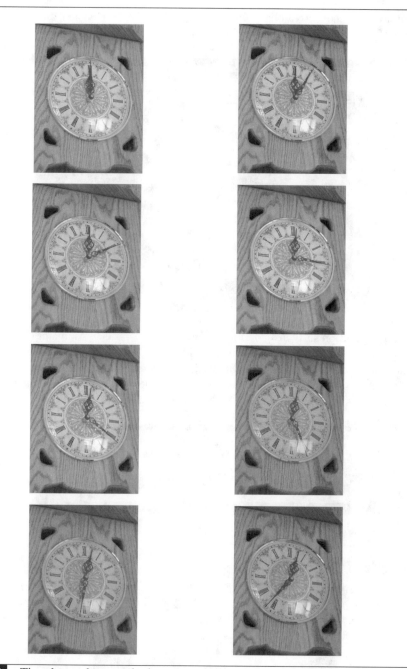

 FIGURE 6-7   Time-lapse photography lets you see changes over a short or long period of time.

can save your movie so it plays "full screen" on the PC or a television, directly from the PC or from videotape. I use MGI VideoWave to do this sort of thing, as you can see here:

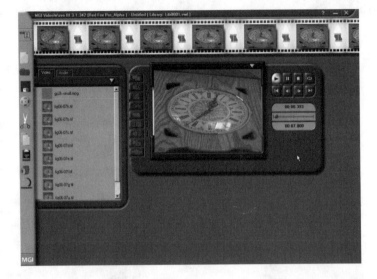

■ **Using animation software** Using a program like Jasc's GIF Animator (included with Paint Shop Pro), you can arrange the individual stills, configure them each to play for a fraction of a second, and save the finished result as an animated GIF or some other kind of animation file that plays in a small window on the computer screen. This technique is better if you want to upload it to a Web site, email it, or just view it on the PC.

Taking Care of Batteries

Digital cameras are battery hogs, plain and simple. You shouldn't expect the batteries in a digital camera to last very long since they are responsible for running a number of key functions within the camera:

- The imaging system, including the exposure system and the zoom
- The LCD display
- The flash
- The image storage system

That's a lot to expect from a set of AA batteries, and, in fact, they don't last long. I recently tested a slew of digital cameras by taking picture after picture with a set of alkaline batteries until they died. These were my results:

Camera	Shots Till Batteries Depleted
Epson PhotoPC 700	157
Ricoh RDC-4200	200
Toshiba PDR-M1	306
Olympus D-340R	140
Kodak DC210 Plus	89
FujiFilm MX-500	307

And while 300 photos may seem somewhat impressive, realize too that this was an absolute best-case scenario. In real life, you'll take some time composing your picture, zooming in and out, reviewing pictures you've already taken, and so on. In other words, ordinarily, the batteries will run out a whole lot sooner—in half the number of shots or less.

Rechargeable Versus Alkaline

Unless you use your digital camera very infrequently, I recommend that you avoid alkaline batteries. Instead, invest in a set of rechargeable batteries. Yes, they're initially more expensive. But they quickly pay for themselves, since you can use rechargeables over a hundred times on average. Do the math: Let's say that you use your camera every weekend for a year, and you have to replace the batteries every other time you use the camera. Here's how the cost stacks up over the course of a year:

AA Alkalines	AA Rechargeables
26 x $3 = $78	$35

The more you use your camera, the more obvious the cost savings become. And once you've bought your first set of rechargeable batteries, additional sets are less expensive because you don't have to buy the charger unit at the same time. So I think you can see how useful rechargeables actually are.

There are actually three kinds of rechargeable batteries:

- ■ **Ni-Cad (Nickel Cadmium)** Ni-Cads are the oldest kind of rechargeable battery and are not commonly sold or used any more. You should avoid Ni-Cads if possible since they suffer from "memory" problems. If you consistently recharge a Ni-Cad battery at the same point in its power curve—such as when it's just half discharged—it will develop a memory for that point and eventually stop discharging beyond halfway. In effect, Ni-Cad memory problems rob you of your battery's full potential. Worse, if you fully discharge a Ni-Cad before recharging it, the battery may not recharge properly. It needs to have some charge left to work properly. Since you need to pay such close attention to how and when you recharge them, they're more trouble than they're worth.

- ■ **NiMH (Nickel Metal Hydride)** NiMH batteries are cost-effective, contemporary alternatives to Ni-Cad batteries. You can get a set of four for about $20 ($35 with a charger), and they last for well over 100 charges.

- ■ **Li-Ion (Lithium Ion)** Better than NiMH batteries, they're also more expensive. Li-Ion cells usually pack more pictures per charge and have a longer overall life. Right now, though, NiMH batteries are usually a better buy.

Get the Most out of Your Batteries

With so many demands on your camera batteries, it's not all that surprising that they don't last very long. But there are certainly things you can do to extend the life of your batteries, making them last longer between charges or replacements. Just follow some of these commonsense tips:

- ■ **Use the optical viewfinder.** If your camera lets you, turn off the LCD display and look through the optical finder instead. The LCD screen is one of the biggest energy hogs on your camera, and you can significantly extend the value of your batteries by not using it.

- ■ **Don't review your pictures.** Likewise, avoid gawking at your pictures on the camera's LCD display. Review them briefly if you need to select images for deletion (to free some room on the camera's memory card) or to see if you need to reshoot a particular picture. But save most of the review for your computer.

- ■ **Disable the flash when you don't need it.** Sure, there are excellent reasons to use it, even outdoors (we talked about fill flash to improve portraits in Chapter 4), but if you are shooting subjects that are 40 feet away and the flash can't possibly help, turn it off. Your batteries will thank you.

- ■ **Leave the camera on.** If you're taking a lot of pictures in a brief time, don't turn the camera off after each and every picture. You might think that you're conserving battery life, but in fact you're burning energy every time the camera has to power on. That's especially true if your camera has to retract the zoom lens every time it powers down and extend the lens when you turn it on again.

■ **Use AC power when it's available.**   When you're transferring images to the PC, don't rely on battery power. You should have an AC adapter to power the camera when you're working at your desk near electrical power. If your camera didn't come with an AC adapter, it's probably wise to invest in one for exactly this reason. The AC adapter might also come in handy if you're shooting a lot of pictures inside a house from a somewhat stationary position. You can save battery life for when you really need it by tethering yourself to an AC outlet.

TIP

If your batteries die in the middle of a shoot and you don't have any spares, here's a trick you can try that might give you a few extra shots: turn the camera off, wait a minute, and then turn it back on. Often you can sneak in a few more pictures before the batteries are completely exhausted.

6

Pack Extra Batteries

Never go anywhere without a spare set of batteries in your camera case. I don't need to tell you how frustrating it can be to run out of energy in the middle of Yellowstone National Park. If you can fit it, I also suggest bringing a charger with you so you can top off your rechargeables as needed. I am particularly fond of slim-line chargers like the one shown here, since it takes up so little space and can be used to hold a second set of batteries without consuming any more precious space in your camera bag:

Part II

Transferring Images

Chapter 7

Conquering File Formats

How to...

- Use image file formats
- Distinguish among formats like JPG, TIF, GIF, and BMP
- Recognize file extensions on the PC
- View file extensions in Windows
- Understand the value of JPG compression settings on the camera
- Select the best image compression on a camera
- Determine when to use the TIF format to capture pictures on your camera
- Know when to save images in various file formats
- Batch-save a large number of images in a different format automatically
- Choose the best JPG compression level on the PC

Like it or not, working with a digital camera means that you are going to have to learn some of the nuances of your PC. That can be bad news. After all, computers can be a pain in the neck, and Windows in particular can be a nightmare.

Nonetheless, the pictures stored in your digital camera are not terribly useful to you unless you understand how to work with them. The images are stored in individual files not unlike the document files you'll find on the computer itself—like word processing files, music files, or the saved game files created by a video game. In this chapter, we will look in some detail at the image files created by your digital camera. We will talk about file formats, image quality, and what you need to know about all of this to get the best results with your camera. Don't worry, though: this is not a computer class, and we won't go into any more detail than you will actually need to manage your pictures.

What Are File Formats and Why Do I Care?

When you take a picture with your digital camera, the camera's CCD acts like film and records a representation of the scene on the camera's memory card. The scene actually becomes a grid, or matrix, of pixels. How many pixels depends upon the resolution of the camera. If you were taking a 1-megapixel picture, for instance, the image's resolution might be 1280 pixels across (the X dimension) by 960 pixels down (the Y dimension). It would look something like Figure 7-1, though obviously there would be a lot more pixels. The picture is a sort of paint-by-numbers grid—just add the right color to each of the pixels in Figure 7-1, and you'll end up with a picture of something.

So far, so good. The problem comes in when you want to save all this data to the memory card. How do you do it? Essentially, you need to save the data in some standardized format so the information will be understandable to software and devices other than the digital camera

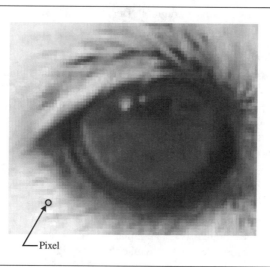

Pixel

FIGURE 7-1   A digital image is little more than a grid of colored pixels.

itself. If the camera stored information about the color value of each one of those pixels however it felt like it, odds are good that only the camera would ever be able to understand that information again.

And that is a somewhat long-winded explanation of why we have file formats. By writing the color information about each of those pixels in a standard and predictable way, each picture that the digital camera saves can be read by your computer's software, even if the software didn't come from the same company that made the camera.

There's more than one file format used by digital cameras and graphics programs—many more. In fact, there are well over a hundred file formats in use by image software on computers today. Only about a half dozen are particularly popular, but even six or eight can be confusing. Why are there so many file formats? Good question. It's not just to confuse everyone. Instead, different file formats exist because some are better at certain tasks than others. Some file formats compress well—in other words, a large picture will only take up a small amount of space on the memory card or hard disk. Other file formats more accurately represent the original image, are optimized for the Web, or are designed to work well on both Windows and Macintosh computers.

The Most Common File Formats

As I said earlier, there are really just a few file formats that most people use most of the time. So while you may occasionally hear about file formats like IFF, IMG, and KDC, you can typically ignore all but just a very few.

By the same token, you really should get to know the most common file formats and use them when it's appropriate. Don't stick to a particular file format just for the sake of using the same format all the time—you will come to regret it. Here is a quick overview of the most common formats and what they are used for:

- **JPG**   Short for Joint Photographic Experts Group (pronounced "jay peg"), this file format is considered *lossy*. That means when you save an image in this format, some of the data is lost. That's because JPG files are compressed to save storage space. Why do people put up with a file format that sacrifices image quality? The answer is that the JPG format does an outstanding job of preserving all the visual information that the human eye can generally see in a picture. When you save a picture in the JPG format, you'll typically have to zoom in quite a bit to begin to see any artifacts or digital noise caused by the JPG format. That's good enough for most people most of the time, and so the JPG format is perhaps the single most common file format in use today for storing digital images.

- **TIF**   Short for Tagged Image File format, this format is also very popular, but for exactly the opposite reason that JPG is popular. TIF files can be saved in two different ways: Using compression, they maintain an extremely high degree of image fidelity while reducing file size a bit. Without compression, TIF files are absolutely *lossless*— they preserve 100% of the information about every pixel in the original image. TIF files are also popular because they are used on both the Windows and Macintosh platforms; that makes TIF a good choice if you need to share files with someone using a different kind of computer.

- **BMP**   This is the old standard bit-mapped file format for Windows users. It can be used for general-purpose storage, for image editing, and as the wallpaper on your Windows desktop, but it isn't generally readable by Macintosh computers. Nor are BMP files used on the Internet. That makes this a relatively unpopular format. Another reason that BMP files aren't particularly popular is that they tend to be quite large, since the BMP format makes no effort to compress the data at all. In general, the only reason you will tend to use this file format is if you want to display a digital image as the wallpaper on the Windows desktop.

- **GIF**   Short for Graphics Interchange Format (pronounced "jiff"), this format was originally developed by CompuServe and is commonly used on the Web, along with the JPG format. GIF has a few advantages over JPG on the Web: You can make the background of GIF images transparent, which comes in handy if you want the area surrounding an irregularly shaped image to be the same as the background of the Web page. You can also make GIF images display in *interlace* mode—that is, in chunks, so that you can get an overall impression of the picture even before it has fully downloaded. That is a valuable feature on the Internet, since many people have slow modem connections. You can also save a GIF image with just a few colors. If you save a GIF image with just 256 colors, for instance, the file will be dramatically smaller and may not look a whole lot different from the original full-color version.

Understanding File Extensions

The many file formats used on computers today are generally referred to by the letters that make up their three-letter extension. Computer files are generally named using a standardized system that looks like this:

filename.ext

The filename can generally be almost anything—a random collection of numbers and letters or a word or two that describe the contents of the file. Filenames also use a three-letter extension that tells the computer what kind of data is within the file. Here are a few common file extensions:

- ■ .DOC   Word processing document (usually created by Microsoft Word)
- ■ .XLS   Spreadsheet document (usually created by Microsoft Excel)
- ■ .MP3   A popular digital music file, commonly downloaded from the Internet
- ■ .HTM   Web page document

In other words, you and I, as users, control the first half of the filename. The file extension, though—the part that comes after the period—depends upon the program that made the file or the file format that the data corresponds to. If you open a folder on your computer and find a bunch of image files, you can immediately tell what format they are in by looking at their extension. *Mypicture.jpg* is a JPG image, while *pretty-flower.tif* is saved in the TIF format.

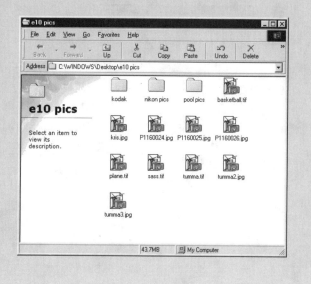

Windows may not be configured to show you the complete filename including the extension. To turn on the extension view, do this:

1. Open a folder on the Windows desktop.

2. Choose View | Folder Options from the folder's menu.

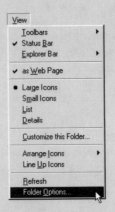

3. Click the View tab so that you can see the Advanced settings.

4. Find the entry Hide File Extensions For Known File Types, and remove the check mark from this selection.

5. Click OK to save this change.

Using File Formats

Now that you understand file formats, you are probably wondering which one you should use on your own system. As in all things, it depends upon how you're going to use your images. Let's look at your choices, and I'll make a few recommendations about how you might want to work with and save your images.

On the Camera

Let's start with your camera. No doubt, you realize that your camera saves images in one of these file formats as soon as the images are taken, but which format?

Actually, this is easy. Most digital cameras save their images in the JPG format. JPG is a pretty good compromise between quality and file size for most users and in most photographic situations. But what you may not realize is that you have a fair degree of control over how aggressively your camera compresses the JPG images. Take a look at your camera, and you will no doubt find that somewhere—whether it is in a menu system or controlled via a button on the camera housing itself—there is a setting for image quality. Note that image quality is quite different from resolution: resolution is a measure of how many pixels are in the image; quality determines how much each image will be compressed, and consequently how much image quality will be sacrificed.

Most cameras tend to have several quality settings, such as high, medium, and low. I recommend that you stick with either the highest or medium setting for your JPG images— the low-quality setting tends to make for some pretty unsatisfactory images. Take a look at Figure 7-2 for a graphic depiction of the difference in image quality between the high and low settings on a typical digital camera. The image on the right—the lower-quality JPG—has more boundaries visible from one color to another. There's a real trade-off to be made here, though: the higher the quality, the fewer the images you can fit on a camera's memory card.

Be sure to check your camera menu for details on setting image quality and resolution. That's because every camera is a little bit different. Some cameras make it easy to distinguish between resolution and image quality because they are set with two different controls. The Kodak DC 4800, for instance, has a self-explanatory menu for choosing among the various image qualities:

FIGURE 7-2   The same image shot with a camera set to high and low image quality

Other cameras offer these two controls in a single, somewhat confusing menu selection. On the Olympus D-620L, for instance, the menu gives you a choice of SHQ, HQ, and SQ. Both SHQ and HQ are the same high resolution, but with different amounts of JPG compression. The SQ setting represents a smaller pixel count.

Likewise, Epson tends to use a series of graphical stars in its LCD display to indicate a combination of resolution and image quality. What do these stars mean? It'll take you a while before you memorize their meaning. Until then, you may have to check the user manual a few times.

Lossless Image Files

It's worth pointing out that many digital cameras have a second file format option—TIF. Remember that the TIF format, unlike JPG, can be used to ensure that the image is absolutely pristine, without any data loss at all. Many cameras have a special setting that you can use to save your images in this lossless TIF format.

You might want to work in TIF if you are shooting a special photograph that you'll want to crop, enlarge, and print. Any professional work probably calls for TIF images. But realize that the TIF format exacts a serious penalty—it's so large that you may only be able to fit one or perhaps two images on the memory card that comes with your camera.

If you want to work in TIF format a lot, you might want to get the largest memory card you can afford. Even with a 128MB Compact Flash card, you might only be able to store a half-dozen images in your camera at one time. How significant is the difference between TIF and JPG? The differences are typically only apparent when enlarged. Figure 7-3 shows details from a pair of pictures. The one on the left was shot and saved in TIF format, while the one on the right was shot with JPG set to moderate compression. The difference isn't significant, but it is most important when trying to print an enlargement on a good color printer.

On the PC

When you transfer your images to the PC, you'll find them in the same file format that the camera used. There's no magical transformation as they go from camera to computer. But just because they arrive in JPG format, that doesn't mean they have to stay that way. You can save these images in any file format you like.

> *When you save a JPG picture in TIF format, you essentially freeze the image at its current level of detail and image quality. That way, when you edit and save it again later, you're not degrading its quality like you would by resaving it in JPG format. But remember—just saving an image in TIF cannot restore quality that wasn't there to begin with. Your image will never look any better than it did as a JPG.*

FIGURE 7-3   JPG artifacts (like those on the right) may not bother you most of the time, but many cameras have a TIF mode to capture the whole truth (the picture on the left) for special situations.

I highly recommend saving any files that you plan to edit or manipulate in a lossless file format like TIF. I have nothing against JPG—it's a great format—but since it is lossy, every time you open, edit, and resave a file, it degrades a bit more. This is very important! Many people assume that resaving a JPG image doesn't affect the image quality, but that's not the case. Think of it this way: A JPG is nothing more than an approximation of the original. Every time you save a JPG file, the JPG compression algorithm runs, effectively making an approximation of an approximation. Figure 7-4 shows the effect of opening and saving the same image a dozen times in an image editing program like Adobe PhotoShop. Notice that the veins in the leaf are much less sharply defined in the image on the right after it has been resaved multiple times using the JPG format.

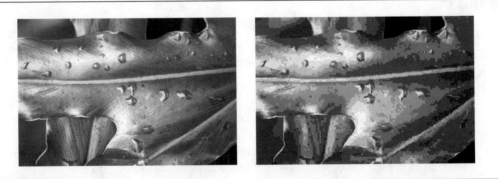

FIGURE 7-4   Every time you click the Save button in an image editor, a JPG file degrades a bit more—the image on the right is a degraded copy of the original.

Change the File Format

When you open an image to crop it, brighten it, or perform some other minor (or major) editing job, you should save your changes as a new file with a .TIF extension. Here's how to do that:

1. In an image editor, choose File | Save As from the menu.

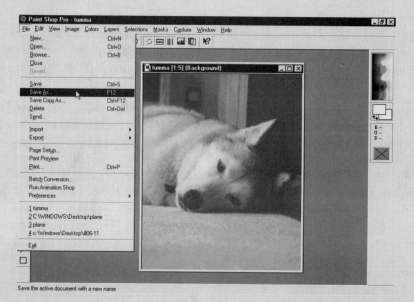

2. In the Save As dialog box, click the list arrow in the Save As Type box, and choose the option for TIF. It is often spelled out as Tagged Image File.

3. Change the filename if you desire, and then click Save.

If you no longer need the original JPG file, you can delete it from your hard disk to save space. You might want to keep it, though, in case you want to go back to the original image (prior to the edits you just made).

Choosing a File Format

The TIF format is great if you plan to print enlargements of your images or if you want to preserve an image precisely, without any compression artifacts. Digital images have lots of uses, though, and that's why there are lots of file formats. Here are a few file format tips you might want to keep in the back of your mind:

- **Web publishing**   If you're posting images on the Web, JPG is usually the best choice. But you might want to test your potential images and see how GIF stacks up as well. That's because GIF is better at rendering text and other images with lines and contrast, as you can see in Figure 7-5. JPG files—like the one on the left—will almost always be smaller, but GIF can sometimes look better.

- **Print publishing**   Creating a newsletter? If you're printing a black-and-white document, such as on a laser printer, it often pays to convert your image to grayscale before you insert it into the page layout or word processing program. There are two reasons for this. First, you can see exactly what you're going to be printing, and viewing it in shades of gray lets you determine whether the image needs brightness adjustment or other edits. Second, you're sending less information to the printer, and the software should work somewhat faster.

- **Enlargement printing**   If you want to print digital images at large sizes, such as 5x7 inches or beyond, stick with TIF.

- **On-screen display**   The JPG format is perfectly adequate for most on-screen applications, including email, slide shows, PowerPoint presentations, Web photo albums, Windows desktop wallpaper, and that sort of thing.

Tweaking JPG

The JPG file format is very flexible. Just as on the digital camera, where you can usually select from several grades of JPG image quality, desktop-based image editing software usually lets you specify an image quality level as well.

FIGURE 7-5   Experiment to see whether JPG or GIF does a better job with certain kinds of images; the GIF on the right looks much better than the JPG version on the left.

Remember the trade-off with JPG settings: the higher the image quality, the larger the file size. In a program like Paint Shop Pro, for instance, you can find the JPG controls in the Save As dialog box:

With the JPG file format selected, click the Options button. You should see a slider control for increasing the compression level. Most people stick with a compression level in the range of 10 to 15. Beyond 15, the compression artifacts start to become quite noticeable, though the file size shrinks dramatically. Check out Figure 7-6, for instance. Here you can see a conservative

FIGURE 7-6 Use JPG compression wisely.

compression of 10, on the left, and an aggressive compression of 50, on the right. The difference is dramatic, especially in the background.

Batch Processing

Some people like to convert their images to TIF (or some other file format) as soon as the images make their way from the camera to the PC. It can be slow and boring to do that by hand—how would you like to access the File | Save As menu item 50 times in a row to save each of your images as TIFs?

Instead, there are various ways to automate the process. One of my favorites is a program called Image Robot from Jasc. This software makes it a snap to automatically convert any number of JPG images into TIFs while you go grab some lunch or do another task on the computer. If you work with hundreds of images at once and frequently need to convert them to another format, investigate this program.

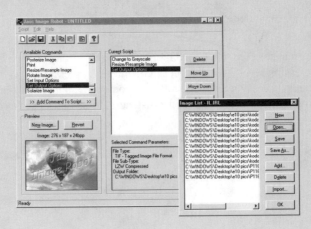

Chapter 8

Working with Digital Film

How to...

- Choose a camera based on its memory card format
- Understand the advantages and disadvantages of various kinds of memory cards
- Use a serial connection cable to copy images from the camera to the PC
- Troubleshoot serial port problems
- Correlate serial ports and COM port numbers
- Use a USB cable to copy images from the camera to the PC
- Solve USB port problems
- Delete images from your memory card
- Care for memory cards

Often you'll hear people describe a digital camera's Charge-Coupled Device (CCD) as the equivalent of a 35mm camera's film—heck, I use that comparison myself pretty often. That's because the CCD behaves like film. It is sensitive to light and is primarily responsible for recording exposure. But in just the same way that 50 different people each stake a claim to being the Fifth Beatle, there's another component in your camera that is "like the film in a digital camera." That's your camera's removable memory, and that's the subject of this chapter.

Removable memory cards like SmartMedia, CompactFlash, and even the good old floppy disk are just like film in the sense that this is where your images are actually stored. If you remove the memory card from your camera and hold it in your hand, you're holding your pictures. If you insert that memory card in your PC, you can transfer those pictures to your computer for editing or printing. And since memory cards can be erased and used again, digital imaging is a lot more flexible and potentially cheaper than 35mm photography in the long run. To learn how to get the most out of your computer's digital film, read this chapter.

The ABCs of Digital Film

All digital cameras have to store their images somewhere—it's the *where* that is the big question. There's no single standard way of storing images in a digital camera; there are almost a half-dozen typical storage schemes in use by cameras today, so what kind of storage system you want to use might actually be a consideration when choosing your camera. Almost all cameras use one of these methods of storing images:

- **Internal memory** Although a few low-priced digital cameras use a few megabytes of internal, nonremovable memory for storing images, this animal is a dying breed. In fact, it's almost extinct. Most cameras include the ability to insert some sort of removable memory. That way you can insert a fresh memory card when your camera is full of pictures. With only internal memory at your disposal, you can't take more pictures with your camera unless you delete a few to free up space or you download your images to the PC—something that can be hard to do if you're shooting snapshots on vacation.

■ **SmartMedia** SmartMedia is a compromise between size and capacity. It's small enough to fit in an adapter that you can insert in a floppy disk drive to transfer images to the PC, yet it can hold up to 64MB of data. An example is shown below. SmartMedia cards are very thin, somewhat flexible, and have exposed contacts on the outside of the card. That makes SmartMedia a bit more easily damaged than other kinds of memory, but its tiny size lets it fit easily in smaller cameras and tiny transfer gadgets like the floppy disk adapter. On the downside, SmartMedia cards come in only a few capacities, and they top out at 64MB. For that reason, you won't often find high-resolution cameras (like 3.3 megapixel or larger) that use SmartMedia cards, because they fill up too quickly.

■ **CompactFlash** The most versatile memory card format on the market, CompactFlash memory is really best for photographers who need to pack a large number of images onto each card. As you can see below, CompactFlash is reasonably small (it's about an eighth of an inch thick), yet it comes in capacities up to 1GB—as much storage space as a computer's hard disk. CompactFlash cards are ideal for high-megapixel cameras and situations in which you can't easily swap out memory cards when the first one is full— underwater photography is an excellent example. Traditional CompactFlash cards come in capacities up to 128MB. To break that barrier, you need to use IBM's Microdrive, which is a tiny hard disk packed into the CompactFlash format. There are two Microdrives available: a 340MB card and 1GB. Not all camera manufacturers certify their cameras to work reliably with the Microdrive, so you should check before investing in one.

■ **Memory Stick**   Originally manufactured exclusively by Sony for Sony products, Memory Sticks are slowly starting to catch on. In fact, Lexar, a popular maker of SmartMedia and CompactFlash memory cards, is now making Memory Sticks as well. Memory Sticks (shown below) resemble a stick of gum and come in a variety of capacities up to 64MB. Sony expects to have 128MB versions of the Memory Stick available next year. The real appeal of Memory Stick–equipped digital cameras is that you can remove the Memory Stick and insert it into any other Sony Memory Stick–enabled device and access the images. Memory Stick products include VAIO laptops, digital picture frames, and the CLIE handheld PC.

■ **Floppy disk**   Many Sony digital cameras use the floppy disk drive as a form of image storage. The advantage: floppy disks are ubiquitous. There are no confusing image transfer procedures, since you just pull the floppy out of the camera and insert it into the PC's floppy disk drive. On the other hand, floppy disks only hold 1.44MB of data— a tiny amount compared to any other storage mechanism. Floppy disks are also fairly slow. Those disadvantages add up to cameras that can't take high-resolution images and suffer a long lag between when the image is taken and when it's written to memory. Serious photographers are well advised to avoid cameras that use a floppy disk drive for storage. And if you're worried that image transfers with other cameras are too complicated, just keep reading.

As I've mentioned, memory devices vary dramatically in size. In Figure 8-1 you can see the relative sizes of the most common memory formats.

It's worth noting that in at least a few cases, you don't have to choose between different memory storage formats anymore. Some camera makers are starting to include both CompactFlash and SmartMedia slots in some of their cameras. Not only does that mean you can pick a camera on features and not worry about whether you like SmartMedia or CompactFlash better, but you can insert two memory cards in the camera at once and switch from one to the other when one card fills up. The Olympus E-10 (seen in Figure 8-2) uses just this system, eliminating the traditional confusion over competing memory card formats.

FIGURE 8-1   Relative sizes of SmartMedia, CompactFlash, and floppy disk storage devices

8

FIGURE 8-2   You can insert a CompactFlash card or a SmartMedia card in the Olympus E-10, or insert both and switch between them for twice as much storage space.

The Mystery of the Fifth Beatle

Everyone, it seems, stakes a claim to being the Fifth Beatle. This is an odd phenomenon that has perplexed me as well as other Beatles scholars for many years. Here's a short list of the most prominent names sometimes awarded the coveted Fifth Beatle moniker:

- Billy Preston, close friend and occasional session musician
- Eric Clapton, close friend, guitar god, and occasional session musician
- George Martin, Beatles producer
- Yoko Ono, wife of John Lennon
- Ravi Shankar, mentor to George Harrison
- Ringo Starr, often acknowledged as the Fourth Beatle
- Stuart Sutcliffe, actual Fifth Beatle in their early pre-EMI days
- Paul Rice, musician and writer widely acknowledged to be too short to be a Beatle

Transferring Images to the PC

No matter what kind of digital camera or removable media you use, eventually you'll need to get your pictures from the camera to a computer (see Figure 8-3). It's there that you'll be able to edit them and print or distribute them. Your digital camera comes with software for transferring

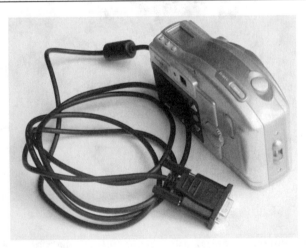

FIGURE 8-3   Transferring images to your PC usually means connecting them with a connection cable of some kind. Your camera probably comes with either a serial or USB cable for this very task.

images and a cable that you can use to connect the camera to your PC. For many users, this in-the-box solution is all they'll ever need. There are two common kinds of transfer cables—serial and USB.

Transferring Images with a Serial Cable

Until recently, most cameras used a serial connection cable to transfer pictures from the camera's memory to the computer. That's because all computers—both PC and Macintosh—have serial ports, and so camera makers were assured that their camera would work with your computer, no matter what kind you have.

On the downside, though, serial connections leave a lot to be desired. Your PC's serial port is slow, meaning that in a worst case, it can take a half hour or more just to copy images from the camera to the computer. The serial port is also kind of stupid; it doesn't know when something is plugged into it, so you have to manually start the software needed to copy images. If you've already got something in the serial port, you might also have to remove that device and disable its software. Most computer manufacturers recommend that you shut off your PC before you insert and remove cables from the serial port, so that also entails a lot of rebooting.

That might sound like a sales pitch to convince you to avoid serial-based digital cameras, and it is. If you're buying a new digital camera, I emphatically recommend looking for a camera that uses USB to transfer images, and I'll talk about that in a separate section shortly.

Connecting Your Camera with Serial

If you have a camera that uses a serial cable, here's a general overview of what you need to do to get images from your camera to the PC:

1. Shut off your PC. Be sure to shut down your PC using the Start | Shut Down menu item in Windows.

8

2. Check the back of your PC. If there's already a serial device (like a modem or Palm cradle) connected, unplug it now. Plug the camera's serial cable into the back of the PC now.

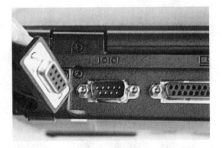

3. Plug the other end of the serial cable into your camera.

4. If your camera has an AC adapter, plug it in now. Serial transfers can be slow and drain a lot of battery life, so avoid transferring images with battery power alone.

5. Start your PC and wait for Windows to appear.

6. Turn on your camera and set it to the data transfer mode, if it has one. If not, you probably want to set it to playback mode. Check your camera manual to be sure.

7. Start the image transfer software that accompanied your camera, and initiate the transfer.

Troubleshooting the Serial Port

If your computer reports that it can't find the camera, there could be any number of problems preventing the PC and camera from communicating. Follow this checklist to help resolve the problem:

■ Is the camera turned on and set to the appropriate transfer mode? The PC won't be able to find the camera unless it is set up properly.

■ Are the batteries fully charged? If you are running on battery power, low batteries can make the camera go into low power mode or act erratically, sabotaging your efforts to connect to the PC. Use fresh batteries or an AC adapter.

■ Is the serial cable plugged into the correct port? Most (but certainly not all) computers have two serial ports, referred to as COM1 and COM2. If your camera isn't found, there may be an autodetection feature in the transfer software that you can use to determine which serial port is connected to the camera. If not, or if the program can't autodetect the camera for some reason, experiment by switching ports or setting the software to use the other COM port. Remember that your camera will need to be turned on and set to its transfer mode for detection to occur.

■ Is software controlling the serial port? This one isn't quite so obvious. Certain kinds of serial devices may use special programs that take total control of the serial port and won't let the camera in even when it's connected. A good example of this is the HotSync cradle for a Palm handheld organizer. If you disconnect the cradle and connect a camera in its place, the HotSync Manager software may still be running, monitoring the port for a signal from the Palm (see Figure 8-4). You'll have to turn off the HotSync Manager from its System Tray icon before the camera will work. Other software can cause the same kind of trouble—in particular, fax and modem software can lock the port and may need to be disabled before your camera will work.

If none of these procedures work, there may be some kind of software conflict on your PC that is preventing your camera from working properly in transfer mode. When all else fails, try reinstalling the camera's software. You might also want to talk to the camera manufacturer's technical support.

Which COM Is Which?

Confused by COM ports? That's not too surprising, especially since they're rarely physically marked on the computer itself to tell you which is which. Nonetheless, if you need to figure out which serial port corresponds to which COM port, you can usually use this little cheat sheet:

This port:	Is usually:
Your computer only has one serial port.	COM1
The small, 9-pin serial port.	COM1
The big 25-pin serial port. (By the way, you may need an adapter, available at any computer store, to use this port.)	COM2
A second port that was installed in the computer's expansion slot.	COM2

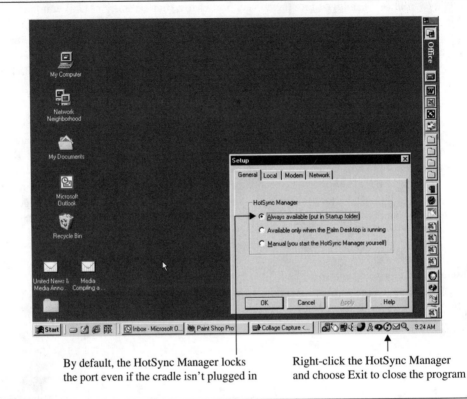

By default, the HotSync Manager locks
the port even if the cradle isn't plugged in

Right-click the HotSync Manager
and choose Exit to close the program

FIGURE 8-4   The HotSync Manager is the bane of many computer users. It locks the serial port, confusing you when your camera fails to work properly.

Transferring Images with a USB Port

USB-enabled cameras are fast becoming a standard for two very good reasons: they avoid most of the headaches associated with serial connections, and they transfer images a lot faster than the old, slow serial ports.

I like USB because it's a lot smarter than serial. Not only is it *hot swappable* (which means you don't need to power off your PC to insert or remove a USB cable), but typically it'll automatically recognize your camera when you connect it and automatically launch the appropriate transfer software.

In addition, USB ports transfer data at up to 12Mbps. That's something like 50 times faster than data transfers with the pokey old serial port. In reality, transfers never reach that theoretical maximum speed, but it's a lot faster than serial nonetheless.

How to ...   **Connect Your Camera with USB**

If you have a USB-enabled camera and PC, the transfer process is a lot easier and less error prone than using a serial port. Here's a general overview of how to do it:

1. Connect the USB cable to your computer's USB port and to the camera. You don't have to turn off your computer to do this, even if you have to disconnect an existing USB device to free up a port.

2. Turn on the camera and set it to its transfer mode. Connect the camera to AC power if you can.

8

3.   The computer should automatically recognize the camera and start the transfer software. Now you can drag the images from the camera to a folder on the computer.

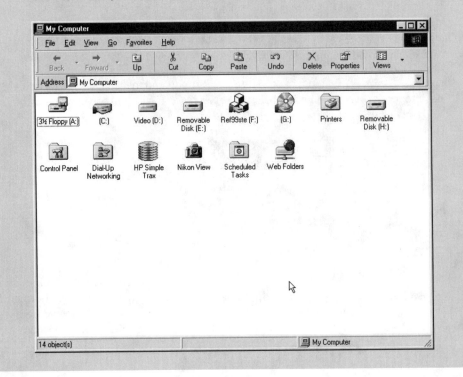

USB Glitches

Though USB is susceptible to fewer problems than serial ports, it has its share of annoyances as well. The main problems? A lack of power and bandwidth, which can hamper USB devices trying to communicate with your PC. Consider these tips:

- **Add more ports**. Most PCs come with only two USB ports. If you have two USB devices connected to your PC, you're already out of ports. Solve that problem by buying a USB hub from the local computer store. A USB port typically turns one USB connection into four, as you can see in Figure 8-5.

- **Power the ports**. While some devices can get power from the USB port itself, many USB devices require more power than the USB port can deliver. That's why it's a good idea to use a *powered hub*—that's a USB hub that you plug into AC power. If your USB devices seem to work erratically or if you get warning messages in Windows, be sure to use a powered hub and keep the hub plugged in.

- **Distribute your bandwidth**. Your PC probably has a pair of USB ports, each of which can transfer up to 12Mbps of data. If you attach a hub to one of those ports, those four

FIGURE 8-5 Belkin's powered USB hub is just one of many devices you can use to connect more gadgets to your computer's limited array of USB ports.

new ports in the hub have to share the original 12Mbps of data. (Each port doesn't get its own independent bandwidth.) If you put four data-hungry devices (like a digital camera, video Webcam, joystick, and speaker set) on the same hub, they can overtax the USB hub and make it perform erratically. So if you have a bunch of USB devices, I suggest that you put a hub on each port and try to move devices around so the most power-hungry ones aren't all connected to the same port.

Memory Card: Fact and Fiction

I've met people with some interesting misconceptions about digital film, so let me try to dispel some myths.

Removable memory cards are nothing more than digital storage for your camera. That means that memory cards aren't designed to store images of a certain size. Some people mistakenly believe that if they want to store images of a larger or smaller pixel size, they need a different memory card. Memory cards are completely standardized and interchangeable, and they don't particularly care what you store on them. In fact, you don't even have to put digital images on them at all. They'll hold sound files, text documents, and more. Your camera won't know what to do with files like that, but you can store anything on a memory card.

There are differences between memory cards, though. The principal difference is speed—cards are rated at 2x (slowest), 4x, or 8x (fastest). The faster ones write data faster and are a good choice if you value speed when taking pictures. They're also good for high-megapixel cameras, since large files take longer to record.

Transfer Shortcuts: Using Memory Adapters

Just because your camera comes with a serial or USB cable, that doesn't mean you have to use it. *Memory adapters* let you easily transfer images to the computer without messing with any cables at all. There are several advantages to using memory adapters:

- You can conserve camera battery power, since the camera isn't used in the transfer.
- You don't have to get to the back of your computer to connect or disconnect cables.
- Transfers may be faster with an adapter, especially if you usually use a serial connection.
- You can usually avoid confusing transfer software, since most adapters let you drag and drop images directly to a folder on your hard disk.

Using a Memory Adapter

The kind of memory adapter you choose depends largely upon the kind of removable memory that your camera uses. In general, they're all more efficient than connecting your camera with a cable.

- **CompactFlash readers**   CompactFlash cards are too thick to fit in a floppy disk drive, so vendors instead make readers for these memory cards that connect to the USB, parallel, or serial ports. CompactFlash readers like the one shown below are available from several companies, including Lexar, SanDisk, and even individual camera manufacturers like Kodak.

- **SmartMedia readers**   The most common way to read the data from a SmartMedia card is by inserting it into a FlashPath adapter (shown below). This device slides into a floppy disk drive and lets you read the images off SmartMedia as if it were a floppy. FlashPath adapters are available from a large number of manufacturers, including SmartDisk and many camera vendors.

- **All-in-one readers**   Just like cameras that are starting to accommodate more than one kind of memory card, readers are becoming more flexible as well. The Lexar Universal Digital Film Reader, for instance, plugs into the parallel or USB port. Slide SmartMedia or CompactFlash memory cards in and read the data as if it were stored on an external hard disk; just drag and drop to move the images to your computer's hard disk.

8

Caring for Your Memory Cards

After you are done transferring images from the memory card to your PC, you no longer need those images. You can delete them to make room for more pictures. There are two ways to do this: you can delete them via the PC, or use the camera's controls to delete images or reformat the card. If your memory card is inserted in the PC via some sort of memory card adapter, using the PC doesn't waste camera battery power, and that's a good reason to do it that way. If you don't have that luxury, it's a good idea to plug the camera into its AC adapter so you don't drain your AA batteries.

To delete images from your memory card via the PC, you can usually just select the files and press the DELETE key on your keyboard; it's just like deleting any kind of file from your PC's floppy or hard disk. A typical interface is shown in Figure 8-6.

```
100olymp                                                              _ □ ×
 File   Edit   View   Go   Favorites   Help
  ←        →        ↑       ✂       📋       📋       ↺       ✕       ☞       ⊞
 Back    Forward    Up      Cut     Copy    Paste    Undo   Delete  Properties  Views
 Address  H:\DCIM\100OLYMP                                                    ▼

  📷       📷       📷       📷       📷       📷       📷       📷
 P2030159  P2030160  P2030161  P2030162  P2030163  P2030164  P2030165  P2030166

  📷       📷       📷       📷       📷       📷       📷       📷
 P2030167  P2030168  P2030169  P2030170  P2030171  P2030172  P2030174  P2030175

  📷       📷       📷       📷       📷       📷       📷       📷
 P2030176  P2030177  P2030178  P2030179  P2030180  P2030181  P2030184  P2030185




                                    ↖



 24 object(s)                      6.09MB                  🖳 My Computer
```

FIGURE 8-6   With your memory card's contents displayed on screen, just select the image or images you want to delete and press the DELETE key on your keyboard.

To delete images using the camera's interface, you'll have to navigate the camera's menu system. Typically, you'll have the option of deleting a single image or all the images on the disk at once. Be careful—this operation cannot be undone.

If you have some very important images on your memory card and don't want them deleted, you can usually use your camera to protect them. Check your camera's menu system for a feature called protect or lock. That way, you can delete all the images on your memory card, and those specially protected images will remain until you explicitly unprotect them.

In addition to deleting images from your memory cards, you should take other precautions to ensure that your cards live a long and fruitful life. After all, memory cards can be expensive. Keep the following tips in mind:

- Avoid putting memory cards in direct sunlight, which can damage them.

- Don't put memory cards in your back pocket or other places where they can get bent or crushed. That's particularly true for SmartMedia cards and floppy disks, which are bendable and can break with moderate amounts of force.

- Keep your cards empty whenever possible. All memory cards look alike, and the last thing you need is to put a memory card in your camera while on vacation only to discover that it's still full of images you never saved to your PC from last time. Transfer images to the PC promptly, and then format or erase the card.

- Never write on memory cards or put any kind of sticker on them to track their contents. That can damage the card or the camera.

8

Chapter 9

Keeping Images on the PC

How to...

- Use the My Pictures folder in Windows 98
- Organize your images in Windows
- Transfer, rename, and categorize your images to reduce clutter
- Use the special My Pictures folder in Windows Me
- Browse images visually with Paint Shop Pro and Image Expert
- Search images by keyword with Image Expert
- Use Quick View to see pictures without opening an image editing program
- Install Quick View from the Windows 98 installation CD
- Estimate file size for TIF and JPG images
- Archive your pictures on CD-ROM
- Install a new hard disk for additional storage

In the previous chapter, we talked about how to get images from your camera or its memory card onto your PC. That's a good start, but if you're anything like me, you need some help getting it all under control. Digital images can be big and hard to organize. After just a few months, in fact, you might discover that your computer's hard disk is essentially full, and the unorganized mess within is largely a ton of poorly named, hard-to-decipher digital images that don't do anyone any good.

In this chapter we'll talk about the essentials of getting your stockpile of digital images under control. There are a lot of things to consider: naming and arranging your images; using special software to better arrange and organize your pictures; understanding the relationship between image size and file size, so you can predict how much space you'll need. And because you might eventually need to add on to your PC's storage capability, we'll talk about how you can archive your images on media like CD-ROMs and additional hard drives.

Managing Your Digital Pictures

Keeping your hard disk organized is essential if you hope to be able to find your digital pictures. In a sense, then, part of this chapter is a tutorial in managing your computer's life.

I know a lot of people who don't worry too much about organizing their hard disk. They just download images from their camera to some folder on their hard disk and assume they can find what they need later. The problem? The images from your camera typically have fairly obscure filenames, like pic00012.jpg or dsc0012.jpg (see Figure 9-1). It's impossible to determine the contents of an image from such an arcane filename. Imagine having hundreds of files like this on your hard disk, and you start to get an inkling of the problem.

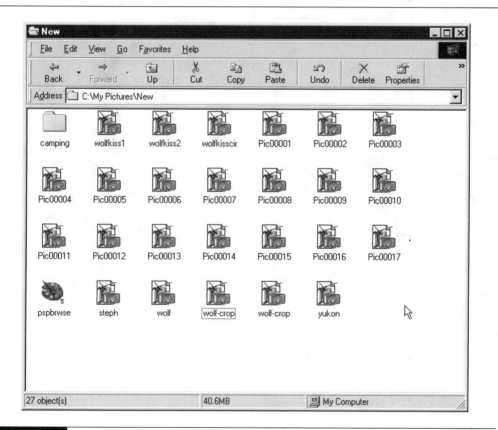

9

FIGURE 9-1   Your digital camera's codelike naming scheme for images is no help when you want to find a specific picture.

Organizing Your Images in Windows 98

Keeping your images organized and easy to find isn't hard, but it takes a little planning. I recommend that you store your images in a single folder or set of folders, instead of spreading them all over your hard disk. Windows 98 and Windows Me users have built-in folders for storing images, and I suggest you use them. In Windows 98, a common place to store your images is in a folder called My Pictures, found in the C: drive.

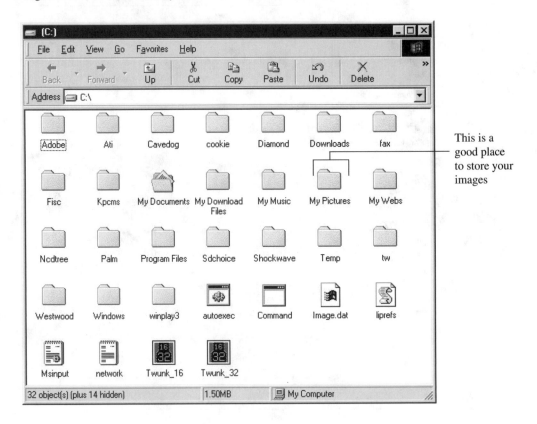

This is a good place to store your images

If the folder doesn't exist, create it yourself. To create a folder to store your images, do this:

1. Double-click the My Computer icon on your Windows desktop. You should see a window that displays all of the devices and drives connected to your PC:

2. Double-click the C: drive. Again, a window should open, revealing all the folders stored in the hard drive.

3. If you don't see a folder called My Pictures, create it. Right-click on an empty space in the C: drive's window. You should see a menu appear.

9

4. Choose New | Folder from the menu. A new, empty folder should appear in the C: drive window.

5. Now it's time to rename the folder. The "New Folder" text under the folder is highlighted, as shown below; just type **My Pictures** and press ENTER. You should see the name of the folder change.

If you click on the desktop before you have a chance to rename the new folder, just right-click on the folder and choose Rename from the menu. Then type the new name of the folder.

If you are using Windows Me, there's a different place to store your images. The folder is still named My Pictures, but it's located inside the My Documents folder. To find it, double-click My Computer, and then double-click the C: drive icon. Next, double-click the My Documents folder, and you should see a folder called My Pictures; it will look like the illustration shown below. We'll discuss that in more detail later in this chapter when we cover Windows Me.

You can store your images anywhere, but I think the My Pictures folder is a great place. It's easy to remember, and many graphics applications will automatically look here for pictures.

Now that you have a main folder for storing your images, you might want to create subfolders, which are folders inside your main folder (like My Pictures) that let you organize your pictures more precisely. As you can see in Figure 9-2, I organize my images into a myriad of folders that help me find specific images by category, event, purpose, and genre.

Renaming Images in Windows 98

Now that you have an organizational system for arranging your images, it's time to think about filenames.

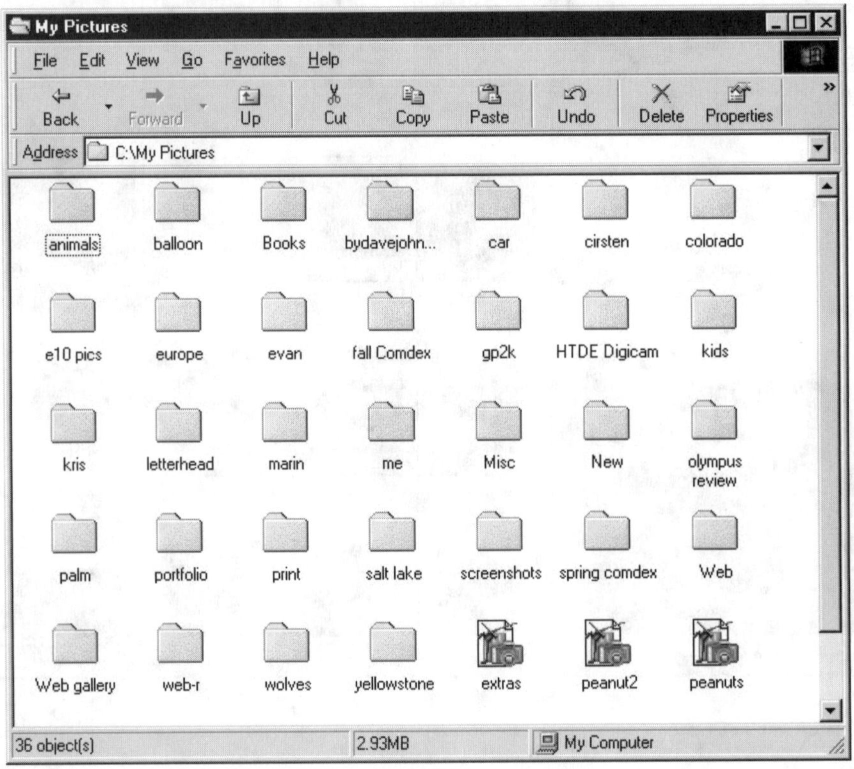

FIGURE 9-2   The more subfolders you use, the easier it should be to find the right image in a pinch.

I suggest that when you transfer your images to the PC, you immediately rename your images and categorize them into specific folders. Don't put this off till later! If you transfer images and opt to rename them later, you'll end up with a few batches of 30 images each that need to be renamed. The task will eventually get too daunting, and you'll have 100 or more pictures with obscure filenames that need to be renamed.

Here's an easy strategy for renaming your images in Windows 98:

1. Open the temporary folder in which your newly transferred images are stored.

2. Right-click the first image in the folder and choose Quick View from the menu.

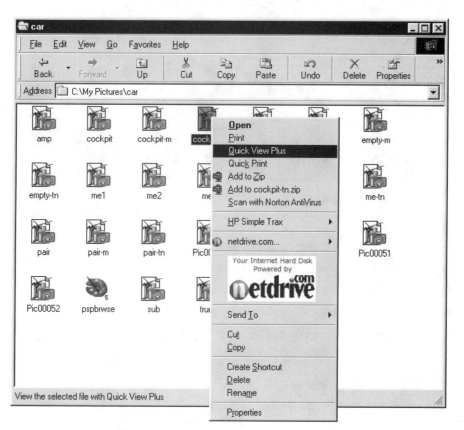

3. The Quick View windows should appear, showing you the image. For example:

4. Close the Quick View window.

5. Right-click on the file and choose Rename from the menu.

6. Type a descriptive filename and press ENTER.

7. Repeat the process with the other images in the folder.

8. When you are done, you can drag images into appropriate subfolders in the My Pictures folder and delete the empty temporary folder.

Working with Quick View

As you can see, I use Quick View to preview images on the PC. It's handy for determining what's in a file when you're ready to rename it, and it's also handy for getting a quick look at pictures in general. But what is Quick View?

Quick View is simply a program in Windows 95 and 98 that lets you see the contents of certain kinds of files just by right-clicking on their icon and selecting Quick View from the menu, as you can see in Figure 9-3. It's a lot easier—and faster—than opening a special graphics program. I recommend that all Windows 95/98 users rely on Quick View for taking a look at pictures on the desktop.

If you don't have Quick View in your menu when you right-click on an image, it isn't installed. But fear not—Quick View is a utility that's included on the Windows installation disk.

FIGURE 9-3   Quick View is a handy tool for displaying images on the desktop without opening a large, slow graphics program.

Quick View is not included in Windows Me for reasons we'll talk about shortly. So don't panic if you look for Quick View and can't find it.

Here's how to install Quick View on Windows 95/98:

1. Choose Start | Settings | Control Panel from the Windows Start menu. You should see the Control Panel window appear:

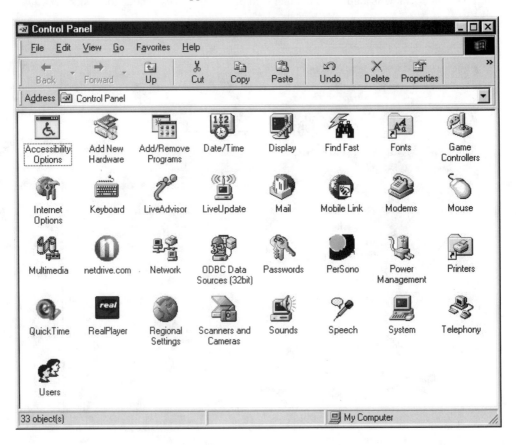

2. Double-click the Add/Remove Programs icon.

3. Click on the Windows Setup tab. This contains a list of all optional software on the Windows installation disk.

4. Click on the entry for Accessories and click the Details button. You should see the Accessories dialog box appear. This contains a list of all the accessory programs in Windows.

5. Scroll down until you find Quick View and click on it, putting a check mark next to the entry. Then click OK.

6. Click OK again, this time in the Add/Remove Programs dialog box. Windows
    may prompt you for the Windows installation CD. If it doesn't, insert it in your
    CD-ROM drive.

After the installation, you should have the Quick View entry in the context menu when you
right-click on icons on the Windows desktop.

> *Quick View is a great program for viewing certain images, but Microsoft endowed it
> with the ability to preview a very limited number of file types. If you want to get more
> out of Quick View, including the ability to see almost any kind of graphic image file
> using the Quick View menu item, you might want to purchase Quick View Plus, from
> Jasc (www.jasc.com). Quick View Plus greatly enhances the capabilities of Quick View.*

Locating and Cataloging Images in Windows 98

Even with a rigorous set of subfolders, it can get difficult to find specific images on your hard
disk. My hard disk contains a few hundred images, for instance, and even with descriptive
filenames and lots of aptly titled subfolders, it can be a challenge to locate one specific file. It's
akin to finding a needle in a stack of other needles. Even though I usually use Quick View, which
gives me the ability to see what each needle looks like, I can only view one image at a time.

Filenames and folders are great, but there's no substitute for actually looking at your images.
That's why I'm going to show you how you can catalog your images with a visual tool—software
that lets you view your pictures directly, all at once, and open the one you need without delay.

View Your Images with Paint Shop Pro

One of the best image editors around is called Paint Shop Pro, from Jasc (www.jasc.com). If you're
not already using Paint Shop Pro, you can try an older version of the program by downloading a free
trial at the Jasc Web site. It has about 75% of the features found in a heavyweight image editor like
Adobe PhotoShop, at a much lower price and a much easier learning curve.

One great reason to use the program is its Browse tool, seen in Figure 9-4. Browse lets you
see the images on your hard disk graphically, with each image represented by a thumbnail. That
means you can use Browse two ways:

■ You want to edit or print an image, so you use the Browse tool to find the image you
    want visually.

■ You just want to review your images, so you use the Browse tool to see your image
    thumbnails.

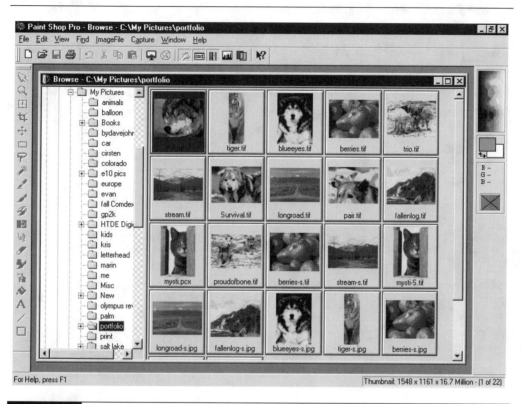

FIGURE 9-4   Paint Shop Pro lets you browse your hard disk visually.

Here is how to use Paint Shop Pro's Browse tool:

1. Start Paint Shop Pro.

2. Choose File | Browse from the menu bar (shown below). The Browse window should appear.

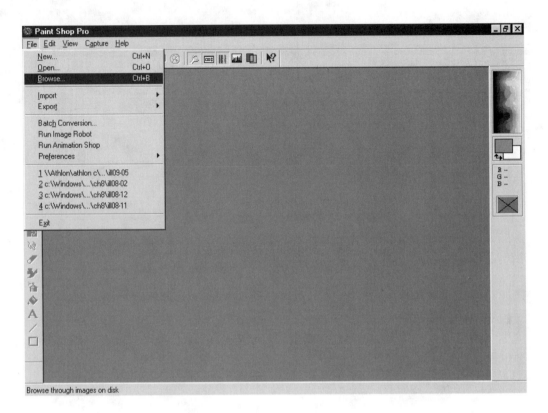

3. Use the folder tree on the left side of the window to find the folder you want to look in. When you click the folder, thumbnail images will appear on the right. To find C:\My Pictures (a common directory to store images), for instance, you would click on the plus sign next to My Computer to expand that folder. Then expand C:, and click on My Pictures, which should be listed under C:, as shown here:

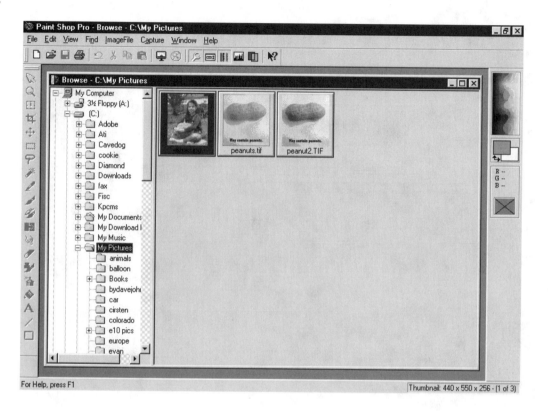

4. To open an image in Paint Shop Pro, just double-click on a thumbnail. The image will open, ready for editing, printing, or just viewing at a larger size.

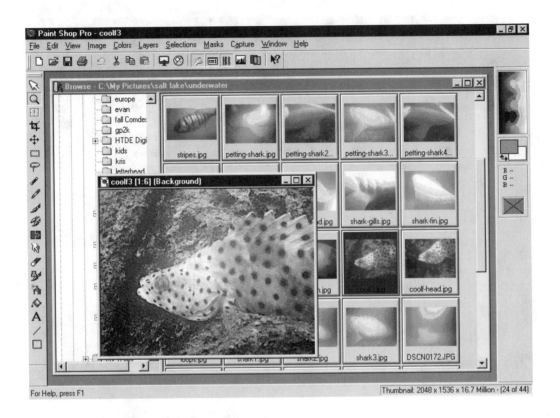

5. You can continue opening additional images from the Browse window. Close the
Browse window when you are done with it.

The first time you browse within a folder, the browse display may update slowly. When you
return to that folder later, though, the display will update significantly faster, since Paint Shop
Pro saves a small catalog file in that folder that helps it display the images more quickly. If you
add or delete images in that folder later, Paint Shop Pro always updates the catalog file so it
displays the most up-to-date thumbnails.

View Your Images with Image Expert

Another great program you might want to invest in is called Image Expert, from Sierra Imaging
(www.sierraimaging.com). This program is not so much an image editing program (though it
does include some of those tools), but instead it is designed principally as a cataloging and
management tool for your digital pictures. Actually, Sierra might disagree with me—they may

think it's an editing program—but as a catalog tool, I think Image Expert, which you can see in Figure 9-5, is without equal.

At first glance, Image Expert looks like Paint Shop Pro's Browse mode. But it can do a lot more than Paint Shop Pro. Specifically, you can search your hard disk for images by name or description as well. If you attach certain keywords to your images, you can use those to track down pictures rapidly.

Notice in Figure 9-5, which is in Browse mode, that there are three main elements in the Image Expert display. You can navigate the directory tree in exactly the same way as Paint Shop Pro to find a specific folder. The folder contents are displayed in thumbnail mode on the right

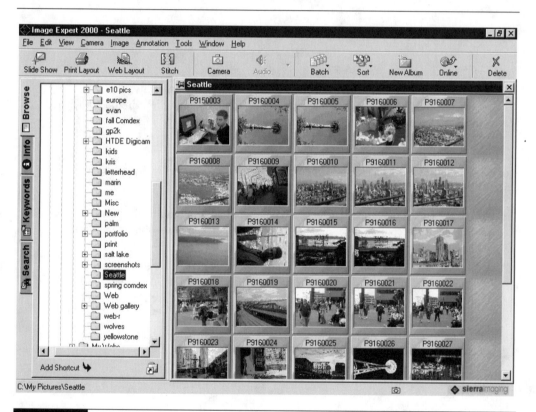

FIGURE 9-5   Image Expert is a good alternative to Paint Shop Pro for reviewing and cataloging your digital pictures.

What's a Keyword?

Keywords are terms that you can use to identify the contents of an image. Suppose you have this picture, for instance:

May contain peanuts.

You might save the following keywords with this image: peanut, funny, macro.

When you search for pictures that have the word "funny" in their description, this image should appear in the list.

side of the screen. But the screen also includes a set of tabs, labeled vertically on the left side of the display. Here's what they do:

- ■ **Browse**   This is the mode in which you can see images in thumbnail form. To see a picture in more detail, double-click its thumbnail. You can also zoom in or out of the picture using the Zoom tool.

- ■ **Info**   The Info tab is where you can assign keywords to the image description. First double-click a thumbnail so an image is displayed on the right side of the screen. Then click the Info tab and enter any descriptive words you want in the Description box. The text is saved automatically.

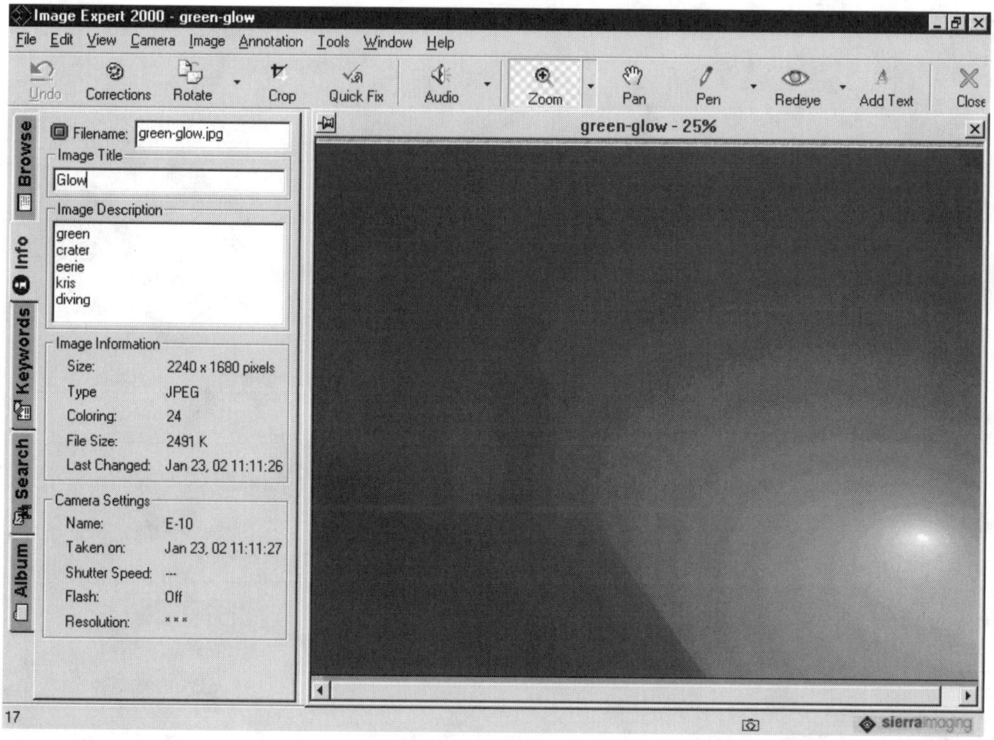

- **Keywords**   This tab lets you search by criteria like the photographer's name or subject.
- **Search**   Click this tab to look for the keywords you entered in the description field of images. Enter a search word and press ENTER. Any images that match your criteria will appear on the right side of the screen. You can double-click them to open the images just like you did in Browse mode.

Search results

Organizing Your Images in Windows Me

If you use Windows Me, you're something of a special case. Congratulations.

Actually, you can use the techniques I talked about for Windows 98, but Microsoft has added a powerful new weapon to your arsenal in Windows Me that makes a lot of that stuff somewhat irrelevant. The addition? Smart folders that display thumbnail images of your digital pictures.

Check out Figure 9-6. Here you can see the My Pictures folder. Each of the images displays a thumbnail in place of the file icon, and if you select an image by clicking it, another image preview appears on the left side of the folder. Using this handy visual tool, you can avoid spending money on extra programs like Image Expert, unless you want the extra features that programs like that provide.

As you can see in Figure 9-6, the left side of the My Pictures folder has a few special tricks of its own. When an image is selected and it is previewed in this location, you can rotate, zoom, and print the picture using the icons.

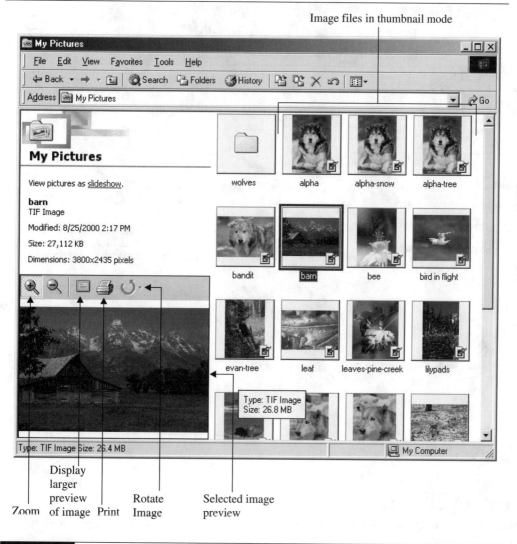

FIGURE 9-6   Windows Me has a thumbnail viewer built into the operating system.

Note that this cool preview feature only works in the My Pictures folder or one of its subfolders. If you store images in other folders on your hard disk, you won't see a folder window like the one in Figure 9-6. Instead, it will look more like the following image.

Estimating File Size

So, you save a lot of images on your hard disk. How many can you pack in before you need more storage space?

That isn't necessarily an easy question to answer. That's because the most common file formats, like JPG, don't always save an image to the same file size. The size that any particular image takes up on your hard disk will vary depending upon how much color information is stored in the image. A single-color image, such as a graphic that's plain, solid blue, will compress dramatically to a miniscule size, while a complex image with thousands or millions of colors will not compress as efficiently. Nonetheless, we can make some ballpark estimates that will help you keep track of storage space if you want to.

Calculating TIFs

Let's start with the easy file formats. There are file formats out there that are considered lossless. (Recall from Chapter 7, that means no matter how many times you open and resave the file, no loss of data will ever occur.) That's because the image isn't really being compressed. Every pixel is preserved forever. The most common lossless file formats are BMP and TIF files. To figure out how much space either of these files will take up, just use this equation:

File size in bytes = x-dimension × y-dimension × 24 / 8

In other words, take the pixel dimensions of your image and multiply them. Multiply that by 24 (because there are 24 bits of color information associated with every pixel in the image), and then divide the result by 8, because we want the answer in bytes, not bits. Divide that answer by 1000 to get the answer in the more popular kilobytes.

Here's an example. Suppose you want to know how much space two dozen images will take up that were shot with your digital camera on its lowest resolution setting (which is 640x480). The camera saves its images in the lossless TIF format. The math would be

$640 \times 480 \times 24 / 8 = 921{,}600$ bytes

Divide that by 1000, and you get 921KB.

Multiply that single image result by 24 (the number of images you plan to shoot), and you get a total storage size of 22,118KB, or 22MB. That's a lot of space.

Calculating JPGs

That's all well and good, but most of the time digital cameras shoot in the lossy file format known as JPG. JPG files can be adjusted to compress more aggressively—that makes the files smaller but the quality lower—or compress less for bigger, higher-quality files.

There's no easy equation you can use on JPGs, since the compression varies not only according to the image quality setting you use on your camera, but also according to the amount of color information and overall complexity of the picture. Nonetheless, I'll take a stab at it. In general, you can assume that JPG files will be about this size, depending upon the quality setting:

JPG Quality	Compression
High (low compression)	Approximately 95% of the original TIF size
Medium	Approximately 75% to 85% of the original TIF size
Low (high compression)	Approximately 25% of the original TIF size

These are ballpark figures, but you would be able to store about 440 average JPGs in the same hard disk space that it would take to store full-resolution TIF files of the same pixel dimensions.

What does this say about how you should store your images? In general, high-quality JPGs are good enough for most applications, and they take up a mere fraction of the space TIFs or BMP files would consume. When you can, use the JPG format, and your hard disk will thank you. Be careful about using too much JPG compression, though. I recommend sticking with a fairly low compression level, or your image quality will suffer.

Archiving Images

Eventually, your collection of digital images may grow too large for your hard disk. If that's the case, you have a few choices:

- Delete nonessential images from your hard disk.
- Archive the images on another storage device, like CD-ROM.
- Add another hard disk for additional storage space.

Deleting images is the easiest route, but it has the least potential. You probably want to save many of your images forever, so there may not be that many images to get rid of. Instead, consider archiving your images to another device. If you have a CD-RW drive, you can copy dozens or hundreds of images to a CD (depending upon the file size) that will last more or less forever. CDs do degrade over time, but they will last for a hundred years or so—longer than the ink on many kinds of photographs.

A CD-RW drive is a kind of CD-ROM drive that can write to blank discs. Most CD-RW drives come with software like Adaptec's Easy CD Creator, seen in Figure 9-7. This software lets you simply drag and drop image files from the hard disk to the CD and then "burn" the disk, a process that takes a few minutes to copy all the data to the CD. After it's done, the CD is playable in any computer with a CD-ROM drive.

When you archive your images, be sure to use CD-R discs, not CD-RW discs. The two media are quite different, and CD-RWs are generally not readable on other PCs. In addition, data copied to CD-RW discs can be deleted, so it's possible to accidentally overwrite your images later on. To be safe, always use CD-R media.

Pixel Potential

If you photograph a plain white background, in JPG format it'll take up almost no space at all on your memory card or computer hard disk. That's because the JPG format stores information about the change in color information from one pixel to another, and if the image is all white, there's very little change data to record. But what about a TIF? The same picture stored as a TIF will be much larger, because the file holds a space for all 24 bits of color data in each pixel. The TIF format isn't concerned about the colors that are actually in the image; instead, it is preoccupied with the potential colors that could be in the image. Even though every pixel is white, the TIF format has enough room to store any color in each and every pixel.

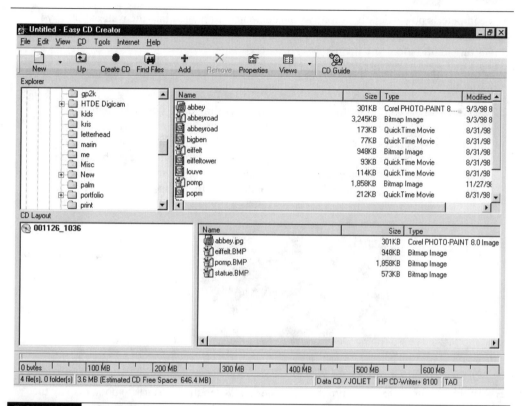

CD-RW software makes it easy to copy images to a blank CD.

Adding Extra Hard Drives

One other option you might consider is adding another hard disk. Hard drives get cheaper and bigger every year, and these days 20GB and 40GB drives are not unusual, nor are they overly expensive. Some people install a second drive and dedicate it for images, video, music, and other multimedia files.

To see if your PC is a good candidate for a second hard disk, shut it down and open it up. Many computers have tool-free cases that you can open easily; other PCs require a small screwdriver to remove the side of the case. In either case, once the PC is open, check to see if there's a spare bay to mount the hard disk. You can mount it in one of the drive bays or perhaps on the bottom or side of the case, where there are some mounts for exactly that purpose. If there's somewhere to put a hard disk, it's easy to install yourself. Once you've found somewhere to put the drive, follow these basic steps:

1. Ensure the PC is off and you are fully grounded before proceeding. You can purchase a static grounding mat or a strap that attaches to your wrist at any local computer shop. Alternately, you can ground yourself by touching the metal cage surrounding the computer's power supply as long as the computer is plugged into the wall outlet. If you leave the computer plugged in for grounding purposes, be absolutely sure the computer is turned off before you open it up and start working.

2. Remove the new hard disk from its packaging and review the instructions that came with it.

3. Set the hard disk's jumper to master or slave depending upon how you are installing it. Essentially, if the drive will share the same IDE ribbon cable as the original hard disk (there are two places to plug hard disks into each IDE cable), then follow the hard disk's directions to set it as a slave drive. If you plan to install the hard disk with its own IDE cable into the PC's alternate IDE port, then configure the drive as a master. The hard drive installation guide will tell you how to configure the jumper.

Change master/slave setting by moving jumper

4. Mount the drive in the PC. Connect the power cable and IDE cable to the hard disk.

5. Without closing the case, turn the computer on. When the PC starts to boot, display the BIOS screen (usually by pressing the DELETE or F1 key as your computer starts to boot) and check to see that the computer recognizes the hard disk. If it doesn't, make sure you have set the master/slave jumper properly, it's connected to the correct IDE channel, and the power cord is fully inserted in the hard disk.

6. If all is well, shut down the PC and seal the case.

7. Finally, use the software that came with your hard disk to format the drive and prepare it for operation in Windows.

As you can see, it's not difficult to install a hard disk on your own. For more details, check out another book of mine, *Upgrading and Repairing Your PC Answers*.

Chapter 10

Turning Prints into Digital Images

How to...

- Understand how a scanner functions
- Distinguish among different styles of scanners, like flatbeds and photo scanners
- Choose scanner resolution
- Shop for a scanner
- Operate a typical scanner
- Increase image sharpness
- Avoid moiré patterns
- Correct for uneven scan brightness
- Decide whether to use print or slide film

Most of this book is about how to take pictures with a digital camera, get those images on the PC, and edit, manipulate, share, and print them. But it would be a mistake to assume that everyone uses newfangled digital cameras all the time. A majority of photographers—both professional and casual—still use good-old 35mm cameras, and 35mm chemical film still sells like hotcakes in every grocery store around the world. Even if you already own a digital camera, odds are good that you still use a traditional film camera sometimes.

So, you might be wondering: how can I take my slides or negatives and get them onto my PC? That's a great question, because you probably have shoeboxes full of pictures that date back years and years, and it would be wonderful to turn them into digital images.

In this chapter, we'll look at bridging the gap between film and digital photography. I'll talk about scanners and how to get the best results from your analog images in the new world of digital. So if you have slides or negatives and want to get them into your PC, take a look at this chapter. If you're already 100% digital and don't need any scanner advice, feel free to move along to Part III of this book. See you there.

Understanding Scanners

A scanner is a device that, like a photocopier, takes a snapshot of whatever document you lay on the platen (also called a scanning bed). A scanner doesn't just make a copy and print that document, though—it converts the data into bits and bytes and stores it on your PC in a digital image file, just as if it came from a digital camera.

In fact, a scanner is kind of like a digital camera that needs a stationary object to work properly. Instead of a digital camera's rectangular, gridlike CCD that captures an entire image at once (as I explained back in Chapter 1), a scanner uses a CCD with a single row of light-sensitive pixels. This linear CCD registers the light value of the image one "line" or "row" at a time, and that information is sent to the computer immediately and is flushed so that the next line can be read.

The resolution of the scanner is partially dependent on the speed and accuracy of the motor that steps the CCD past the document, or the document past the CCD, depending upon the kind of scanner you have.

There are actually several different kinds of scanners around. You're probably already familiar with the most common kind of scanner, the flatbed. It's a good all-around scanner for most kinds of scanning jobs, but it isn't necessarily the best choice for photo scanning. Here's an overview of the kinds of scanners that are around:

- **Flatbed scanner**   A flatbed is typically a long, narrow tray (usually either 8.5x11 inches or 8.5x14 inches) on which you place your document. An example is shown in the following illustration. The scanning head travels the length of the bed to create a digital image of the document. Different flatbed models connect to your PC in different ways; some use the parallel port, others use a SCSI adapter, and still others rely on USB. Flatbeds generally make high-quality images and accept options like automatic sheet feeders; so you can copy lots of pages at once. They can also scan almost any size document, from tiny business cards and 35mm slides all the way up to legal-sized documents. On the downside, they have a big "footprint," so they're hard to integrate into a small office. The major limitation of flatbeds, at least as far as photographers are concerned, is that they can't scan with sufficiently high resolution to make good enlargements of slides and negatives.

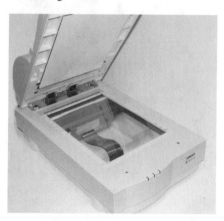

10

- **Sheetfed scanner**   This is a much smaller scanner that does away with the traditional moving optics and flat scanning bed. Instead, sheetfeds stand upright and pull documents through the unit—right past the stationary scanning head—to offer a compact scanning solution. Their advantages include a low price and a compact footprint and a design that's optimized for scanning sheets of paper and small snapshot photos. Of course, you can't scan thick objects like books or magazines unless you first separate the pages from the source. And some low-grade sheetfed scanners can introduce imperfections in the scan due to the imprecise motor that pulls the page through. While this kind of scanner may be fine for text documents, I highly recommend you avoid it for photographic work.

■ **Photo scanners**   Photo scanners are designed to scan just pictures—usually 3x5-inch or 4x6-inch pictures, though some also can handle prints as large as 5x7 inches. If all you need is the ability to convert 35mm prints into digital images, this is a decent solution. Some photo scanners even fit in an empty drive bay of your PC, taking up no room at all. You insert the print in this kind of internal scanner much as if you were inserting a floppy disk in your PC. On the other hand, these scanners are completely useless for scanning anything except small pictures.

■ **Film scanners**   Here is the choice of serious photographers. Film scanners (pictured below) vary dramatically in price—anywhere from about $500 at the low end to several thousand dollars at the high end—but they can give you outstanding results. Film scanners are designed to accommodate slides and negatives and can usually scan at a very high resolution—as much as 3000dpi—which gives you rich, detailed digital images that you can print at full enlargement sizes.

Choosing Resolution

Scanners come in a vast array of resolutions, from a paltry 300dpi all the way up to about 3000dpi. Which resolution do you need? If your printer is a mere 200dpi device—as are most inkjets—why would you ever need to scan a file at a resolution beyond 200dpi? In general, there are several principal reasons to choose a scanner with a higher resolution:

■ High-resolution scanners typically discern greater detail in the images they scan, particularly in the lightest and darkest portions of the image, whereas lower-resolution scanners can't take enough samples to resolve the image properly.

■ Higher-resolution scanners let you scan small images and print them larger than actual size. For instance, you can scan a small picture or a negative and then print it larger than its original dimensions.

■ You can scan an image at high resolution and then crop it. The result can still have enough information to enlarge, though if you scanned it at 200dpi initially, you would have to print the entire image without cropping, or risk seeing pixels in the final image.

Why go with lower-resolution scanners? That's easy—they're less expensive. Not everyone needs 2400dpi, or even 600dpi. If your main goal is to scan images for Web pages, for instance, a 300dpi scanner may be as much as you need.

Shopping for a Scanner

So you want to convert your slides or prints into digital files and need to purchase a scanner. There are a lot of features you can look for, but the most important things to consider when scanner shopping are the scanner's fundamental specifications. In a nutshell, you should consider resolution and color depth. Remember these rules of thumb:

■ **Resolution**   Scanners are rated by the resolution at which they can convert documents into digital images. Inexpensive scanners are typically 300dpi. Often, you'll see a rating like 300x600dpi. The first number is the optical resolution of the imaging system; the second number is the resolution of the motor that moves the scanning head across the document. Since the optical resolution is always lower than the number of discrete steps the motor can perform, the first number—the actual resolution of the optics—is more important. You should use that number to compare scanners when you shop.

10

Hewlett Packard, a major scanner manufacturer, typically doesn't publish the "Y" resolution—that is, the motor's stepping accuracy—of any of their scanners.

■ **Color depth**   Most inexpensive scanners are 24-bit scanners, meaning they can digitize as many as 16.7 million colors, which also happens to be about as many colors as the human eye can see. More sophisticated scanners work at 30 or 36 bits per pixel, meaning they can distinguish among billions of colors. Those scanners with more than 24-bit accuracy have more colors to choose from when resolving dark regions and images with lots of rapid color changes. This adds up to a high-quality image. If you are serious about scanning your photos, keep an eye on color depth and choose your scanner accordingly. If you're scanning snapshots or posting images on a Web site, color depth isn't as important to you.

You might also want to consider other features, like convenience tools. Most scanners are fairly dumb; you need to activate them by choosing Acquire from the menu of your image editing program. Some scanners, though, place a button right on the front of the scanner, like the one in Figure 10-1. If you press it, the document in the scanner is automatically imaged for you.

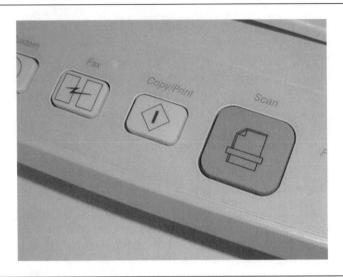

FIGURE 10-1   A scanner button, like the one on the front of this Visioneer One Touch flatbed, turns the scanner into a push-button appliance instead of a complicated peripheral.

Some scanners even go this one better: they start the scanning software as soon as you open the cover to set a new document, or feature multiple buttons on the front for automatic faxing, copying, printing, and emailing.

Are these features essential? Not in a million years. But they do make your scanner just a little bit easier to use.

Finally, you should also consider the scanner's interface. As I mentioned earlier, scanners come in all shapes and sizes, and while many connect with the USB port, a lot connect with parallel or SCSI too. Which is best? USB is the easiest, and parallel can be slow and might conflict with your printer. SCSI is the traditional interface for high-end scanners, and it is generally the fastest. SCSI can be a challenge to install, though. You'll need to open your PC and insert an expansion card in an available PCI slot, and SCSI software is finicky on some computers. Weigh all these issues before selecting a scanner.

Almost all scanners that use a parallel port also include a "pass-through" port so you can use your printer at the same time. There are occasionally compatibility problems with certain combinations of PCs, scanners, and printers, but this system generally works without a snag.

Scanning and Correcting Your Images

Scanning is generally a straightforward process. Typically, you'll just need to access the scanner software from an image editing program like Paint Shop Pro or Adobe PhotoShop, set the scanner to preview, and then scan the photo in the scanner. Figure 10-2 shows a typical scanner program.

Determining the Right Resolution

What resolution should you use to scan your image? Your scanner is probably capable of capturing images at a wide variety of resolutions—perhaps from under 100dpi all the way up to 3000dpi or so, depending upon what kind of scanner you own. Which one should you pick?

In general, it's a trade-off between file size and image quality. On the one hand, you might want to scan everything at the scanner's maximum resolution so you're prepared for anything, but that has practical limitations. The files will be huge, and that adds up to a lot of wasted disk space. In addition, large files slow down your PC, sometimes dramatically so.

FIGURE 10-2   The Minolta Dimage software is typical of the software used by many scanners.

How to ... Scan an Image with a Typical Scanner

1. Start the scanner software. In Paint Shop Pro, choose File | Import | TWAIN | Acquire from the menu, as shown below. The scanner software should appear.

2. Make sure the photo is properly positioned in the scanner, and then click the Preview button. After a few seconds, you should see the image on screen. It has been quickly scanned in low resolution so you can adjust the image before the final scan.

3. Crop the image if you don't want to scan the photo in its entirety.

4. Adjust colors and brightness if necessary. In this scanner program, there's an auto-adjust tool, or you can tweak various color and brightness settings by hand.

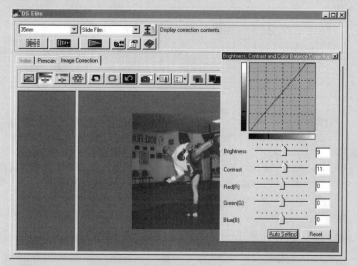

5. Adjust the scan resolution. Scan the image at a resolution high enough for your final application (such as printing or Web publishing), but don't overscan the image. You'll just waste disk space and slow down the overall process.

6. When you're happy with the result, press the final scan button.

After the software is finished scanning the image, it'll either save it to your hard disk under a filename you specified, or open it for editing in an image program.

The solution is to attempt to match the scanned resolution to the resolution of the required final output. So a newsletter that will be printed on a 300dpi printer, for instance, should incorporate images scanned at 300dpi. Use this table as a guideline for choosing the appropriate resolution:

Document	Scan Resolution
Fax documents	200dpi line art or grayscale
Pictures for Web pages	75dpi
Color or grayscale images for print	The easy answer is to scan at the resolution of the intended output, so a 300dpi printer would require scans at 300dpi as well. Images for inkjets should be scanned at about 200 or 250dpi.
	A more accurate method of printing to laser printers, however, is to look up the line screen frequency (LSF) and scan at twice that value. If you have a 300dpi printer, the LSF is probably about 70.
Line art for print	Scan at the printer's resolution (frequently, 300dpi)

But there are yet other wrinkles. Suppose you scan an image but intend to print it larger than the original. For instance, suppose you have a 3 × 5-inch picture that you want to print at 4.5 × 7.5 inches in a newsletter. You need to scan it at a higher resolution in order to keep enough information to make a high-quality print. Otherwise, enlarging the scanned image results in a low-res, jaggy image. Use this formula for figuring out what resolution to scan:

Scanner resolution = final dpi × (intended image width / original image width)

So, let's say we wanted to print the 3 × 5-inch picture enlarged to 4.5 × 7.5 inches at 300dpi. The resolution would be

300 × 4.5 / 3 = 450dpi

You would set the scanner's control panel to 450dpi before scanning the image.

Likewise, suppose you want to crop a scanned image and only include a smaller detail of it in the finished product. If you end up choosing to enlarge the detail, you need to consider the dimensions of the cropped image at the outset, not the size of the entire image, and increase the scan resolution accordingly.

Calculating Scanned Image Size

How much space will your scanned image take up on your hard disk? Some scanning software will tell you before you commit to the scan, others won't. If you are short on disk space, or you want to know if a few scanned images will fit on a Zip disk or CD-ROM, you can use this equation to determine how big your scanned images will be

File size = (resolution × horizontal size) × (resolution × vertical size) × scan mode

where size is measured in inches, and scan mode refers to the color depth you used in the scan:

Color Depth	Scan Mode
Line art	1/8
Grayscale	1
Color	3

Using this equation, you can see that scanning a full-color 5x7 image at 300dpi is about 9MB, but scanning that same image at 600dpi is over 36MB. If you're trying to carry images on a 100MB Zip disk, this formula comes in handy.

Tweaking Your Images

Today's scanners usually do a good job of reproducing photographs. Of course, you get what you pay for: a $1000 scanner will create dramatically better images than a $100 scanner, almost without exception. But there are things you can do to improve your images.

Sharpen a Soft Image

Some photographs are a tad soft to begin with. Others lose their edge in the scanning process because the scanner's focus isn't razor sharp. (Again, this is often an issue with the scanner's quality.)

Sharpening is a process that your scanner software can use to increase the apparent sharpness of an image, as you can see in Figure 10-3. Sharpening filters typically increase the contrast along edges in the image, making the image seem sharper than it actually is. Some sharpening filters leave most of the image alone, only mucking with edges. Some sharpening filters increase the contrast of the entire image instead.

These days, the most popular sharpening filter is called Unsharp Mask, and it's typically built into scanning software as well as image editing programs like Paint Shop Pro and Adobe PhotoShop. Do you need to use sharpening? Not always. Here's a guide to when to use this feature:

- Images with lots of edges and detail benefit more from sharpening than images that lack detail. Close-up pictures of people, for instance, are less likely to benefit from sharpening than a real estate profile of a house.

- High-resolution images benefit more from sharpening than low-resolution images since there's more detail for the sharpening filter to work with.

10

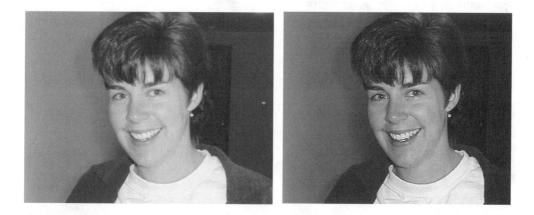

FIGURE 10-3   The image on the right has had a sharpening filter applied to increase the apparent sharpness.

■   Sharpening is more advantageous in printed images than in screen-based images.

■   If in doubt, scan the image both ways and use the one that looks best. Too much
    sharpening can actually ruin an otherwise good image.

*You might want to disable sharpening in the scanning software and sharpen in an
image editing program instead. That way you'll have more control over the process,
and you can readily compare the before and after.*

Eliminate Moiré

You may encounter a problem scanning certain pictures: photos that have already been through
the scanning process once before, such as newspaper and magazine images, may suffer from
something called a moiré pattern. A moiré pattern is caused by the interference of your scanner's
screening overlaid on top of the original screening pattern, as the example in Figure 10-4 shows.

To avoid this ugly moiré pattern, you can use the descreening tool found in most scanners' control
software. Descreening adds time to the overall scan, but it's necessary with these kinds of images.

Correct for Uneven Brightness

Some scanners have a lot of trouble evenly lighting the entire platen, and that sometimes creates
images that are brighter in the center than at the edges. This problem seems to be getting worse,
in fact, as some really cheap scanners hit the market. Usually, this isn't apparent, but it might be
obvious with some photographs.

There are generally only two ways to avoid this problem. You can upgrade to a higher-
quality scanner, or arrange your documents in the center of the scanner and avoid the edges. The
disadvantage to this method is that it can sometimes be more difficult to ensure the document is
placed squarely on the tray without using the edges.

FIGURE 10-4   The moiré pattern is caused by scanning not an original photo, but one that was
originally in a magazine or newspaper.

Eliminate Scanner Aberrations

As with any optical system, you may need to clean the glass scanning bed occasionally; otherwise, it'll get dirty and show up as smudges, streaks, spots, and lines in the scanned images. Use a damp cloth and wipe the surface of your scanner bed, but don't spray water or cleaning solutions directly on the glass. (They can leak into the mechanism through the edges of the glass.)

Surprisingly, dust can accumulate on the underside of the glass (inside the mechanism) after months or years of use. You may be able to remove the glass to clean it, but beware—that can void the manufacturer's warranty, so check first.

Slides, Negatives, or Prints?

As most photographers will tell you, you'll get best results from your scanner if you start with slides. That's because the slide format is, at its core, the most accurate representation of what you *tried* to photograph to begin with. Negatives and prints have been tweaked by the photo shop, and they may not reflect what you intended to shoot. Given a choice, I recommend that you shoot on 35mm slides and scan those.

Slides have disadvantages, though. Most importantly, they have a fairly narrow exposure range and are less forgiving when used improperly. So a photo that might look just fine when over- or underexposed on print film might look terrible on slide film.

10

Part III Editing Images

Chapter 11

Quick Changes for Your Images

How to…

- Determine what the system requirements are to edit images on a PC
- Choose an image processing program
- Open and edit images in Paint Shop Pro
- Change the resolution of digital images for email, Web, and other applications
- Change the number of colors that can be displayed in an image
- Save an image in a different file format
- Crop images to improve composition
- Crop and copy an image into a new file
- Create an irregular crop
- Rotate images taken with the camera on its side
- Fix a crooked image
- Change the brightness in an image
- Correct the color balance in a picture

One of the most exciting advantages of using a digital camera is the flexibility and control it gives you for tweaking and improving your images. Don't like your composition? Change it. You can crop your pictures just a little to subtly improve their appearance, or radically change the look of a picture by turning its orientation from landscape to portrait. You can fix a crooked horizon, resize an image for email, tweak the colors or brightness of an image—it's all up to you.

These are things that until recently you needed a darkroom and a whole lot of practice to do right, and every attempt would cost you money in photo paper and chemicals. These days, you can experiment endlessly. It never costs you a penny until you're ready to print the final result, because it's all done with pixels on a computer screen. As long as you're careful not to save over the original file, you never have to damage or change the original image, either.

In this chapter, we'll get started with image editing. This is the place to turn to for the most common kinds of corrections—simple things you can do to your images without learning a whole lot about the art and science of image editing. For more sophisticated things you can do to edit your images, check out Chapters 12, 13, and 14, which get into the topic a little deeper.

How Much PC You Need

You're probably expecting me to tell you that you should have the fastest PC you can afford—a 10GHz Pentium 5 is just about right. Aside from the fact that computers haven't gotten that fast yet, you don't really need quite that much speed. To be perfectly honest, you *should* work with the fastest PC that you can afford. Image editing, especially with high-megapixel images, is a horsepower-intensive task. The more computer that you've got pushing pixels around, the more fun you'll have. A slow PC might frustrate you, since it'll take a long time to perform editing operations and even take a while to redraw the screen.

Here's what I think you should have to do image editing without getting an ulcer:

- **Pentium II processor**   I used to do image editing on a 200MHz Pentium (now known as a Pentium Classic), so it can obviously be done. But it's slow.

- **128MB of RAM**   Here's where spending just a little extra can really pay off, though. If you upgrade to 256MB of RAM (which typically costs about $100 more, and you can install it yourself), image editing will seem much faster, even on a slower processor. That's because high-megapixel images occupy lots of room in memory, and if they can't fit there, Windows stores parts of them on the hard disk. That can make something as simple as a screen redraw drag on forever.

- **20GB hard drive**   They're really cheap now, so you should have lots of room to store your images. A CD-ROM drive or some other kind of media for archiving old images can come in handy as well.

Choosing an Image Editor

Before you can get started editing images, you need an image editing program. Any one will do, at least at first. For the most part, all image editors give you the ability to do certain things, such as:

- Resize your images
- Apply paint to your image, using a set of brushes and other paint tools
- Add text and other graphics
- Delete parts of the image, which you can use to "crop" and change the composition
- Combine multiple images into a new composition
- Use filters to change aspects of your image, like the brightness and contrast

That's certainly a quick overview of image editing, but the point is that there are a lot of image editors around that will get the job done. Which one is for you? Well, you might want to start with a free one. If your digital camera came with an image editor of some sort, you might want to give it a spin and see if you like the way it works.

Ultimately, though, you may be dissatisfied with the bundled software and decide to invest in a better program. There are two sorts of image editing programs that you're likely to encounter: automatic and manual packages.

Automatic packages include a lot of wizards and automated processes to change your image for you. These programs can adjust the colors and brightness in an image, remove red eye in flash photography, and perform a host of other minor miracles without any real input from you. In Figure 11-1, for instance, you can see Sierra Imaging's Image Expert 2000, a program that can correct a host of problems with your image with a single click. The downside, of course, is that the final result is not always what you expect, and often such automated attempts to fix your

11

FIGURE 11-1   Image Expert 2000 is an image editor that can run all sorts of corrections on your image automatically, though the results are not always as good as you can achieve by hand.

photos don't quite hit the spot. Use them with care, and always remember that you can use the Undo button to revert to the original image. These programs are really aimed at novices who don't want to learn the ins and outs of an image editing program, but want immediate results.

If you're reading this book, I suspect you are probably more interested in getting your hands dirty, so to speak, with a more manually operated image editing program. These programs give you more control and power, but of course you have to master the interface before you can see improvements in your images. Perhaps the most famous image editor of all time is Adobe PhotoShop, seen in Figure 11-2. Available in full-strength form and in a weaker Limited Edition (LE) version, PhotoShop is the choice of many professionals. The downside is that the program has a somewhat steep learning curve.

Instead of PhotoShop, I actually recommend Paint Shop Pro from Jasc (www.jasc.com). This image editing program has about 75% of the features found in PhotoShop, but at a fraction of the

FIGURE 11-2   A great choice is PhotoShop, though its power can be intimidating.

cost and with a much simpler interface. Throughout the rest of this book I'll use Paint Shop Pro to illustrate techniques. Keep in mind, though, that you can use any software you like, but the actual mouse and keystrokes will differ depending upon what program you choose to use.

> **NOTE** *You can download a trial version of Paint Shop Pro from the Jasc Web site at www.jasc.com. If you're also interested in digital video editing, my book* How to Use Digital Video *comes with a copy of Paint Shop Pro on the included CD-ROM.*

> **NOTE** *Throughout the rest of this book I've used Paint Shop Pro Version 7 to illustrate how to perform many common image editing tasks. You can use an older version of Paint Shop Pro or another program entirely, but keep in mind that the menu items and tool locations will be different.*

11

How to ... Open an Image in Paint Shop Pro

Since I'm going to spend a lot of time in Paint Shop Pro over the next few chapters, let's take a quick look at how to use the program. Start Paint Shop Pro by choosing it from the Windows Start menu. There are three ways to open an image in Paint Shop Pro—you can use whichever method you find easiest.

■ Choose File | Open from the main menu and navigate your way to the image you want to open in the Open dialog box. Double-click on the file, or select it and click the Open button.

■ Choose File | Browse from the main menu. The Browse window appears, which shows a set of thumbnails in the right pane and a directory tree of your hard disk on the left. An example is shown below. When you select a hard disk folder, its contents appear on the right. Just double-click an image to open it. The Browse window remains open in case you want to open more images in this way.

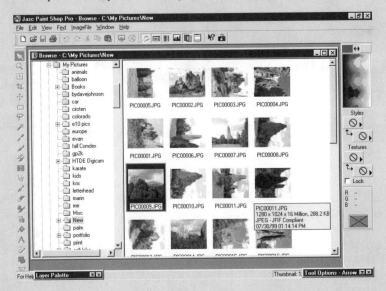

■ Open the folder with the image you want to open directly on the Windows desktop, and drag the image file from the folder to the Paint Shop Pro window. If Paint Shop Pro isn't on top, you can do this instead: drag the image file out of the folder and hold it over the Paint Shop Pro button in the task bar at the bottom of the Windows desktop. Don't let go of the file yet; just hold it there for a few moments. Paint Shop Pro should pop to the front. Finally, just move the file up to the Paint Shop Pro window and let go.

Tweaking the File Format

Much of the time, you'll only need to make minor changes to your images to get them into email, on the Web, or into other documents and applications. In the next few sections, I'll show you how to make changes to the file itself, like resizing, changing the colors, and changing the file format of your digital images.

Shrinking Your Images

As Jebediah Springfield, founder of the animated city in "The Simpsons," once said, "A noble spirit enbiggens the smallest man." If the Simpsons can make up a word, so can I—so this section is all about de-biggening your pictures.

Why would you want to do that? Well, high-res megapixel images are great, but they're just too big for certain applications. Suppose you want to post some images to a Web site, for instance. Or say you want to email some pics to friends and family. A 3.3-megapixel image, which measures about 2048x1536 pixels, is just too big for these kinds of applications. What you need is to de-biggen your images. In other words, shrink them down to a manageable size that others can appreciate—to a size smaller than the computer monitor, for starters, so people can see your image all at once without panning around.

TIP *Some cameras have the ability to resize images even before they're transferred to the PC. The Sony DSC P1, for instance, is a cool little camera that can automatically make a second, email-friendly copy of every image you take. That way you can skip this de-biggening step when you want to email or upload your pictures.*

How small is small enough? I suggest that for Web-based or email images, you shrink the file so that its longest dimension—either length or width, depending upon the orientation of the image—is no more than 500 pixels. Here's how to do it:

1. Open Paint Shop Pro and load the file that you want to resize.

2. Choose Image | Resize.

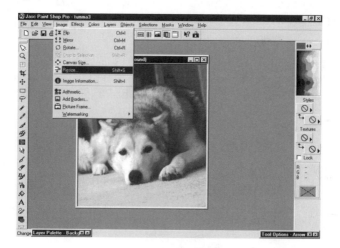

3. Since we want to make the image a specific pixel size, make sure Pixel Size is selected in the dialog box. We could also change the size of the image based on percentage or print size, but we don't need those options now.

You'll usually resize images by pixel size

Check this box or your image might be deformed

4. Make sure the dialog box is set to resize all layers and to maintain the aspect ratio of the image. Also set Resize Type to Smart Size. This tells Paint Shop Pro to use the best algorithm for resizing the image to generate the best final result.

5. Finally, enter the new dimensions for your image. You only need to enter the height or the width, and since the aspect ratio isn't changing, Paint Shop Pro will fill in the other number for you automatically. Assuming we started with a 1024x768-pixel image, enter **500** for the width and you'll see the height change to 375 pixels.

6. Click OK to resize the image.

7. You should see the image shrink on the screen. You can now save your image over the original—destroying the original—or save it as a new file so you retain the original's larger pixel size. To save it as the old filename, choose File | Save from the main menu. Otherwise, choose File | Save As and give the image a new name.

CAUTION   *You may have noticed that you can make images bigger using this procedure as well. Avoid increasing the size of your images, though, since all you can really do is stretch and manipulate the pixels already in the images. The result is generally unattractive.*

Changing the Color Depth of an Image

Sometimes you'll want to change the number of colors in an image. Every file format supports a specific number of colors. JPG images, for instance, can display 16 million colors, the number needed for photo-realism. GIF, on the other hand, supports just 256 colors.

Suppose you have a GIF image that you want to combine with a JPG for a special effect (such as putting someone from one image into a scene in another picture). You'll need to convert the image into a format that can accept more colors.

> **NOTE**   *The JPG file format only works with 16 million color images. That means that even if you convert a 24-bit image into an 8-bit image, if you later save it in JPG format, it'll automatically be considered a 24-bit image again. That's usually OK, since JPG files are quite compact.*

Increase the Colors in an Image

Here's how to increase the number of colors in an image:

1. Open an image in Paint Shop Pro. GIF and PCX can have just 256 colors, so load one of those if you have one on your hard disk.

2. Choose Colors | Increase Color Depth. Choose 16 Million Colors from the menu.

3. The image will be immediately converted into a format that has the space for additional color depth.

Notice that the image didn't really change visually. All this operation does is allow the image to display more colors if possible, but it can't add more colors into the image all by itself.

Suppose you had a four-color cartoon panel; by adding more color depth, you've created the ability to insert a photo-realistic image into the cartoon. We'll talk about how to do that kind of thing in Chapter 13.

Decrease the Colors in an Image

Now let's consider the other possibility. Suppose you have an image with 16 million colors, such as a JPG. If you want to turn the image into a Web graphic (like a push button, for instance) you might want to reduce the number of colors and save it as a GIF image. You might also want to reduce the number of colors to achieve an artistic effect, or to save disk space (a BMP with 256 colors takes less space than one with 16 million, for instance).

The process for decreasing the colors in an image is similar to increasing the colors, though there's an extra step. Here's how to do it:

1. Open a JPG image in Paint Shop Pro.

2. Choose Colors | Decrease Color Depth. Choose 256 Colors from the menu.

3. In the Decrease Color Depth dialog box, choose Optimized Median Cut and Error Diffusion, and then click OK. Those options will choose the best colors to give you the most accurate depiction of your image.

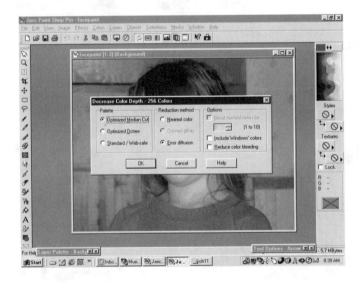

4. Click OK. The image should be rerendered with fewer colors. Unlike the case of increasing the color depth in an image, in this case you should be able to see a difference, since the image has to be painted on screen with fewer colors, and therefore less accurately. Check out the difference between the two images in Figure 11-3, for instance. One was saved as a 16-million-color image, and the other is just 256 colors. The difference is particularly apparent in full color.

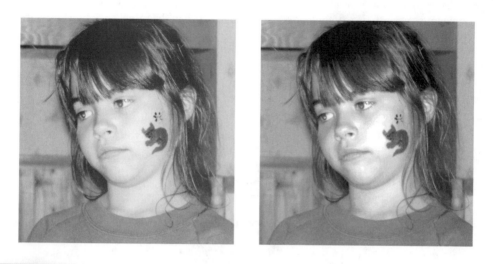

FIGURE 11-3   Using just 256 colors can rob an image of its photo-realism.

11

TIP
Many pictures look good enough in 256 colors to be converted from 24-bit without a serious compromise in quality for situations in which fewer colors might save some disk space or connection time.

Saving Images in Different File Formats

One of the most common things that I do with my images is change their file format—usually from JPG to TIF. Why do I do that? Usually, to preserve image quality. Every time you resave an image in JPG format, it loses a little quality. TIF is immune from that kind of compression punishment, though, so as soon as I start to edit an image, I save it in the TIF format to (as they say in the zip-lock bag industry) lock in the image quality.

Why don't I just take pictures in TIF format right from the start, you must be wondering? Well, even though my digital camera can take images in TIF format (as most can), it's an almost useless feature. Even with a large memory card, I can only take a few images in the huge, space-consuming TIF format. Since the image quality difference between TIF and high-quality JPG is small, I take the pictures in JPG format and convert them to TIF afterwards, when they're on the PC. It's a compromise, but a sensible one.

There are a number of reasons why you might want to change image file formats on the PC. Here are some of the most common:

- You convert a JPG to TIF to preserve image quality before repeated edit-and-save sessions.
- You convert TIF to JPG to save disk space or make an image small enough to upload using the Internet.

■ You need to import an image into a program that doesn't support the file format that the image is currently in; so you convert it into a file format the program does work with.

For a more in-depth discussion of file formats, check out Chapter 7. Saving images in different file formats is easy, though. Just follow these steps:

1. Open the image in Paint Shop Pro.

2. Choose File | Save As from the main menu.

3. In the Save As Type drop-down menu, choose the file format you need.

4. If necessary, click the Options button to fine-tune the file format. The Options button lets you specify the amount of image compression, number of colors the image will be saved in, and other properties.

5. Click OK to save the file.

After saving the file, you'll have two copies—one called myfile.jpg and one called myfile.tif, for instance. You can delete the older file, or if you might still need it, keep both copies. Of course, when you look at two files with the same name but different file extensions on the Windows desktop, it can be hard to tell them apart. If in doubt, right-click on the file and choose

Properties from the menu, as you can see below. Verify the file extension before you possibly delete the wrong file.

— File type

Improve Your Composition

In the world of 35mm photography, editing your composition is not always easily done. To crop an image or change its composition, you typically need your own darkroom or a local photo shop with which you can work closely to dictate crop marks and reprint photos to your personal specifications.

Of course, there are exceptions. In many large photo shops, you can insert your negative into a kiosk and the image is scanned and displayed on screen. Then you crop the image on the screen and print the result minutes later. These new image editing stations are just big, in-store versions of the image editing software you have on your PC.

In other words, you don't have to drive across town and pay money to do it in a store anymore. Now you've got the tools to do it yourself at home.

Crop Your Image

I wouldn't be surprised if this were the single most common edit made to digital photographs. Since you can crop and recompose your images so easily on the computer, the need to compose your shot perfectly in the viewfinder is somewhat diminished. Instead, you can tweak the shot to your heart's content afterwards, when you have time to think about it and evaluate your options.

Even if your shot is close to perfect to begin with, a little cropping can very likely make it better. Here's how to do it:

1. Load an image into Paint Shop Pro. Adjust it so that you can see the entire image on screen at once. To do that, you may need the Zoom tool, shaped like a magnifying glass. Click on it, and then click on the picture with the right mouse button to shrink it, or the left button to enlarge it, until it comfortably takes up most of the screen.

Zoom tool

Crop tool

2. Click on the Crop tool, shaped like the thick frame.

3. Click in the image, and, holding down the mouse button, drag the crop tool until you've drawn a rectangular outline around the part of the image you want to keep.

4. To move the crop box around within the image, move the mouse inside the box so that you see the mouse pointer change into a four-way arrow. Click and drag the box around the image.

5. To change the size of the crop box, hold the pointer over the box outline. You should see a two-way arrow. Now just click and drag to change the height or width of the box.

Resize crop marks

11

6. When your crop box represents the picture as you want it composed, click the Crop Image button in the Tool Options - Crop dialog box. The image will be immediately cropped down to size, which you can save as a new file or save to replace the older image.

If you don't see the Crop dialog box, it may not be activated. Choose View | Toolbars and select the Tool Options Palette. Then click OK. It should now appear on screen. Notice that this dialog box changes depending upon which tool you have selected.

Cropping by Cutting and Pasting

Not all image editing programs have a cropping tool. In fact, even in Paint Shop Pro there's another way to crop—one that you should learn. In this alternate approach, you actually select and copy a portion of the image, then paste it into a new image document. Here's how to do it:

1. Load an image into Paint Shop Pro and configure it so you can see the entire image.

2. Click the Selection tool (that looks like a dotted rectangle). Be sure the Selection Type is set to Rectangle in the Tool Options dialog box.

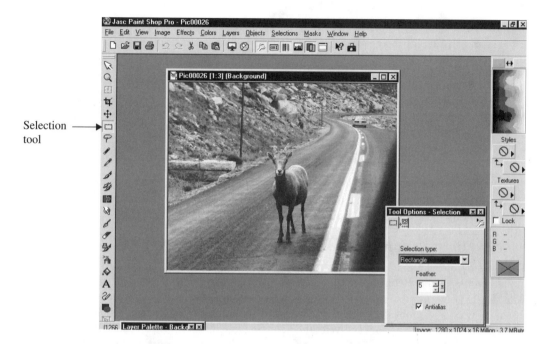

Selection tool

3. Draw a rectangle around the part of the image you want to keep. Note that you can't move or resize this selection rectangle in the same way that you did with the Crop tool. If you don't like the result, click elsewhere in the image to change the selection, and then try again.

4. When your selection is complete, choose Edit | Copy from the menu. This copies the selected region into the Windows clipboard.

11

Using Cut and Paste

The Cut, Copy, and Paste tools are just like the ones in Microsoft Word and other programs, though you have a bit more in the way of options. These tools allow you to grab a selection—some part of the image—and paste it in a variety of ways. The most important options? You can paste selections elsewhere in the same image (which lets you add a second copy of yourself to a photo, for instance), in another photo (so you can shake hands with Elvis, for example), or even into a new, blank image.

5. Choose Edit | Paste | As New Image. The selected region should appear in a new image window, which you can then save to the hard disk.

Special Effects with Irregular Cropping

Why would you want to use this process instead of the Crop tool? For starters, as I mentioned, not all programs have a convenient cropping tool built in, so you may have to copy and paste your way to compositional excellence. But there are other reasons. You might want to create several new compositions, for instance, all based on the same original image. When you crop an image, the original data disappears. With the Selection tool, though, you can keep going back to the original image and copying different, even overlapping parts and pasting them into new files. It's a way to make an unlimited number of new compositions based on a single photograph.

Last, but not least, you can make irregular crops with this technique—something that's just not possible with the cropping tool. What do I mean? Check out Figure 11-4. Here, you can see that I created an image by creating a crop of connected geometric shapes. How does this work? It's easy—just try this out:

1. Load an image into Paint Shop Pro and choose the Selection tool.

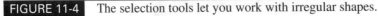

FIGURE 11-4   The selection tools let you work with irregular shapes.

2. Draw a rectangular selection in the image.

3. Hold down the SHIFT key and add another selection to the image. The SHIFT key is a modifier that combines selections in the image.

4. Hold down the CTRL key and drag another rectangle in the image, this one intersecting at least part of one of the selections already in the image. The CTRL key is a modifier that removes overlapping selections from the image. You can use the CTRL key to take the edge off a rectangle or even to turn a selection into a "donut" by giving it a hole!

11

5. Keep adding and removing selections until you're happy with the result. Choose Copy | Edit from the main menu.

6. Now we need to create a new home for this image: choose File | New from the main menu. In the New Image dialog box, make sure that the width and height of the new image are at least as big as the selection you just made, and then click OK. You should see a new, empty window appear on screen. This is where we're going to paste our selection.

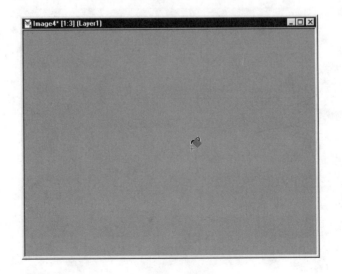

7. Before we do that, let's paint it. Click on the Fill tool (the overturning paint can).

8. Click on a color from the color palette in the upper-right side of the screen. Now click in the empty white image, and you should see it fill up with the color we just selected. In this illustration, you can see the Fill tool as it paints the entire image window a single color.

9. Finally, it's show time. With the new image window still selected, choose Edit | Paste | As New Selection. The irregularly cropped image should move around under your mouse pointer. Decide where you want it to be in the new image and click. It will pop into the new image, with the strange shape clearly visible against the colored background.

That little exercise is just scratching the surface of what you can do with selections in Paint Shop Pro (and other image editing applications). Here are a few other tricks you can try out:

■ **Create a vignette crop.**   Have you ever seen oval-shaped images? It's easy to do with the Selection tool. Just choose Ellipse from the Tool Options dialog box after you choose the Selection tool. When you make your selection in the image, it will be in the form of an ellipse that you can customize depending upon how you drag your mouse.

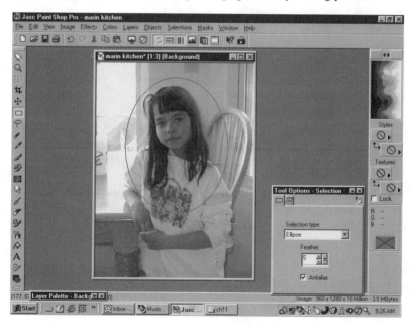

■ **Feather the edges.** When you paste an image into another image, you can smooth the transition from the selection to the background using the Feather tool in the Tool Options dialog box. The larger the number, the more feathering you'll get. Be sure to select the Feather option before you select your region though, or it won't have any effect.

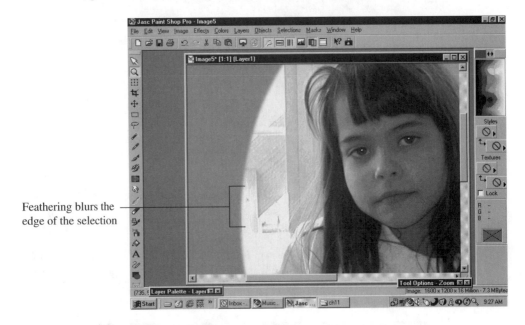

Feathering blurs the edge of the selection

■ **Invert your selection.** One cool trick you can try is to create a selection in your image and then choose Selections | Invert from the main menu. You should find that you got the exact *opposite* of the selected region. It's an easy way to select everything except the middle of an image, for instance.

Rotate Your Perspective

Not all your shots are going to be plain old, horizontal shots—especially if you took my advice in Chapter 3 and went nuts with camera position and perspective. If you have images from your camera that are sideways—you took the pictures sideways, so you have to turn your head to look at them on the PC—you should fix those images right away. It's a snap.

Some image editors, in fact, even have one-click buttons for rotating your images to the left or right by 90 degrees. Paint Shop Pro doesn't have that, but it's not much more difficult. Here's what you need to do to fix a sideways image:

1. Load the sideways image in Paint Shop Pro and decide which way it needs to be rotated—right (clockwise) or left (counterclockwise).

2. Choose Image | Rotate. The Rotate dialog box appears.

3. Specify how you want to rotate the image. Click Left or Right and make sure the button for 90 is selected; then click OK.

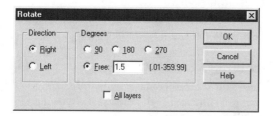

4. The image should rotate such that it is oriented properly; if you made a mistake, choose Edit | Undo and try again.

There are other ways to reorient your image as well. If you took the picture with the camera upside down, for instance (and stranger things have happened, trust me), you can choose Image | Flip from the menu. Likewise, you can flip it left-to-right, giving you a mirror image of the original shot, by choosing Image | Mirror.

Level a Crooked Picture

There's nothing quite as annoying as a crooked picture. Especially when the horizon or some other straight line is visible in the image, a crooked shot can ruin an otherwise great picture. Even if the horizon is only off a little, it can be annoying, but you can use the principle you learned in the last section, on rotating sideways images, to fix this annoyance. Here's what you need to do:

1. Load the crooked image into Paint Shop Pro. Decide which way it needs to spin to correct the error, and estimate by how many degrees. Most errors, even seemingly egregious ones, are typically less than 3 degrees.

2. Choose Image | Rotate.

3. Specify the direction (left or right) and enter a number in the Degrees box. You can type in a decimal, such as .5 (which is half of a degree), if you want. Click OK to see the result.

4. Inspect the result. If you aren't satisfied, choose Edit | Undo and try again with a different angle of rotation. When you are happy, save the file.

CAUTION *Don't apply rotation on top of rotation, or the image quality will suffer. Undo the first rotation completely to get back where you started, and then apply a different rotation angle to get where you're going all at once.*

Improve the Color and Brightness in Your Image

These edits require the most artistic skill, so I saved them for last. Fixing elements of your picture like bad color or poor exposure can be done, but it'll take some practice before you can make your images really look right. But don't worry about that; time in your image editor is free, and if you stick with it, you can fix some badly mangled shots!

Brighten Gloomy Shots

Everyone has a stockpile of too-dark images. The flash didn't reach the subject, or perhaps the camera underexposed the subject because of a bright background. Back in the first part of the book, I told you how to avoid those kinds of problems "in the lens" when you take the picture, but you can also repair some of the damage in postprocessing.

There are three primary ways of adjusting the brightness in an image:

■ You can use the Brightness control (in some programs, it's called luminance). Brightness raises or lowers the entire image's luminance value indiscriminately, whether all areas need it or not. On the other hand, if just one portion of an image needs to be brightened, you can select it using the Selection tool and then add brightness. When part of an image is selected, operations you perform on the image occur in the selected region.

TIP *Use the Selection tool to add or remove brightness only where it's needed.*

■ Alternately, you can use the Gamma control. Gamma affects the midtones of an image more than the extreme bright and dark regions; that means you can brighten a dark skin tone without washing out a dark shadow nearby. Gamma affects a limited range of brightness in the image, so you can better target your changes.

■ Finally, and perhaps the best way to tweak the brightness of an image, is with the histogram. This is an intimidating-looking tool that tells you the distribution of lights and darks in an image, and it's a powerful way to correct your shots—as long as you're willing to invest a little time to learn how to use it.

Correcting with Brightness and Contrast

Let's start with the brightness and contrast controls, though I suggest that you don't rely on this technique often. Play with it, certainly, but I recommend that you get familiar with the other two techniques, gamma and the histogram, and use them.

The process for changing brightness in an image is similar regardless of software, but we'll use Paint Shop Pro, as usual, for our example. Here's the general procedure:

1. Load the offending image into Paint Shop Pro.

2. Choose Colors | Adjust | Brightness/Contrast. The Brightness/Contrast dialog box appears.

3. Use the Brightness slider to adjust the image. You can see the effect of the change in your image immediately by clicking on the Proof button, which is shaped like an eye in the middle of the dialog box.

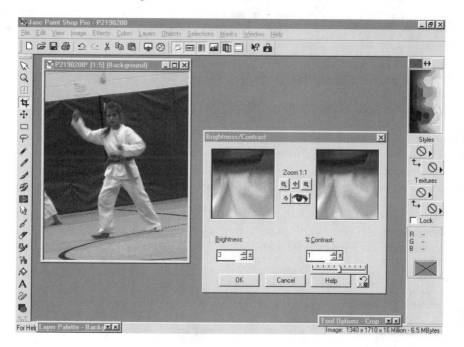

4. Typically, you'll need to change the contrast in proportion to the brightness to keep the image from getting washed out. Experiment until you see the result you want.

5. When you're satisfied with the results, click OK. Your image will be updated with the new brightness value.

Better Corrections with Gamma

As I mentioned, gamma is often a better remedy for fixing an overly dark or overly bright image. Personally, I tend to reach for the Gamma control first. I've found it's often the midtones in a picture that need enhancement, and brightness tends to wash out dark regions and increase the intensity of the highlights—overexposing them. The Gamma control, on the other hand, doesn't affect the brightest and darkest parts of an image, so you can't wash out shadows with this tool, for instance. So as a general rule, you should see if gamma gets the job done.

To tweak the gamma, just choose Colors | Adjust | Gamma Correction, and move the sliders. Unless your image is very poorly exposed, you shouldn't need to change the gamma value above 1.5 or below .5.

Generally, you'll want to change the gamma of all three color channels (red, green, and blue) simultaneously, so be sure that the Link box is checked on the Gamma Correction dialog box.

Fine-Tuning Images with the Histogram

Perhaps the most precise and powerful way of correcting your images is with the histogram. The histogram is a graph that shows the relative amount of information stored in each color channel in your image; or, in plain English, it displays how many pixels are dark and light in your image. The left side of the graph represents the darkest part of the image, while the right side is the lightest. A graph like the one on the left in Figure 11-5 has a lot of midtones, while the one on the right is mostly filled with dark pixels. We can use that information to tweak the brightness and contrast.

Programs like Paint Shop Pro and PhotoShop have a cool tool for adjusting the levels in your image using the histogram and a few sliders. In Paint Shop Pro, it's found at Colors | Histogram Functions | Histogram Adjustment. In general, the way you use this tool is to move the sliders under the histogram to set the white and black points and adjust the gamma. The various controls are explained below.

Suppose you have an image like the one in Figure 11-6. Here's how you would correct the image using the histogram:

1. Since the histogram curve drops off before reaching the right side of the graph, that tells us that there are few pixels with very bright colors. As a consequence, you should drag

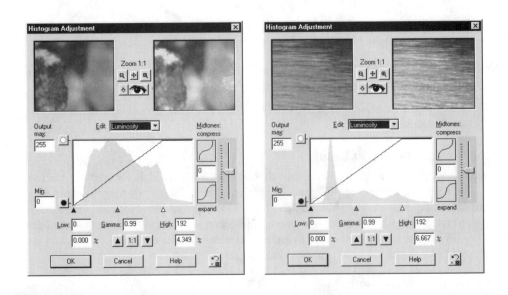

FIGURE 11-5　Histograms tell a lot about the amount of color information in an image.

FIGURE 11-6   The Histogram Adjustment tool is the most precise way to adjust brightness and contrast.

the white point slider to the left to meet the point where the graph really ends. That sets this point in the image as white, and should brighten the image.

2. Do the same for the black point, if necessary.

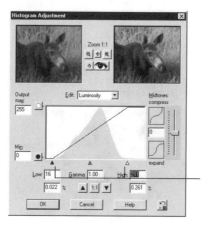

Move these sliders to set white and black

11

3. Now use the gamma slider to adjust the overall brightness level in the image's midtones.

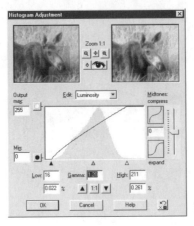

TIP
If you're using Paint Shop Pro, you also have a pair of sliders for compressing or expanding the midtones. Use this for oddly shaped histograms, such as when the curve peaks at the ends (compress the midtones a bit).

Add Snap to Your Colors

There are a few ways to add life to washed-out, flat, or bland pictures. One way is to use the Contrast control. Since bland pictures are often a result of low contrast, you can increase the contrast in the image and make the scene look much "punchier." To do that, simply find the Contrast control and work the slider. In Paint Shop Pro, you can find the contrast in Colors | Adjust | Brightness/Contrast.

TIP
Contrast can work the other way to good effect as well. Want to create some artificial fog? Just reduce the contrast in a picture by about 50%, and the image seems obscured by a dense fog.

Another way to improve your image is with the Saturation tool. Saturation increases or decreases the intensity of colors in an image, much like the saturation control on your television.

Brightness Only Goes So Far

You need to know the ugly little secret of brightness and gamma control. You can only take it so far, because you can't add detail to an image that wasn't there when you originally took the picture. A black shadow, for instance, will only become gray as you continue to increase brightness—you'll never see the authentic Bigfoot creature that was hiding in the thicket of trees. That's why it's important to start with the best exposure you can, although you can always try enhancing it afterwards. You can sometimes salvage an otherwise throwaway image.

Too much saturation can make the picture look like it was taken on Mars, but it can add life to an otherwise bland picture.

In Paint Shop Pro, the Saturation control is found in Colors | Adjust | Brightness/Hue/Saturation/ Lightness. Experiment with the Saturation tool—it's fun. You can bleach all the color out of your picture by reducing the saturation to zero, for instance, or hyperactivate the colors by going in the other direction.

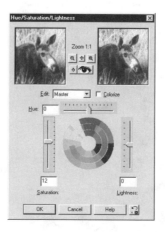

Do you have a people picture that's a little too red? This doesn't happen often, but can occur when you take indoor pictures in artificial light. Back off on the saturation slightly to get a more natural skin tone.

11

Correct the Color Balance

Quite often, the colors in some pictures won't come out quite right for some reason. Some cameras, for instance, tend to shift the whole image toward one end of the color spectrum under certain lighting conditions. You can change the color balance in an image in many programs as easily as sliding three controls marked Red, Green, and Blue.

To fix out-of-synch colors, open the color balancing tool in your image editing program. In Paint Shop Pro, you can find it at Colors | Adjust | Red/Green/Blue. You'll see a dialog box in which you can slide the three primary color controls to the left (less) or right (more) to bias the colors in your photo. For best results, use the color balancing tool very conservatively, and be sure to preview your work before clicking OK. You'll rarely need to change the colors in your image by more than about 15%.

If your image is too blue, however, you won't necessarily get the effect you're looking for just by backing off on the blue slider. Use this chart to fine-tune your image:

Problem	Solution (x is the amount you move the slider)
Too red	Decrease red by x, then increase both green and blue by x / 2.
Too green	Decrease green by x, then increase both red and blue by x / 2.
Too blue	Decrease blue by x, then increase both red and green by x / 2.

Easy Color Correction with Variations

A better solution is regrettably not available in Paint Shop Pro, but other programs, like Adobe PhotoShop, do offer this feature. Let's take a quick look at the Color Variations tool in PhotoShop since it's so useful.

If you have PhotoShop, open it and load an image. Then choose Image | AdjustVariations. You should see something like this:

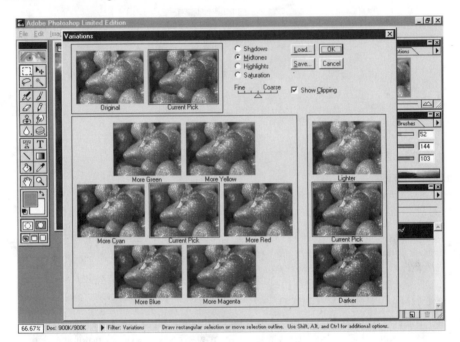

Here's how you use this busy little dialog box:

1. Start by tweaking the brightness. If you want to make the image darker or lighter, click the appropriate thumbnail on the right side of the screen. All the images will immediately change to show you the effect of the change. (The Original thumbnail at the top left will remain the same, so you can compare your changes to it.)

2. Next, decide what color channel you want to change. If you want more red in the image, for instance, click the box marked More Red. The change will appear immediately.

3. Continue tweaking the image until you are satisfied with the result. At any time, you can revert to the original by clicking the Original thumbnail.

Chapter 12

Cleaning Up Your Images

How to…

- Sharpen blurry images
- Blur the background to enhance apparent sharpness
- Use the painting tools in your image editor
- Choose foreground and background colors
- Make selections based on color, region, and by hand
- Remove ugly red eye from flash photos
- Eliminate distracting objects with airbrushing
- Repair tears and scratches on photos
- Create a panorama from a series of photos

In the previous chapter, we looked at easy and fast techniques you can use to gussy up your images—stuff like how to rotate or resize your images, correct bad colors, and even save them in different file formats.

But there's so much more that you can do. In this chapter, we'll go one step beyond and learn how to fix your images with techniques that actually change reality. You'll see how to remove red eye caused by flash photography, for instance, how to sharpen (or blur) a picture, and how to airbrush away distracting elements from a scene and move elements around within a picture.

This chapter is filled with techniques that sit between what I would call elementary quick changes and special effects. We're not adding Elvis to your holiday pictures, but we're certainly going beyond color correction. Strap in and have fun with your images and your favorite image editor!

Sharpening Blurry Pictures

I know what you're thinking. Wow! I can sharpen my blurry pictures! Technology is great!

Well, let me begin by saying that as great as digital imaging is, you can never add detail or information into a picture that wasn't there to begin with. That's why I'm always amused when I see a movie in which the spy takes a surveillance videotape and enlarges the image enough to read the phone number on a piece of paper across the room. No matter how much they enlarge images in the movies, those Hollywood computers can always seem to sharpen the focus perfectly.

With that said, there is some hope for your slightly blurry images. There are actually two ways to sharpen an image: a direct way, using the Sharpen tool in your image editing program, and an indirect way, which amounts to blurring the background so your subject doesn't look quite so bad. I'll show you how to do both.

Using the Sharpen Filter to Enhance Your Picture

The easiest way to sharpen an image is with the Sharpen tool. What this tool does is increase the contrast between pixels, making the image seem sharper, as you can see in Figure 12-1. If the camera jittered madly while you took the picture, though, no amount of sharpening will hide the result.

In most graphics programs, there are a few different kinds of sharpening filters available. These are the most common options:

- **Sharpening**   This affects all the pixels in your image indiscriminately. Sharpen More is a common alternative, which is just somewhat more intense.

- **Edge Sharpening**   This effect only increases the contrast along edges in your picture, where a lack of sharpness is most obvious. It is usually more effective than Sharpening, and it is less damaging to the rest of the image.

- **Unsharp Mask**   This variation of Edge Sharpening adjusts the contrast of pixels that neighbor an edge in addition to the edge itself. This is the most common sharpening filter, and in fact it's pretty standard practice for photographers to run the Unsharp Mask filter on most images that they scan into digital format from a slide or print.

FIGURE 12-1   Digital sharpening can make almost any picture look just a little snappier.

12

In Paint Shop Pro, the Sharpen, Sharpen More, and Unsharp Mask filters are available from the Effects | Sharpen menu.

Which one should you use? Not all programs offer all three filters, but if you have a choice, Edge Sharpening is almost always more effective than the plain old Sharpening filter. Unsharp Mask works best of all, but it sometimes takes some tweaking on your part. You'll generally get to set at least three options, as you can see here:

- **Strength** This is the intensity of the sharpening effect.
- **Radius** This determines how many pixels around the edges are also affected by the filter.
- **Clipping** This determines how different the pixels need to be before they're considered an edge.

TIP *Start with 100 for Strength and 1.0 for Radius and watch the way the filter changes as you change Clipping. A Clipping of 0 is the most harsh effect; beyond about 30, changing Clipping has no real effect on your image. Likewise, raising Radius beyond 1.5 rarely has an attractive effect on your image.*

Blur to Sharpen

Using the Sharpening filter is certainly one way to make your image look sharper, but there's another, more subtle, and arguably more "artistic" way to enhance the apparent sharpness of your image—blur the background. This process works best when you're photographing something quite distinct from the background, like a portrait.

To blur the background of your image, you'll need to isolate the subject so the blurring only happens in the rest of the picture. Once your subject is selected, you need to invert the selection so that the Blur filter happens to everything except the subject. Finally, you can run the Blur filter on your image. In Paint Shop Pro, you can find Blur by choosing an option from the Effects | Blur menu. Once you've blurred your background, turn off the selection and save your image.

That's the quick overview. Here's how to actually pull off this feat of digital trickery:

1. Load a slightly blurry portrait that you'd like to sharpen into Paint Shop Pro.

2. Select the Freehand tool and set it to Smart Edge. Set the Feather value to about 5—that way the transition from the subject to the background won't be abrupt.

3. Trace the outline of the subject's face or body, being careful to stay along the edge.

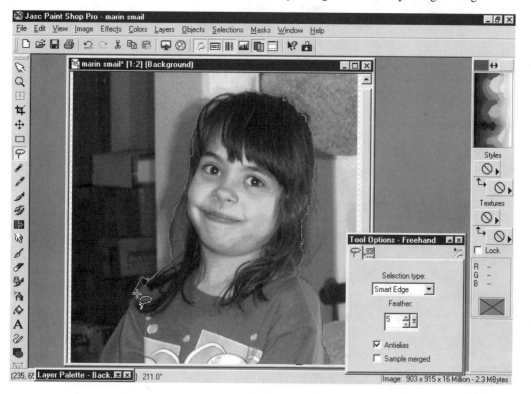

4. When you have completely selected the subject, choose Effects | Sharpen | Unsharp Mask to sharpen the subject but not affect the background.

Simulating a Shallow Depth of Field

You wanted to take a picture with a sharp foreground and a shallow background, but your automatic camera settings didn't cooperate. Well, it's easy to simulate the out-of-focus effect that a wide-open aperture gives your background by using the select-invert-blur technique we used to give the subject more apparent sharpness. You'll need to heap on liberal amounts of blur for this technique to work, though.

5. Next, choose Selections | Invert from the menu. This "flips" the selection so the subject isn't selected, but everything else is.

6. Choose Effects | Blur | Blur More. You should see the background blur slightly. If you're not happy with the result, blur it again. In fact, you can repeatedly use the blur effect until the background is sufficiently blurred.

7. Finally, when the image is complete, choose Selections | Select None.

Hopefully, the subject now looks better, especially in comparison to the background. Compare the two images in Figure 12-2, for instance, for a look at this effect in action.

FIGURE 12-2   Blurring the background slightly can make the subject look sharper.

Painting on Your Pictures

Some of the techniques we'll be discussing through the rest of the book require a little, well... painting. And if you take a look at your image editor—especially a full-featured one like Paint Shop Pro or Adobe PhotoShop—you'll see a complete set of painting tools. These digital gadgets allow you to change the colors in an image on a pixel-by-pixel basis. How do they do that? Take a look at Table 12-1; there, you can see the most important tools in Paint Shop Pro's Paint toolbar. These are fairly typical tools as image editors go; you'll find their equivalent in most other programs.

Tool	Description
	This tool is used to move image windows around within Paint Shop Pro. It's a safe default setting to use since it won't do anything to your image if you click in the picture.
	Zoom into the image by left-clicking; zoom out by right-clicking.
	We used this tool in Chapter 11. It lets you cut out unwanted bits of your picture.
	We used this tool in Chapter 11 as well; it lets you select portions of an image for further editing.
	This is another way to select portions of an image.
	This tool selects a region for editing based on color. Since photos have lots of similar colors, you can click on a region and the wand will select everything nearby that's a similar color. It's an easy way to select, for instance, a person's face.
	This tool determines the color of the currently selected pixel and makes that the current foreground color for painting and editing.
	This is just what it sounds like. It lets you paint on the image, not unlike the way you'd paint with a real brush. It's a lot more flexible than a real brush, though, since you can change features like the size and shape of the brush, as well as the amount of paint that you can spread at once.
	This tool lets you paint with pixels found elsewhere in your image, effectively cloning a part of your picture as you paint.

TABLE 12-1   Highlights from the Paint Tools Palette in Paint Shop Pro

12

Tool	Description
	This great painting tool actually puts the power of many of the program's effects—like brightness and hue changes, effects filters, and more—into a brush so you can paint them on.
	This automated tool erases scratches from scanned photographs.
	This tool allows you to paint with the currently selected foreground and background colors.
	You can configure this tool to splatter paint on your image like an airbrush.
	Pours paint into a region. The currently selected color will run right up to whatever color edges exist. Like the Magic Wand, you can set the color tolerance.
	This tool lets you write text anywhere in your image, in any color and any font. We'll talk about this tool in Chapter 14.
	Use this tool to draw straight and curved lines in your image.

TABLE 12-2 Highlights from the Paint Tools Palette in Paint Shop Pro *(continued)*

Choosing Colors

So, let's say that you want to do a bit of painting. We'll keep it simple: you just want to paint a solid-colored rectangle in the middle of an image. Before we do that, you'll need to know how to select colors in Paint Shop Pro.

There are actually two important colors in any imaging program: the foreground color and the background color. These are usually displayed prominently on the screen (as in Figure 12-3) for easy access and reference.

The foreground color is the color you'll paint with when you use the left mouse button. The background color can often be used by painting with the right mouse button, and it appears if you use the Eraser tool on your image.

In Paint Shop Pro, you can choose a color directly from the color palette by moving the mouse over the palette and clicking on the color you like. A left click selects the foreground color; a right

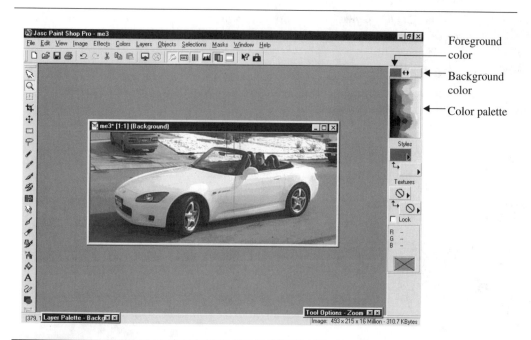

Foreground color

Background color

Color palette

FIGURE 12-3   The color palette is an important feature in most image editors, since it lets you select colors for painting and editing.

click sets the background. You can also set these colors directly from an image; to do that, select the Dropper and click with it on the part of the image you want to grab the color from.

TIP   *Since colors can change from pixel to pixel in a digital image, you will have better luck with the Dropper by zooming in before you select a color with the Dropper.*

Applying the Paint

Once you've selected colors to serve as the foreground and background colors, it's time to lay down some paint. In Paint Shop Pro, do this:

1. Click on the Selection tool and make sure that the Selection style is set to Rectangle in the Tool Options dialog box.

2. Click and drag the Selection tool in the image to create a rectangle.

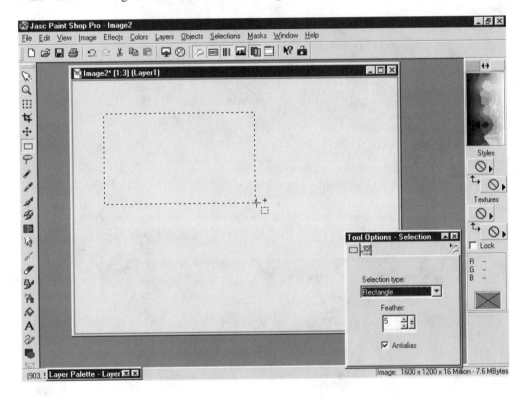

3. Click on the Flood Fill tool.

4. Set the fill style to solid color. To do that, click on the right arrow on the Styles box in the color palette. You'll see several options representing color, gradient, pattern, and no style at all. Click on the first option, shaped like a paintbrush.

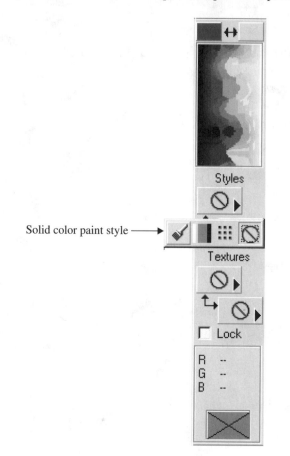

Solid color paint style

5. Finally, click inside the selection with the Flood Fill tool. You should see it fill with a solid color—the same one you selected in step 4. If you like, right-click in the selected rectangle as well. You should see it change to background color.

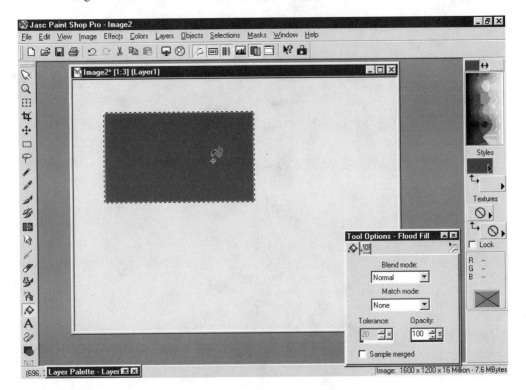

Paint a Gradient

While we're here, let's fill the rectangle with a gradient. A *gradient* is a rainbowlike spread of colors that range in hue from the foreground to the background. Here's how to paint in such a gradient in Paint Shop Pro:

1. Select the foreground and background colors that you want to serve as the extreme values in your gradient.

2. Click on the Flood Fill tool.

3. Set the fill style to gradient. To do that, click on the right arrow on the Styles box in the color palette. Choose the second option, which looks like a spectrum of colors.

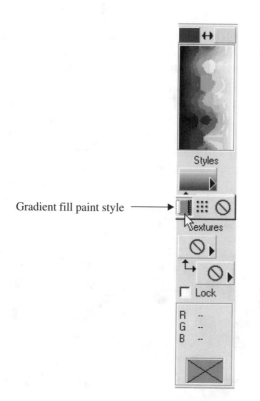

Gradient fill paint style

4. Click in the selection with the Flood Fill tool. If you right-click in the selection, you'll paint it a solid color again—the background color.

> **TIP**
>
> *To paint freely anywhere in the image (as we're about to do in the rest of the chapter), you need to get rid of the selection. As long as there's a selection in the image, you will only be able to paint inside it; that's a powerful tool for making sure you only affect specific parts of the image. To turn off the current selection, choose Selections | Select None.*

Painting More Accurately

You've got the basics of painting down—selecting colors and clicking in the painting. But what if you want to paint a precise set of pixels? The rectangular Selection tool won't get the job done. Instead, there are a few other tricks you can rely on:

■ **Paint Brush** For lots of detail work, the old-fashioned Paint Brush is all you need. Select the Paint Brush, and you'll see you have a variety of options in the Tool Options dialog box. Of particular importance is the Size slider. By changing the size, you're specifying the number of pixels that will be affected every time you click on the image with the brush. To test this tool, just select it and click and drag in the image. You can paint by drawing freehand lines or just dab the screen to make small dots of color.

■ **Magic Wand** If you want to change the color (or perform some other kind of edit) on a region of the image that is somewhat similarly colored (such as a person's face), use the Magic Wand to select all the like-colored neighboring pixels. You can make the wand more or less sensitive to color changes by moving the Tolerance slider. To test this tool, choose the wand and click in a region of your image that has a somewhat consistent color. A Selection region will appear; you can then use Flood Fill or the Paint Brush in this area.

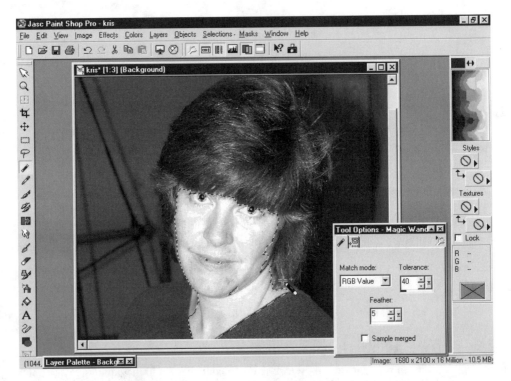

■ **Freehand** The Freehand tool is a great choice when you want to select part of the image, but it's irregular in shape and hard to select any other way. Perhaps the most powerful way to use the Freehand tool is to set it to Smart Edge mode. Here's how it works:

■ Select the Freehand tool and change the Selection Type to Smart Edge in the Tool Options dialog box.

■ Find a region that you want to select. Ideally, it should have a fairly well defined outline, since the Smart Edge tool will snap to high-contrast changes in the image.

■ Click on the edge of the region and move the mouse pointer. You should see a box extend away from the point you clicked.

■ Following the outline of the region, click again on the edge some short distance away.

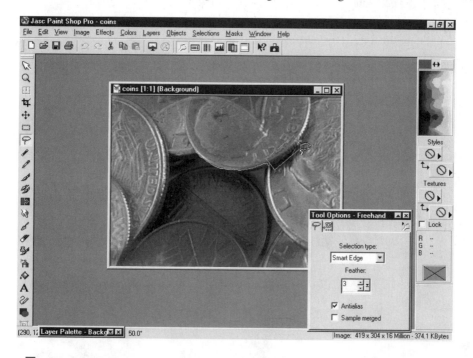

■ Continue clicking with the Smart Edge tool as you work your way around the region. When you reach your starting point, double-click to close the region into a complete selection.

Repairing the Evil Eye

Back in Chapter 4, we talked about how to avoid getting red eye into your pictures to begin with. Red eye, of course, is the phenomenon that occurs when the camera flash reflects off the subject's wide-open pupils in a dark room. If you've got red eye, either because you didn't take the necessary precautions or because you've just scanned an old picture that has red eye, you can correct it on the PC fairly easily.

Using Automatic Red Eye Removal

First, check to see if your image editing software has an automatic red eye removal feature. Some red eye removal software is completely automated: just draw a box around the eyes, and the software does the rest. Somewhere between automated and completely manual is the red eye removal system in Image Expert 2000. Here's how you do it in that program:

1. Zoom into the face of your subject so the red eyes are clearly visible.

2. Click the Redeye button in the toolbar. You may have to click OK in a dialog box that explains the procedure.

3. Use the paintbrush mouse pointer to darken the red region. Dab or paint in circles enough times that the red eyes turn dark.

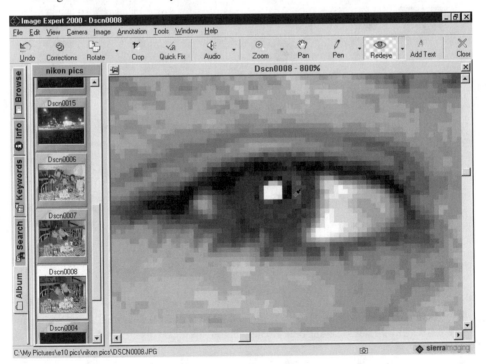

4. Zoom out and check your handiwork. If they still look red, zoom in and try again.

you can change the size of the Redeye brush by clicking on the down-arrow next to the Redeye button in the toolbar.

Removing Red Eye the Old-Fashioned Way

If you're using Paint Shop Pro or some other image editor that doesn't have red eye removal built in, you'll have to take it out yourself. It's easy, actually, and it doesn't even take a steady hand. Here's what you should do:

1. Load the offending image into Paint Shop Pro and zoom way in so the eyes fill most of the screen.

2. Click the Magic Wand tool and click in the red part of the eye. Hold down the SHIFT key and keep clicking until you've selected all of the red in one eye.

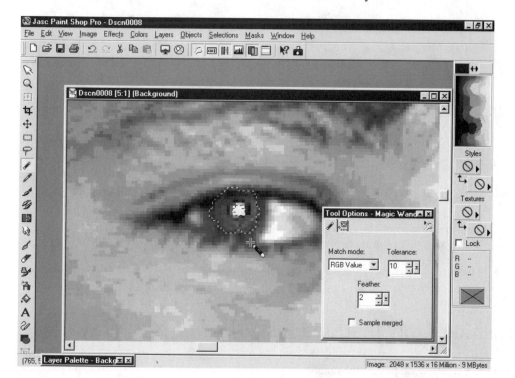

If the wand grabs too much of the image—like parts of the face outside the red—then the tolerance (found in the Tool Options dialog box) is set too high. Adjust it to about 25.

12

3. With the red area selected, select the Paint Brush or Flood Fill tool and choose black as the foreground color. Click in the red to turn it black.

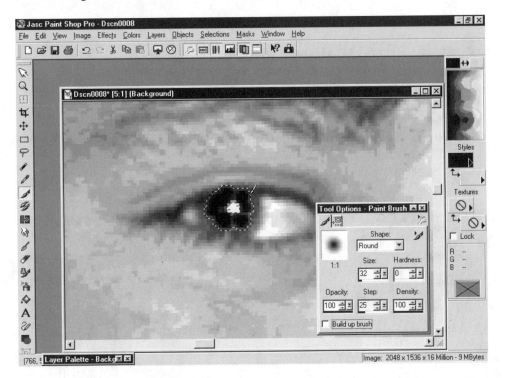

4. Choose Selections | SelectNone from the menu and evaluate your work. If you can still see red around the fringes, you can take the Paint Brush and change the remaining to red on a pixel-by pixel basis. To do that, you might want to reduce the brush size to just a few pixels. (This setting is found in the Tool Options dialog box.)

TIP   *Be sure to leave the white spot in the middle of the eye, or you'll have created a portrait of a space alien.*

Airbrushing Away Distractions

Have you ever taken a great landscape shot only to realize—far too late to reshoot the picture—that there's a telephone pole in the middle of what should be serenity? Or a tourist in a loud shirt right behind your family shot that you wanted to frame? Don't worry—this section will show you how to eliminate those kinds of distractions with a little digital airbrushing.

The tool at the heart of this magical process is the Clone tool. This handy feature, found in most image editors, allows you to copy pixels from one region of your image to another. That means you can "airbrush away" distracting aspects of a picture—like power lines, hotspots, and so on—by duplicating a similar or nearby part of the image (see Figure 12-4). Typically, smaller and more isolated distractions are easier to airbrush away than larger ones (or objects that cut through the main part of your picture); but if you're patient, you can get great results from a surprising number of photos that you thought you'd have to throw away.

To use the Clone tool in Paint Shop Pro just do this:

1. Click on the Clone tool in the tool palette. It looks like a pair of paintbrushes.

2. You'll need to find a region in your image that is similar to the area you want to cover. If you want to airbrush away a power line that runs through the air, for instance, you can look for a nearby patch of sky that's similar enough that you can paint over the power line with this other section of sky.

3. Set the source for your cloning operation. In Paint Shop Pro, just position the mouse pointer over the area you're going to steal color from and either right-click or hold the SHIFT key and click.

FIGURE 12-4   The image on the right looks better without the distraction of a tall pole.

4. Move your mouse over to the area you want to airbrush and start painting. Don't try to cover the blemish all at once; paint a little, pick up the mouse, and paint again. This reduces the chances that a recognizable pattern will appear as a result of your painting.

The Clone tool works best in small areas, because you can start to tell that something is wrong with the area you're cloning to if you paint over too large a region.

TIP   *The Clone tool has two different modes. In one mode, when you pick up the brush and paint elsewhere, the source stays where you put it: this is called "non-aligned." If you pick up the brush and start painting elsewhere and the source moves the same relative distance from where you first started, this is the aligned mode. Some pictures work better with one mode or the other. Experiment to see which is best in each situation.*

Clean Up Old and Damaged Pictures

An unexpected benefit of digital imaging and editing has been the ability to restore old pictures—heirlooms and keepsakes that you may have written off as too badly damaged to be of much value anymore. Some of the techniques I've already mentioned can be used to fix these old prints on your PC. First, of course, you'll need to scan these images into the PC. I talk a bit about scanning in Chapter10, but basically, you'll want to scan your old prints at the highest resolution you have available. That'll make it easier to print them later. From there, it's just a matter of applying digital editing techniques to repair them.

Remove Picture Scratches

After a particularly bad moving experience a few years ago, one of my wedding pictures got a few nasty scratches due to the way the glass broke and slid down the print. The image was essentially irreplaceable, so I turned to digital editing to make a repaired duplicate. There are several approaches you can take to fixing scratches, depending upon where they are in the image, how prominent the scratches are, and their relative size with respect to the rest of the image:

- ■ In some cases, you can select and copy an undamaged area of the picture that is similar in color and overall texture to the damaged portion; then paste it over the damaged area with a liberal amount of feathering to smooth the edges. This is particularly effective in fairly uniform backgrounds such as the sky.

- ■ Another alternative—and the more common solution, actually—is to use the cloning tool (see the earlier section on airbrushing for more details). Select the cloning tool and use a nearby, similar, but undamaged section of the image to paint over the mar. Remember to use short, dabbing motions to paint, or you'll introduce an undesirable pattern into the image.

- ■ Finally, you can use the automated scratch remover found in many image editors. Paint Shop Pro's Scratch Remover (it looks like a trowel) lets you drag a selection box over a long, straight scratch. It then removes the scratch by painting over it with nearby colors automatically. This technique doesn't work well for wide scratches or scratches that curve or bend—it's off to the Clone tool for those.

Remove Dust, Dirt, and Digital Noise

Your images can be filled with little specks that come from grainy, high-speed 35mm film, from bad scans, or from using a digital camera in very low light. Whatever the reason you get specks on your image, most image editors have a Despeckle tool. In Paint Shop Pro, you can find it at Effects | Noise | Despeckle.

Make a Panoramic Photo

A panorama is an image that's wider than the ordinary images produced by your camera, such as the one in Figure 12-5.

Panoramas are typically used to take landscapes, since they provide the wide, sweeping vistas that look so impressive. You can take a panorama of anything, though—a school play, the inside of your home, or some other scene. The key to making something into a panorama with a digital camera, though, is that you'll need to take two or more images and "stitch" them together on your PC. That means that the scene shouldn't change much between photographs, or you won't be able to match them up. So if you're taking a landscape, for instance, the same cars, people, and other objects shouldn't move as you rotate your camera and take successive shots.

FIGURE 12-5   You can connect a number of images to make a wide (or tall) panoramic shot.

I first talked about panoramas back in Chapter 6. In that chapter, I explained how you can use your camera to take the panorama's raw ingredients—the individual shots. In this chapter we'll pick up where we left off and talk about how to stitch those together on the PC.

As I mentioned in Chapter 6, there are two steps to taking a panorama: photographing the scene and stitching the images together afterwards. When shooting the pictures, keep these tips in mind:

- You'll need to take a series of pictures that overlap. Try to get at least 25% of each image to overlap into the next picture to make it easier to stitch them together.

- In order to keep each image's perspective identical, you'll need to keep the camera's rotational axis the same. In plain English, that means you need to take all the pictures from the same location. Don't drift a few feet as you photograph, and take the shots on a tripod if at all possible.

- Avoid using a wide-angle lens, since this can distort the images and make it difficult to line up edges.

Now it's time to make the panorama. There's a hard way and an easy way; which way you choose depends upon how much enthusiasm you have for delicate editing and how much money you have to spend on yet another image editing program.

If you're game for doing it the easy way, you need to purchase a panorama program that automates the entire process for you. My favorite is Enroute Software's QuickStitch. Using this program, all you need to do is drag and drop the individual images in the proper order (see Figure 12-6). The software matches the edges all by itself, and does a good job even with low-quality digital cameras, wide-angle lenses, and other technical difficulties.

Stitching Photos Together by Hand

If you don't have a program like QuickStitch, you can still make a panorama by hand. It just takes a bit longer (and your results will not be quite as good as what you get from most automated software).

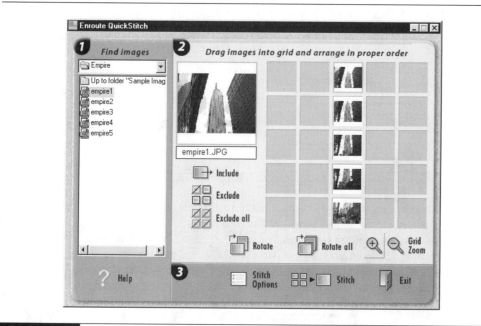

FIGURE 12-6   Automatic panorama software is a convenient way to stitch images together into impressive panoramas without the muss of lining up images by hand.

Here's how to do it:

1. Calculate the finished image size by finding the size of your individual images. If you don't know the resolution of the individual shots, load one into Paint Shop Pro and choose Image | Image Information from the menu. Close the image after you've determined its size.

2. Create a blank document by choosing File | New. For image size, make sure it is the image width times the number of images (such as 640×3 images, or 1920 pixels). For height, make it about 50% bigger than the starting image height, such as 720 pixels for a 480-pixel image. This gives you some room to maneuver if the images turn out to have some vertical offset, and you'll crop out the extra white space at the very end. You'll want the image type to be a 24-bit image (16 million colors).

3. Add the first image to the panorama, working from left to right. An easy way to do that is to leave the Browse window open and simply drag each image, as you need it, into the new image.

4. Take the next image and add it to your panorama document. As you add the images, line them up with the image to their left. If you use a program like Paint Shop Pro that supports layers, you can make the new image somewhat transparent to help you see where it should line up with the previous image. For a quick introduction to layers, see the sidebar "Combining Images with Layers."

Drag the second image to line it up with the first

5. Repeat this process until all your images are inserted and lined up.

6. When you're done, be sure that you reset all the layers to 100%, or they will look transparent in the final image.

7. Use the Crop tool to crop the new panorama so that any irregular tops and bottoms aren't in the image.

8. Save your file.

Combining Images with Layers

More sophisticated editing tasks, like combining multiple images in a panorama, benefit from the Layers feature found in Paint Shop Pro and other image editors. Here's the basic idea: your picture can be made up of many different images and selections, each occupying a different layer. Each layer has its own unique characteristics, including transparency. So you can add a ghost to an image by using the image of a person in a layer with a high level of transparency.

There are two ways to add images to a picture in layers:

- Drag images directly to an image window from the Browse window.
- Use the menu option: Edit | Paste | As New Layer.

Once an image is considered a layer, you'll need the Layer Palette dialog box to control it. If it isn't already on screen, choose View | Toolbars and select the Layer Palette; then click Close.

The layer palette shows you all the layers in an image. To vary their transparency, use the slider to the right side of the dialog box. To make a lot of layers easier to manage, you might want to rename them—just right-click on the layer name on the left side of the dialog box and choose Rename.

Chapter 13

Creating Special Effects

How to...

- Simulate a Hollywood-style bluescreen effect
- Create chromakey effects like a news-show weather map
- Create perfect selections using masks
- Insert friends and family into pictures of celebrities
- Take science fiction shots of laser battles
- Add artistic and paintlike effects to your photos
- Decolorize your photos
- Make a stop-motion animation

When I was a kid, I remember going to the movies and being wowed and amazed by special effects—stop motion, bluescreen, animated laser combat, matte paintings—and while I'm sure a lot of people were just thinking things like "wow" and "cool," I was thinking "I wish I could do that." I was intrigued by the possibilities of trick photography, and I wanted to be able to do it myself.

Such special effects have always been possible for anyone with the time, money, equipment, and determination. I had none of the above. But when I got my first image processing program back in 1987, I realized I could finally do what I'd always wanted to—special effects and trick photography on a budget.

Indeed, digital photography opens a lot of doors for us mere mortals. In this chapter, I'll tell you how to do some of the tricks that can make your images go beyond simple reality. You may not want to try all the techniques in this chapter, but I think there's a little fun in here for just about everyone.

Using a Hollywood-Style Bluescreen

What is a *bluescreen*? Well, it's the generic term for a technique in which action is photographed or filmed in front of a solid-colored backdrop (see Figure 13-1). Later, in postproduction, special-effects technicians substitute a different scene in place of the bluescreen. So a scene that looks like it happened in midair or in France or on the moon actually happened in front of a blue tarp. Separate footage is added in place of the tarp, and voilà. That's movie magic.

We can achieve the same kind of results ourselves. It helps to use a real bluescreen—a solid-colored backdrop that you can "paint out" afterwards with a different image—but it's also possible to achieve good results with no preplanning at all.

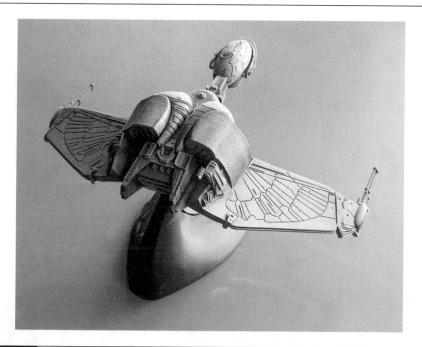

FIGURE 13-1   This model is photographed in front of a backdrop. Later, the backdrop is painted over with a different image.

> **NOTE**   *Though the term is bluescreen, the color of the backdrop doesn't have to be blue. In fact, it's commonly green. For the most part, the bluescreen can be any color you like.*

13

Make a Weather Map

Let's start with the kind of shot we plan ahead for, which makes it a tad easier to get good results.

First, think about the evening news. You've seen the weather forecaster stand in front of a map of the United States and point to cold fronts a million times before, but have you ever thought about how that bit of TV magic happens? Obviously, the forecaster isn't standing in front of a real map. Instead, it's a bluescreen—a solid-colored rectangle. The engineer uses a technique called *chromakey* to replace the rectangle with video from another source. What happens is this: the engineer selects the color of the bluescreen and identifies it as a "key." The second video source then overwrites anything in the scene that has the key-valued color.

You can create your own chromakey weather map effect yourself. Here's how to try it.

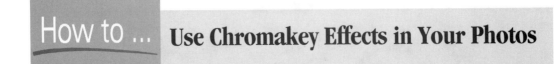

How to ...   **Use Chromakey Effects in Your Photos**

1. Start with a piece of solid-colored board. Hobby stores sell foam boards in a variety of sizes in a number of bright, primary colors, and I use them frequently for projects like this. Tack the board on a wall or have your subject hold it, like this:

2. Since the board is a relatively solid color, we should be able to select all of it with the Magic Wand tool. Choose the wand and click in the board. You should see a selection appear around it.

3. If the board isn't selected in its entirety, hold down the SHIFT key and click in the region that didn't get selected in the previous step. Repeat as necessary until the entire board is selected.

4. Open a second image in Paint Shop Pro. This will be the image that we insert into the first image as a sort of weather map effect.

5. With the second image selected, copy the image to the clipboard by choosing Edit | Copy.

6. Choose Edit | Paste | Into Selection. You should see the second image pasted, or chromakeyed, into the first image.

You can use this technique in all sorts of ways. You can make a window look out over an unusual vista. You can have a plain board become a famous painting. You can use it to create your own news or weather effects. Experiment—it's fun and very easy to do.

Bluescreen Without a Screen

As I've mentioned, in the movies they need to film in front of a special color matte in order to know which pixels to eliminate from the final scene. Our lives would be easier if we could always shoot in front of a bluescreen too. You could simply use the Magic Wand tool to select the whole background with just a few clicks. But since we don't live on a sound stage, sometimes it's a slightly more convoluted process to get a bluescreen effect using Paint Shop Pro.

Suppose we want to place a subject in a completely different scene than the one in which it was photographed. In the movies, an actor would be filmed in front of a bluescreen, and then a matte or second video source would be substituted in place of the bluescreen in postproduction. Here's how we can do it in Paint Shop Pro:

1. Open the image of the person or subject that will be transplanted into another scene.

2. Create a selection area around the entire subject that you want to transplant to another scene. Most of the time, the Freehand tool set to Smart Edge works best, but you might also have good results with the Magic Wand.

3. When the selection is complete, choose Edit | Copy from the menu.

4. Open the second image.

5. Choose Edit | Paste | As New Selection. The selection should appear in the second scene. Reposition the selection until it looks about right, and then save the finished image with a new name.

Fine-Tuning the Selection

The technique I just described works fine a lot of the time, but it's just not accurate enough to create a truly convincing special effect. There are two other ways to get even better results.

First of all, you can invest in a professional edge-detection program that largely automates the process of creating accurate selections for this kind of special-effect work. One of the best is a program called KnockOut by Corel (www.corel.com). You can see KnockOut in Figure 13-2. This program can isolate individual hairs on a person's head; so it's great for this kind of image transplant.

Alternately, you can make your own masks. A mask is similar to a selection; just like the regular Selection tool, masks isolate the area that you want to change, or protect from change, when you apply color, filters, or other effects to an image.

Masks are significantly more powerful than ordinary selections, though. They have three attributes that selections don't offer in most imaging programs:

- A mask is actually a 256-level grayscale image that sits on top of your picture. A selection area is either on or off, but you can use a mask to select the degree to which an effect will occur. Black parts of the mask block all edits, white parts allow changes to occur at 100% strength, and gray areas are something in between. It's as if you were spray painting a model in your basement and using some sort of mask to block unwanted paint. In this case, though, the mask is made of a porous material like gauze that lets you control how much paint gets through.

FIGURE 13-2   KnockOut is a masking program that allows you to cut a subject out of a scene precisely.

■ You can fine-tune the mask with ordinary paint tools. A selection area is only as accurate as your ability to draw with the mouse, but you can create a mask, zoom in, paint pixel by pixel, and make sure it looks exactly the way you need it to.

■ You can create a mask and save it to disk, meaning that you can reuse it in many different images.

That said, let's talk about how to actually use a mask. Usually, unless your selection area is well defined with a narrow range of colors conducive to using the Magic Wand (such as if you're trying to enclose a solitary object against a high-contrast background), a selection is only as accurate as your ability to draw with the mouse. Thus, you might want to try your hand at using a mask instead.

This technique relies on your imaging program's ability to turn a selection area into a mask (though most programs do allow this) and then turn a mask back into a selection area (which not all can do). You can do this in Adobe PhotoShop and Paint Shop Pro. I'll show you how to do it in Paint Shop Pro:

1. Load the image you want to use as the basis for your mask.

2. Draw a selection area around your subject as accurately as you can. But don't spend all day on it, since we'll use the mask tools to fine-tune the selection.

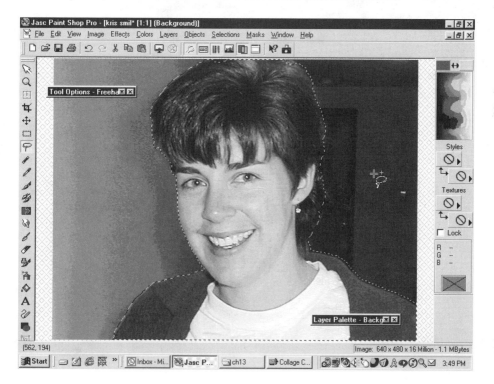

3. Turn the selection into a mask by choosing Masks |New | Show Selection.

4. Turn off the selection outline by choosing Selections | Select None.

5. Enable mask editing by choosing Masks | Edit.

6. Now you can fine-tune the size and shape of the mask using ordinary paint tools. If you choose a paintbrush, for instance, you can edit the mask, pixel by pixel if necessary, until it perfectly matches the subject you're trying to duplicate. You can use the Zoom tool to get a close look and alter the paintbrush's diameter to get just the right amount of detail. It's not quick and easy, but it works, even for including single strands of hair from a person's head.

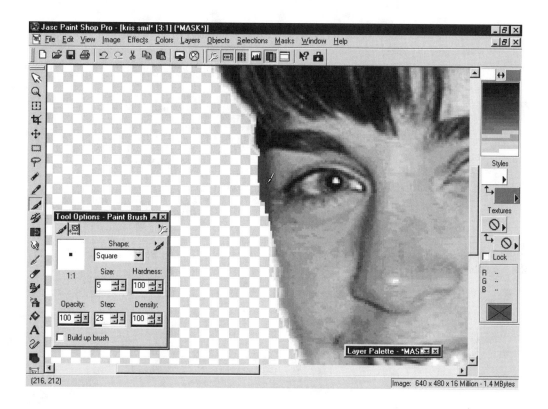

Regardless of the color your program uses to display the mask, the mask is really just a grayscale image, and you need to paint with black, white, and shades of gray. Use white to erase the mask and black to paint the mask. If you want to manually insert various levels of transparency in the mask, use levels of gray.

13

7. When the mask is just the way you like it, convert it back into a selection area by choosing Selections | From Mask.

Select All		Ctrl+A
Select None		Ctrl+D
From Mask		Shift+Ctrl+S
From Vector Object		Shift+Ctrl+B
Invert		Shift+Ctrl+I
Matting		▶
Modify		▶
Hide Marquee		Shift+Ctrl+M
Convert to Seamless Pattern		
Promote To Layer		Shift+Ctrl+P
Load From Disk...		
Load From Alpha Channel...		
Save To Disk...		
Save To Alpha Channel...		
Float		Ctrl+F
Defloat		Shift+Ctrl+F

8. Choose Edit | Copy to copy the selection to the clipboard.

9. Open the new image that you want to paste the subject into.

10. With the new image selected, choose Edit | Paste As New Selection.

11. Position the subject in the new scene. Voilà, you're done!

Shake Hands with Elvis

Now the moment you've been waiting for—the opportunity to combine pictures of yourself or friends with famous celebrities and historical figures. It's not really all that hard, especially now that you know the basic principles from working with bluescreens. Let's suppose that your friend, Kristen, has always wanted to meet Elvis. It's too late to set up a meeting, but you can do the next best thing. In the following steps, I'll show you how to combine a picture of her with an old shot from the Nixon administration (see Figure 13-3).

1. First, you need a suitable picture of Kristen—one in which she's more or less the same size as Elvis. Load the picture of the King into Paint Shop Pro and choose Image | Image Information to find out how tall Elvis is in the selected image.

Current Image Information   ☒

| Image Information | Creator Information |

Source file
File name: C:\WINDOWS\Desktop\ch13\fig13-03.tif
File type: Tagged Image File Format

Image
Dimensions: 602 x 402 Pixels
                    8.361 x 5.583 Inches

Status
Has been modified: No
Has a selection: No

Pixels Per Inch: 72
Pixel depth/colors: 8/256

Number of layers: 1
Number of alphas: 0

Memory used   On disk   In RAM
Image: 238K
Selection: 0K
Masks & alpha channels: 0K
Undo: 0K   0K
Total: 0K   238K

        OK   Cancel   Help

2. Armed with knowledge about Elvis, load the picture of Kristen and crop her so that she's
only seen from the waist up—like Elvis—and resize the image, using the Image | Resize
menu, until she's about the right height.

3. Now for a little housecleaning. You need to erase as much of Nixon as you reasonably can, using the Clone tool and techniques covered back in Chapter 12. In this case, I copied the flag to Elvis's immediate left over the flag that was immediately behind Nixon, then copied the surrounding wall to get rid of as much of the former president as possible. I don't have to erase all of him, because we're going to position Kristen over part of this image. This is what it looked like when I figured it was good enough to paste in Kris:

4. Now for the tricky part. You need to use a selection tool to copy Kristen, but avoid including any of the background. You can use the Magic Wand, Freehand tool—whichever you're most comfortable with. Try the Smart Edge tool, which often gives fairly good results in situations like this.

5. Once she's selected, it becomes obvious that the transition from Kristen to the background is too sharp to be believable. That means it won't look realistic in the final picture. Use the Feather tool to smooth out the edges of the selected region. Choose Selections | Modify | Feather and choose a value of about 4 pixels.

6. Copy Kristen to the clipboard, and then switch to the other image. Choose Paste | As New Layer. She'll appear onstage next to Elvis.

7. Position her in the new image, arranging her so their hands meet.

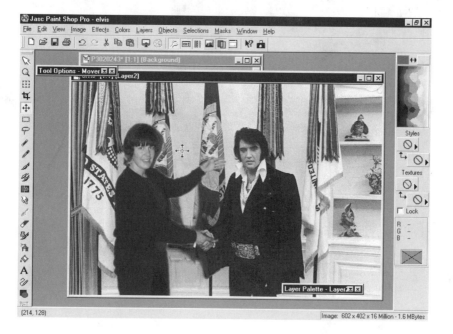

8. There's something a bit squirrelly about their handshake. If you arrange the image so that Elvis's arm appears over Kristen, you can mask her badly cropped appendage with a bit of Nixon's leftover hand and create a slightly three-dimensional effect—she's in front of his left shoulder but behind his arm. To do that, copy Elvis's arm to the clipboard and paste it back into the image as a new layer, exactly over the old arm. The only difference is that it'll end up lying over Kristen's hand, making it look more like they're in the same picture.

To make the illusion more convincing, you can try to sharpen or blur Kristen a bit to match the original Elvis photo before you copy and paste her. The CIA might know it's a fake, but it's probably fine for your purposes.

Shoot a Sci-Fi Firefight

When I was in college, I took my love of *Star Trek*, added a dose of photography, and came up with a hobby that could pretty much only be done around 3:00 a.m. Although it didn't help my grades very much, it was a lot of fun to create special effects like phaser blasts and disintegration halos. The best part? It was all done "in the lens"; so you can try it yourself if your digital or

FIGURE 13-3   The final result of our project—combining a picture you took with a stock photo of a celebrity

35mm camera supports very long exposures. So that you can compare techniques and see if the digital way is easier, here's how I did it in college:

1. Set the camera up on a tripod in total darkness and start a long exposure.

2. Using a flash, expose the subject (like someone holding a phaser) and the target person. The flash does not need to be mounted to the camera—you can just take a flash unit and hold it in your hand, flashing the subject once or twice.

3. Get behind the subject, and, pointing a flashlight directly at the camera, walk to the target of the phaser blast, trying to keep the flashlight moving in a straight line so it traces what will look like a solid laser beam on the film.

4. Outline the target with the flashlight, again pointing it at the camera.

5. If you want to make the target look like he or she is disintegrating, ask the subject to leave the scene and then flash the rear wall once.

6. Stop the exposure.

That's a lot of work, and the results are often hit or miss. Against all odds, you can sometimes get a half-decent one, as in Figure 13-4.

13

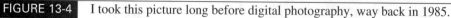

FIGURE 13-4   I took this picture long before digital photography, way back in 1985.

The Disintegrating Subject

With a digital camera and a program like Paint Shop Pro, you can create this special effect a lot more scientifically. Here's an alternate way to create a similar image:

1. Take a picture of two people posed to be the aggressor and the target. *Star Trek* clothing is optional.

2. Load the image into Paint Shop Pro and immediately store a copy of the image in the clipboard by choosing Edit | Copy.

3. As a first step toward making the target glow, carefully create a selection region around the subject, and then set it to get bigger. To do that, choose Selections | Modify | Expand and select perhaps 10 or 20 pixels. Then feather the selection in the same way—choose Selections | Modify | Feather and set the feather to 5 or 10 pixels.

4. Now it's time to add an effect to make the subject glow. Choose Colors | Adjust | Brightness/Contrast and jack the brightness up to maximum. Click OK, and you should see a pure white region where the subject used to be.

5. Next, add the copy as a new layer into your image. Choose Edit | Paste As New Layer. The glow should disappear, since the copy of the original, unretouched image is now on top.

6. In the Layers Palette dialog box, reduce the layer's transparency until you get the effect you like—it'll probably be in the neighborhood of 10% to 30%.

You can also do variations on this. To get the target to disintegrate, take two pictures using a tripod so you have identical framing. In one image, include the subject; in the other image, just shoot the background without the subject. When you combine the images using the layer strategy I discussed above, it'll look like the subject is evaporating.

The Laser Blast

We've now made a pretty convincing disintegration scene, but what about the phaser blast? As I've already mentioned, using a flashlight is a very inexact science—it's hard to get a straight line, as you can see in Figure 13-5.

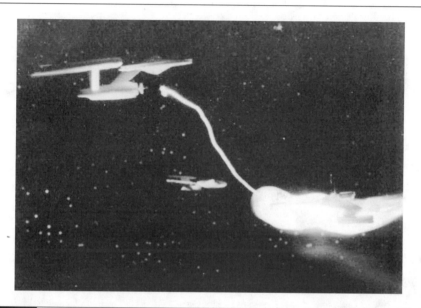

FIGURE 13-5 It's fiendishly difficult to "draw" a straight line through the air with a flashlight doing this the old-fashioned way.

With a paint program, though, you can get a perfectly straight beam. In some paint programs, holding down the SHIFT key while you draw a line actually locks the brush into following a perfectly straight path.

In Paint Shop Pro, click once for the starting point, and then move the brush to the end point. Then hold down the SHIFT key as you click. The program draws a perfectly straight line between the two points. To make it look like a beam of light, make the color a bright white, red, or yellow and add a touch of feathering to the effect. You can see the final result in Figure 13-6.

Paint Like Van Gogh

An easy way to transform your images into unique works of digital art is with the filters that are built into image editing software like Paint Shop Pro and Adobe PhotoShop. A filter is graphics-talk for a tool that allows you to edit or manipulate your image. It's called a filter because when you run it, software changes your image according to a specific mathematical process, filtering the original data in a certain way to deliver a modified image. A common and relatively boring example of a filter is Sharpening, which adds contrast to the pixels in an image, increasing the apparent sharpness.

Filters can do a lot more than just sharpen (or blur) your images, though. There are hundreds of filters out there, and many programs (like Paint Shop Pro) come with a few dozen. The best way to find out what a filter does is to experiment. I say that because it's one thing to read an

13

FIGURE 13-6   Create your own sci-fi effects in about 10 minutes with an image editor.

explanation of the filter, but it's quite another thing to actually process a picture with each filter to see the effect. In general, you probably won't use many of these filters very often. But it pays to try them out, because you never know when a certain effect will be just what you're looking for. Table 13-1 provides a quick summary of the most common filter types you might run across.

Filter	Description
Blur	Blur filters average nearby pixels to give the impression of blur, poor focus, or motion.
Sharpen	Sharpen filters increase apparent sharpness in an image by increasing the contrast between pixels, either throughout an image or only along edges.
Edge	Edge filters typically enhance and trace edges—regions defined by high-contrast borders between pixels.
Noise	These filters can add or remove "noise" in an image. Noise manifests itself in digital images as specks of high-contrast color, like snow in a TV transmission.

TABLE 13-1   Common Filter Types

Filter	Description
Geometric effects	These tools let you distort and skew parts of an image. They're good for displaying an image in a different perspective. You can change the orientation of an image in three dimensions or perhaps distort images within circles, cylinders, and other shapes.
Artistic effects	This is the general name for a slew of filters that do everything from add bas relief, watercolor, charcoal, mosaic, and more to your images. This is where you should go when you want to make your image look like it was hand-painted or give it a unique, nonphoto-realistic look.

TABLE 13-1   Common Filter Types *(continued)*

There's no limit to the kinds of effects you can achieve with filters, though beware: many of them are somewhat clichéd. Use your judgment when applying them. Check out Figure 13-7. Here you can see the original strawberries, as well as what they look like with Brush Stroke, Glass Mosaic, and Sunburst filters applied. In Paint Shop Pro, you can find all of these effects—and many others—in the Effects menu.

FIGURE 13-7   The original image (upper left) has been modified with a number of artistic filters.

What Is a Plug-In?

Many image editors, including Paint Shop Pro, can use something called a plug-in, or a plug-in filter. These are filters that were originally designed for Adobe PhotoShop. PhotoShop filters have become something of a standard in image editing software, and many programs can use these filters. You can download filters from the Web, purchase them in stores, or get them with other image editors. Back in Chapter 6, for instance, I talked about a program called LensDoc, which lets you straighten images that got distorted due to wide-angle and fish-eye lenses. Well, LensDoc is a plug-in for PhotoShop. It's a filter that processes your image within an image editor.

Decolorizing Your Pictures

This effect is a lot of fun. Surely you've seen television commercials in which everything is black and white except for one item—a person, perhaps, or the featured product—which is in full color. It's an effective trick because your eyes are drawn to the color image in a sea of gray.

On television, this effect is typically done with two cameras. On the PC, though, we can do it after the fact with a single image—you didn't even have to have this effect in mind when you originally took the shot. Best of all, it's not very hard to do. It's particularly easy if your image editor supports layers. The basic idea is this:

- Stack two copies of the image in separate layers.
- Convert one to grayscale.
- Select most of the image in the color version.
- Delete the selection, leaving a small color subject on top of the grayscale image.

Specifically, here's how to do it in Paint Shop Pro:

1. Open the image you want to use and make a copy of it by choosing Edit | Copy. Don't paste it anywhere yet; just let it stay in the clipboard.

2. Select the image and convert it to a grayscale picture by choosing Colors | Grayscale. Then turn the image into a 24-bit file by choosing Colors | Increase Color Depth | 16 Million Colors.

3. Rename this image's layer to Grayscale so it's easier to keep track of. To do that, open the Layer Palette dialog box and right-click on the layer name. Choose Rename. In this illustration, you can see the layer has been renamed.

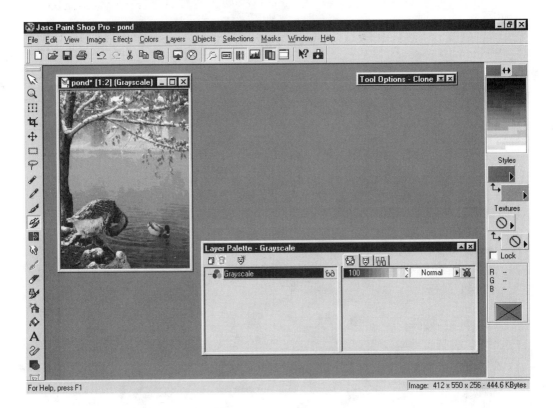

4. Now add the color image on top of this one. Select the image and choose Edit | Paste | As New Layer. You can prove it actually worked by sliding the transparency control of the top layer until you can see the grayscale image peeking through. Now the second layer sites on "top" of the grayscale layer, as you can see in the Layer Palette dialog box:

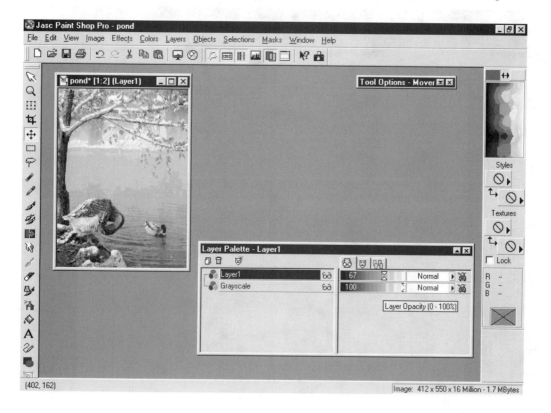

5. With the new color layer selected, use the Selection tool to trace out the subject you want to keep in color. Trace as carefully as possible. If you need to, create a mask to fine-tune the area, and convert the mask into a selection.

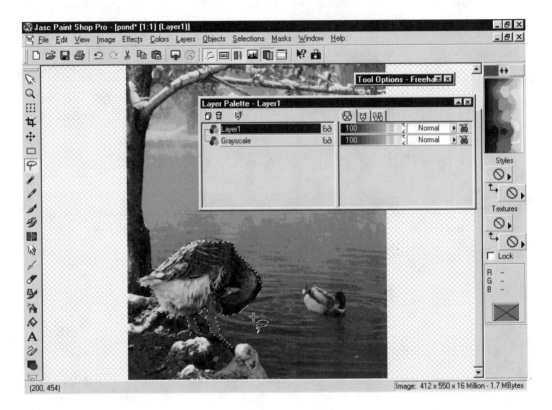

6. When you're done, choose Selections | Invert to select everything *except* the color subject.

7. Choose Edit | Cut to cut most of the color image away.

8. Choose Selections | Select None to finish.

You should now have a grayscale image with a single element in color. Save the image with a new name.

Colorize an Image

You can create an interesting work of art using the Colorize tool. Colorize converts your image into a picture with uniform hue while maintaining the original brightness levels, and that means you get a monochrome image that isn't grayscale. Instead, it's bluescale, redscale, or whatever-scale you happen to choose. Want to get an image that looks like it was photographed through night-vision goggles? Try to colorize it with a hue of 75 and a saturation of 80. But keep experimenting—some images can look very dramatic when rendered in just a primary color.

Create Stop-Motion Movies

The last cool thing we can do with a digital camera is to take stop-motion movies. This is a lot like the time-lapse photos we talked about back in Chapter 6; it's shooting the same scene over and over with a certain time interval between each shot, so that when you play the images back later in sequence, it's like a movie. There's an important distinction between the two, though: in time-lapse photography, we let the camera's automatic time-lapse mode shoot the same scene over and over. The effect? Accelerated time.

In stop-motion photography, we aren't speeding up time. Instead, we're creating animations by moving the objects in the scene ourselves between each shot that is manually fired. You can use stop-motion photography to make inanimate objects move around for fun or to tell a story.

Stop-motion photography is a lot of fun. Just review these tips before you start:

- **Plan your shot.** If necessary, sketch out a short storyboard so you know what story you're trying to tell.

- **Use a tripod.** Set the camera up on a sturdy platform so you can concentrate on setting up each shot. The tripod guarantees that the background won't move, and you'll get a more credible result.

- **Be consistent.** When you take your shots, plan out the motion. If something is supposed to be moving at constant speed, for instance, make sure that your subject moves about the same distance from shot to shot. If you want to show acceleration or deceleration, the distance between shots should vary more dramatically, as seen in Figure 13-8.

13

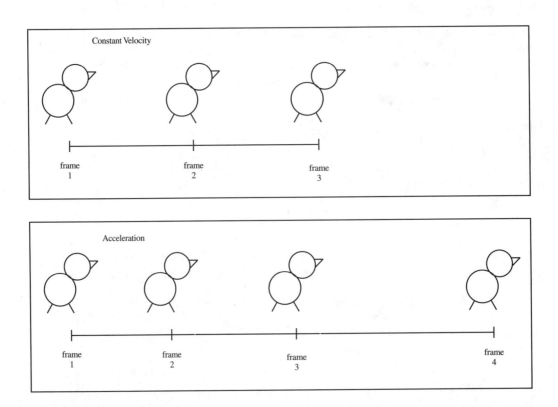

FIGURE 13-8   The distance that you move an object in stop-motion photography determines how fast it appears to move in the final shot.

- **Make short motions.**   Very little should change from one shot to the next. If there's too much change in any given shot, the shot just won't look right.

- **Keep the lighting consistent.**   Be sure that the lighting doesn't change from shot to shot. Remember, the goal is to make it look like a few hundred individual shots are all frames of a film that were taken in the space of a few seconds. If the light is visibly different between the first and 100th shot, it'll be obvious that it isn't a film.

- **Start fresh.**   Make sure you have plenty of room on your camera's memory card to take your series. You might want to start with a blank card and reduce the resolution of each image to a manageable 640x480 pixels. If you plan to take a lot of pictures, be sure the camera batteries are fresh (so you don't run out of gas halfway through the series), and perhaps start with a large memory card.

Chapter 14

Working with Text and Creating Projects

How to…

- Add text to digital images
- Fill text with color gradients
- Fill text with other images
- Create text drop shadows
- Turn images into wallpaper for the Windows desktop
- Add small images to letterhead in Word
- Create greeting cards on the PC
- Make your own newsletter

Over the course of this book, I've shown you how to do all sorts of things to your images—everything from the mundane, like sharpening, cropping, and brightening your images, to adding sophisticated special effects like chromakey and abstract effects.

Sometimes, though, all you really want to do is add a caption, or turn a picture into a birthday card. In this final chapter on image editing, let's talk about the various ways you can add text to your images to turn them into true multimedia works of art. I'll even show you some simple tricks for creating stuff like Windows wallpaper, greeting cards, and letterhead with your images.

Adding Text to Pictures

If you're used to using a word processor like Microsoft Word, you may be surprised to find that most image editors don't allow you to type directly onto the canvas as if you were writing a letter to Mom. Instead, you need to type your text into a dialog box and then paste that text into the image. In fact, the Text tool plays by a few unusual rules:

- You can't type directly into the image. Instead, most image editors require you to type your text in a dialog box, then transfer it to the image when you're done. You can see the Text Entry dialog box used by Paint Shop Pro in Figure 14-1.

- The color of the text will usually be painted in the currently selected foreground color, so make sure it's set to the right color before you click the Text tool.

- In most image editors, text is an editable object when you first position it. That means you can position it, stretch it, and transform it, and so on—but only right away. If you change tools and do something else, that text typically becomes a permanent part of the image.

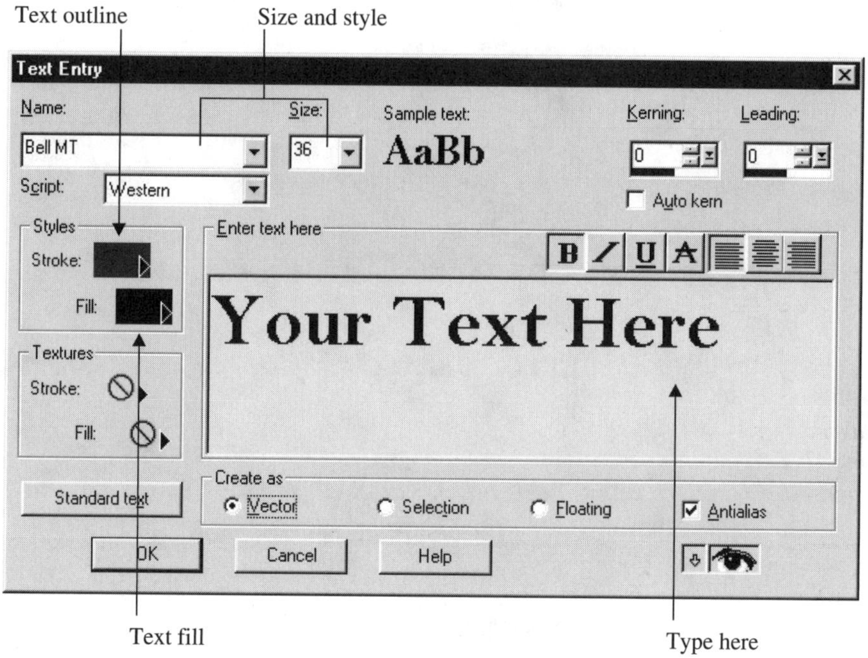

Text outline   Size and style

Text fill   Type here

FIGURE 14-1   The Text Entry dialog box lets you specify the style, color, and size of text you add to a digital image.

■ As soon as you deselect the text, it is embedded permanently into your image and can no longer be modified separately from the rest of the image.

In Paint Shop Pro, here's how to add text to a picture:

How to ...   Add Text to a Picture

1. Change the foreground color to whatever you want the text to be.

2. Click on the Text button in the tool palette. The mouse pointer will change to the letter *A*.

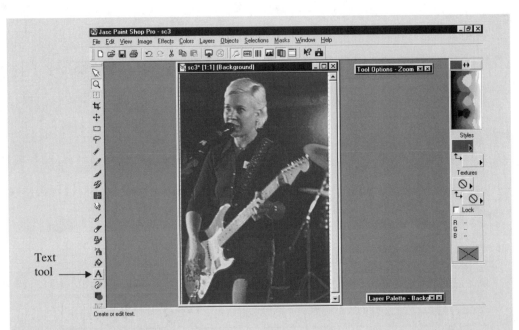

Text
tool ⟶

3. Click in the image where you want the text to be positioned. The point that you click will be the lower-left corner of the text box.

> **NOTE** *The timing of this step varies in different programs. In Adobe PhotoShop, for instance, you don't position the text until the end.*

4. When the Text Entry dialog box appears, choose a font and font size, and type your text into the space provided.

5. Click OK. The text should appear in the image at the place you positioned it in step 3.

6. For the moment, the text is treated as an object that you can edit. You can resize the text by dragging the small boxes in the sides of the text box. You can reposition the text by dragging the box that's in the very center of the text box. See Figure 14-2 for details.

7. When you're satisfied with your text, choose Selections | Select None.

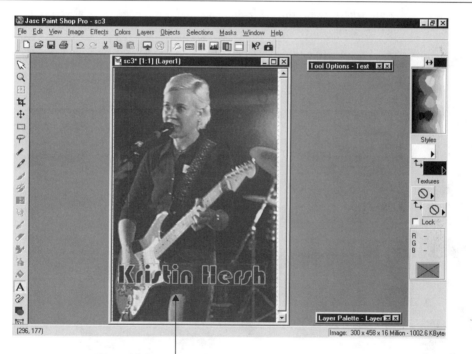

Drag this box to reposition text

  The control boxes in the text object let you edit the text, but only while the text is selected.

Special Effects with Text

There's a lot you can do with text in an image—so much more than just pasting letters down in some primary color. Attractive text, in fact, is what makes or breaks documents like posters and greeting cards. A lot of text tricks are so easy to do that you can experiment and create your own. I've got a few you might want to start with, though.

Create Gradient-Filled Text

The first thing we'll do is fill the text with something other than a boring, solid color. You can create gradient text very easily. In Paint Shop Pro, for instance, here's what you do:

1. Using the color palette, select the foreground and background colors that you want to make up your gradient.

Select colors here

2. Click on the Text button in the tool palette, and then click in the image where you want to position the text. The Text Entry dialog box should appear.

3. In the Styles box, change the Fill item to Gradient. This will fill the text with a gradient fill.

4. Enter your text in the entry box and specify a big, fat font so the gradient will be clearly visible.

5. Click OK to paste the text into the image. You should get a result similar to Figure 14-3.

FIGURE 14-3   Gradient fills add an interesting effect to boring old text.

You can do a lot of things to customize this gradient text. You can gradient-fill the Stroke style instead of the Fill style, for instance, and the result will be a gradient in the outline of the text instead of the inside of the text. You can also change the *direction* of the gradient fill. To do that, click in the center of the gradient fill style in the Text Entry dialog box. The Gradient dialog box will appear, and you can rotate the gradient arrow to force the fill to occur on any angle, instead of the usual top to bottom.

Create Picture-Filled Text

That's not all, though. One of my favorite tricks is to make an image show through the text, as if it were a digital stencil. In Figure 14-4, for instance, I've made the word "Halloween" out of a photo of a pumpkin, in a seasonal photo. It's more interesting—though you can't really tell in this book—because the image of the girl is in black and white, while the text is a vibrant pumpkin orange. This is an interesting exercise in creating an eye-catching picture, so let me show you how to do this yourself. Here's how:

1. Open the image that you want to show through the text.

2. Click on the Text icon and click in the spot where you want to grab the photo as text.

3. Enter the desired text, and set the font and size that you want the text to appear in. You'll need to make the text big and fat in order for this effect to work. Try, for starters, a font like Bauhaus, and set the size to at least 48 points.

4. Choose the Selection option. This will create the text as a selection instead of as solid-colored text.

You can use text as a stencil to show another image through the letters.

Creates a
selection
region from
the text

5. Click OK. The text appears as a selection in the image.

6. If necessary, reposition the text so it's over the correct part of the image. You can move the text by positioning the mouse pointer in the middle of the selection; the pointer will turn into a four-position arrow.

7. Copy the text to the clipboard by choosing Edit | Copy.

8. Open the image to which you want to add the text.

9. If you want to try my fancy "black and white with a splash of color" trick, you'll need to turn the picture into an image now. Choose Colors | Grey Scale from the main menu. Then choose Colors | Increase Color Depth | 16 Million Colors (24 bit), or else the text will be rendered in grayscale as well when you paste it in.

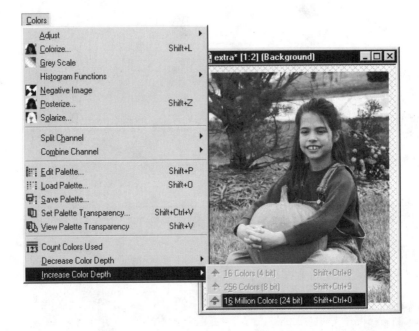

10. Choose Edit | Paste | As New Selection from the menu. The text should appear in the image.

11. Position the text to your liking and choose Selections | Select None.

Add Drop Shadow

Drop shadows, seen in Figure 14-5, are a cool embellishment that can add a lot to the visual appeal of your text. They can even make it more readable, particularly on certain kinds of images. Some programs come with a drop shadow tool built in, making it a snap to add drop shadows to your text.

But if your program doesn't have a drop shadow feature, you can achieve similar results simply by making two copies of the text in different colors and arranging them by hand so they look like text and shadow. Try this:

1. In the color palette, set the foreground color to black. This will be the color of our shadow text.

2. Click the Text button in the tool palette and click on the image to specify where you want it to appear. The Text Entry dialog box should appear.

3. Make sure the Stroke and Fill styles are set to solid color—they should look black—and enter the text, font, and size.

FIGURE 14-5   Drop shadow is an easy effect to achieve, and it looks great.

14

4. Click OK, and then position the text precisely where you will want it in the finished image.

5. Now go back to the color palette and change the foreground color to white.

6. Click the Text button in the tool palette again and click in the image. You don't have to be precise about where the text will go right now, since we'll move the text with the mouse in a few steps.

7. In the Text Entry dialog box, don't change anything. You'll want the font, size, and text to be exactly the same as the shadow text we've already entered.

8. Click OK to paste the text into the image.

9. Position the mouse pointer over the center of the text, and then drag the text until it is positioned over the shadow text, offset just enough that it looks like a drop shadow.

10. Choose Selections | Select None.

Combine Image and Drop Shadow

This last text trick is so simple you're going to say it's hardly a trick at all, but I'm including it to show you how easy it is to come up with cool effects with very little effort. The effect: text filled with a picture, like we've already done, but this time the picture is the same as the one that the text is in. How can you see the text at all, you wonder, if it's filled with the same image as the background? The text is bordered—on two sides, at least—by a dark drop shadow. Check out Figure 14-6.

Here's how to do it:

1. Change the foreground color to black using the color palette.

2. Click on the Text button in the tool palette and click in the image to specify where the text will be pasted.

3. In the Text Entry dialog box, make sure the Stroke and Fill styles are set to solid color, and choose Selection in the Create As section of the dialog box.

14

4. Enter the text and specify a font and size.

5. Click OK to paste the text into the image.

6. You should see a selection shaped like the text. Just grab the text and drag it a short distance. In place of the text you should see black lettering that will serve as your drop shadow. Don't move the text too far, or the image text will get "lost" in the surrounding image.

FIGURE 14-6   This is a subtle but effective text trick.

Projects for Your Digital Images

Now that you know how to edit, manipulate, and embellish your images, you probably want to apply those skills by using images in projects that go beyond emailing images to your friends. One of the benefits of digital images, of course, is the ease with which you can incorporate them into projects like posters, greeting cards, newsletters, and business cards. Let's take a look at how you can get started doing this yourself.

Using Digital Images as Wallpaper

Let's start with something that's not only easy but will make your PC a bit more fun. Your Windows desktop can display any kind of image as long as it has been saved in a JPG, GIF, or BMP format. If your desktop still has that same old blue background, you can use an image from your digital camera to brighten things up.

To display your image on your desktop, do this:

1. Make sure your image is in JPG, BMP, or GIF format. As you know by now, most digital images save images in JPG format, so you're probably ready to go. If you are using Windows 98, you can select a JPG or a GIF image, but you will have to enable the active desktop. Otherwise, you can use a BMP file.

14

2. Right-click on the desktop and choose Properties from the context menu. The Display
Properties dialog box appears.

3. On the Background tab, click on the Browse button to choose the image.

4. If you want the image to be centered in your display, choose Center in the Display
drop-down menu. If you'd prefer the image to repeat itself all across the display, choose
Tile instead.

5. Click OK to close the dialog box.

NOTE   *You might want to resize the image in a program like Paint Shop Pro to match the screen
resolution you run on your PC. That way, the image will take up the entire screen.*

If your image is too small for the display, it'll either be tiled to fill the screen or centered in the display with a lot of blank desktop around it. For photographs, I think centering looks good—tiling photographs is just too busy and annoys me (see Figure 14-7). Of course, you can experiment and arrange your display any way you like.

Adding an Image to Letterhead

If you use Microsoft Word and send a lot of letters, you might want to try this next project— creating your own personal letterhead with an embedded digital image. Here's what to do:

1. Open Microsoft Word. If you don't already have a new blank document open, click on the New Document icon in the toolbar.

FIGURE 14-7 The same image shown centered, tiled, and stretched.

2. Design the letterhead any way you like. You should set your formatting to single space and try to keep your text smaller than about 11 points.

3. To insert an image from your digital camera, choose Insert | Picture | From File and locate the image you want to include. The image will appear in your document.

4. To make the image easier to move around and position on the page, you'll need to put a frame around the picture. Right-click on the image and choose Format Picture.

5. Click on the Layout tab and choose Tight.

6. Click OK.

7. Position the image in the letterhead region of your document, such as to the left of your name. Notice how the text moves to accommodate the image.

8. Finish the letterhead off by drawing a thin horizontal line under the text and image (see Figure 14-8). To do that, activate the drawing tools by clicking on the Drawing icon in the toolbar. Then click on the Line tool and drag out a horizontal line, holding down the SHIFT key at the same time. The line will snap to the horizontal automatically.

Creating Your Own Greeting Cards

There are two ways to make greeting cards using your computer: the easy way and the not-as-easy-but-still-not-very-hard way. The easy way is by using one of the many greeting card

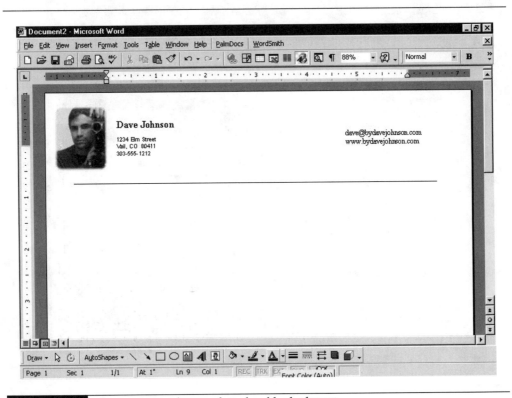

FIGURE 14-8   Images can make your letterhead look elegant.

software packages on the market (see Figure 14-9). Not only can you import your digital camera images into these programs, but they also come with a considerable collection of clip art and premade card templates.

If you don't have one of those programs, you can still make your own greeting cards in a page layout program or Microsoft Word. Since Word is the lowest common denominator—almost everyone has it—let's create a card in that. Before we get started, though, it's worth pointing out that there are two common methods for making a greeting card on the PC: the single-fold and the dual-fold.

Single-fold cards are simply made from 8.5x11-inch paper or cardstock and folded once down the middle so that the card measures 5.5x8.5 inches. This is a slightly oversized card, but

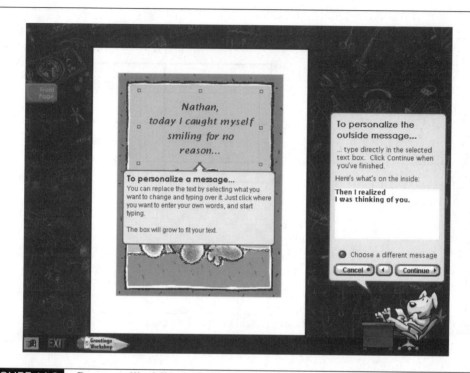

FIGURE 14-9   Programs like Microsoft Greetings Workshop let you import your own digital images into their greeting card templates.

it's a good size and the one I usually use. The alternative is a dual-fold card that is folded once lengthwise and again widthwise, for a card that measures 5.5x4.25 inches. The disadvantage to this kind of card is that it's a bit small and it has a potentially amateurish double fold along one edge (see Figure 14-10).

You can't really make dual-fold cards in Word, since that kind of card requires one of the panels to be printed upside down. So Word is best at single-fold cards, as in this example:

1. Open Word and create a new document.

14

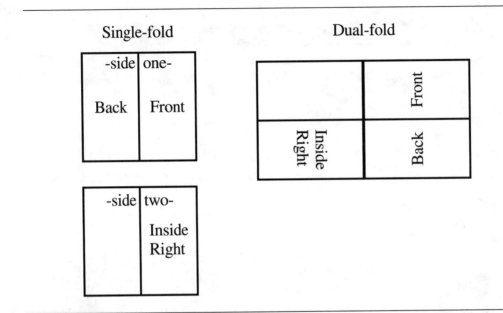

FIGURE 14-10
You can make either single-fold or dual-fold cards on your PC with almost any program.

2. Change the document into a landscape orientation. Choose File | Page Setup. The Page Setup dialog box appears.

3. Click on the Paper Size tab and select Landscape from the orientation section. Click OK.

4. Now we need to give the document two columns. Each column will be a panel on the finished card. Choose Format | Columns.

5. In the Columns dialog box, select Two and click OK.

6. Now you can enter your text. The left column on the first page is actually the rear of the card. If you want to, you can add something to the bottom of the rear panel like commercial greeting cards have. Just press ENTER enough times to get to the bottom of the page.

7. Now it's time for the front of the card. That's the right column on the first page, so press ENTER to get there. You'll probably want to insert an image there using Insert | Picture | From File. You can place text above or below the image, or integrate the text in the image in a program like Paint Shop Pro first. Be sure to experiment with large and stylish fonts for this card.

TIP

Microsoft's WordArt is a cool way to dress up a greeting card in Word. Choose Insert | Picture | WordArt to insert WordArt into your project. WordArt lets you turn plain text into a fancy 3-D piece of art, as seen in Figure 14-11.

8. The inside of the card is on the second page. The left inside panel is the left column, and the right inside panel is the right column. Enter text and images as necessary to lay out the card you want to create.

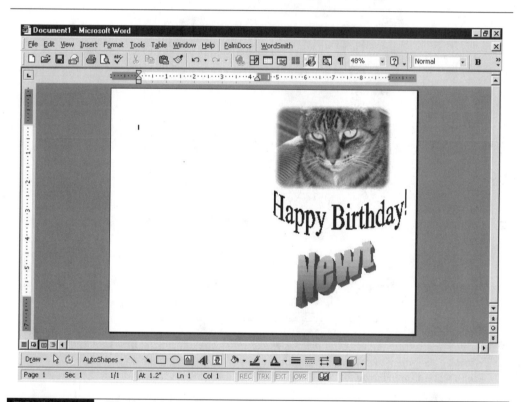

FIGURE 14-11   Word can be used to make quick and easy greeting cards, though a dedicated card program is a better bet.

14

9. When you're done, you'll need to print your card manually so that it doesn't print the second page of the document on a second sheet of paper. To do that, you have two choices:

- Only load a single sheet of paper in the printer. When the first page is printed, turn the paper over and load it back in for the second pass, *or*

- Change the printer settings. In Word, choose File | Print. Choose Properties to open the Printer Properties dialog box and change the printer's paper source to Manual.

TIP *If you're printing on an inkjet printer, make sure you wait for the first side to dry before turning the paper over and printing the second side. See Chapter 15 for more information on printing.*

Create a Newsletter

Equipped with Microsoft Publisher, you can create professional and attractive newsletters for the office, family, or your club or organization. Publisher comes in most versions of Microsoft Office, and I highly recommend it for generating your own newsletters (as well as business cards and other projects). Publisher is a wizard-based program. All you have to do is follow the directions to set up the overall look and feel of your document, and then fill in the text and replace the placeholder images with your own pictures.

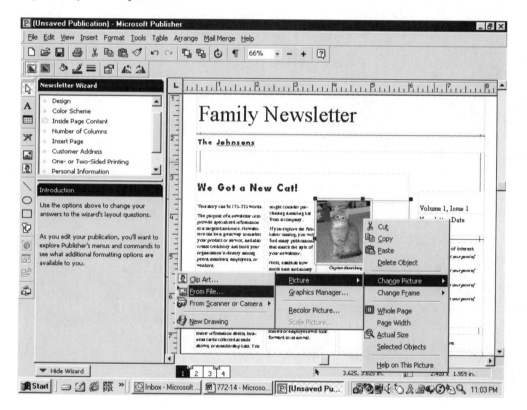

Part IV

Using Your Images

Chapter 15

Printing Your Pictures

How to...

- ■ Choose the printer that's right for you
- ■ Distinguish among laser, inkjet, and dye sublimation printers
- ■ Shop for a printer
- ■ Match resolution to print size
- ■ Choose the right kind of paper for your print job
- ■ Print an enlargement with Paint Shop Pro
- ■ Configure your printer for paper and quality
- ■ Determine what side of the paper to print on
- ■ Care for prints after they come out of the printer
- ■ Send your images to someone else for printing

A lot of the time, it all comes down to this: no matter how versatile the digital medium is, a digital camera isn't very useful unless you can make prints. Great prints. Prints that look every bit as good as what you can get from a 35mm camera and the local photo shop.

If that sounds like you, you're in luck. Recent advances in print technology have made it possible to make your own prints that look every bit as good as what you can get from a 35mm camera. In some ways, the results can be better. With a digital image you can tweak it so it looks exactly the way you want it to, and you can print it any way you like, from wallet sized all the way up to near-poster 13x19 inches.

In this chapter I'll talk about everything you need to know to get great prints from your digital images. When you're done, you'll be able to frame your creations, and no one will be able to tell that the pictures came out of a computer printer.

Using the Right Printer

There was a time not all that long ago that computer printers had a reputation for, shall we say, substandard output. Of course, everyone thought the printers looked pretty good at the time, but there was no way anyone would mistake what came out of a computer printer for a real photograph. Printers couldn't depict enough colors. The resolution was too low. Obvious bands of different intensity colors ran through images like venetian blinds on a window. And those were just the most vexing of the output problems.

Then, a few years ago, it all started to change. Around the same time that scanners became affordable and digital cameras began to hit the scene, printer manufacturers had new incentives to make their products work better. By the late 1990s, most mainstream printers could create passable prints from computer images, and the top-of-the-line printers made prints that were essentially photo-realistic.

In the last few years, not a lot has changed dramatically. For most practical applications, it's not possible to make prints look any better to the casual viewer, so printer manufacturers have turned their attention to other aspects of digital printing, like making the prints last longer before they fade. I'll discuss this area in more detail a little later in the chapter.

Choosing a Printer

Before we get started printing, let's talk about the printers themselves and how to choose the right one. Buying a printer isn't an easy decision because not only are there many different brands of printers competing for your attention—and lots of different models from each manufacturer—but you also have to figure out what kind of printer you want. If you're serious about printing digital images, I suspect you'll want an inkjet printer. But to be sure, let me tell you about the variety of printers you can choose from.

Laser Printers

Laser printers are like specialized photocopiers. Using the digital image in the computer's memory as a template, they electrically charge a piece of paper. The printer then allows toner—a fine inklike powder—to come into contact with the paper. (See Figure 15-1 for a look at a typical toner cartridge.) The toner sticks to the paper in places where it has an electrostatic charge, and the toner is finally permanently melted into the paper by a very hot fusing wire.

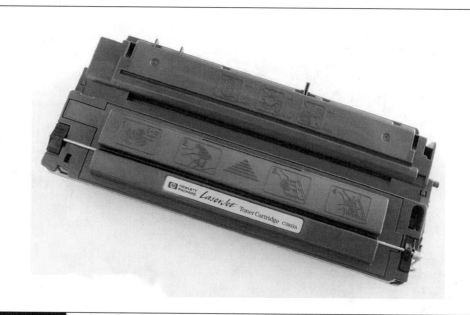

15

FIGURE 15-1   A laser printer's toner cartridge is generally good for several thousand prints.

Laser printers have a lot of advantages. They can print quickly (many personal laser printers can generate as many as 8 or 10 pages per minute), and the toner lasts a long time, yielding a very low cost per page. My HP LaserJet 6P (see Figure 15-2), which has served me for many years now, prints about 3000 to 5000 sheets of paper for each $80 toner cartridge. Those advantages add up to a good all-around office printer that handles most common print jobs pretty well. Personal laser printers can be had for between $200 and $500.

Unfortunately, laser printers tend to be better at printing text than graphics. That's mainly because most laser printers are black-and-white devices, able to generate just shades of gray. Color laser printers are available, but since they tend to cost $2000 or more, they're beyond the reach of most people. Even if you could purchase a color laser printer, I wouldn't recommend it for printing digital images for framing. Color laser printers tend to produce a shiny, artificial look, and they limit you to a print size of 8x10 inches.

Laser printers can certainly be used to print images, and they can do it well, as long as your needs don't include color. You can print a large quantity of family newsletters with a laser printer faster than with an inkjet, for instance.

Inkjet Printers

If you want to print images, I think inkjet printers (such as the one in Figure 15-3) are the best all-around printing solution for most people. They produce excellent color output, but can also print text at a reasonable speed—as long as you don't need to print a lot of it.

FIGURE 15-2   The HP LaserJet 6P

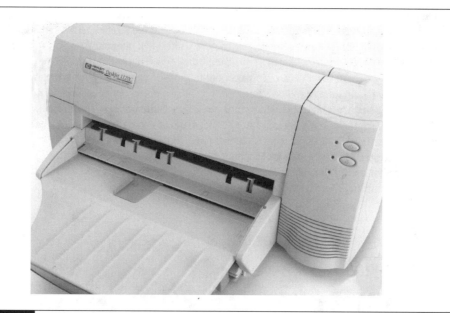

| FIGURE 15-3 | The HP DeskJet 1120C inkjet printer |

Inkjet printers are, in some ways, a simpler technology than laser printers. Simply put, they work by spraying microscopic droplets of ink onto paper. You can see an inkjet's internals—complete with ink cartridges—in Figure 15-4. Of course, it gets a lot more complicated than that. Printer

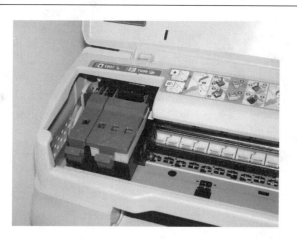

| FIGURE 15-4 | The print head slides back and forth across the page, spraying dots as it goes. |

15

manufacturers exert a lot of effort making sure that the dots are small; that they combine with other dots to mimic thousands of distinct colors; that they dry fast enough so they don't spread, run, or smear; and that the paper is optimized to handle the ink's chemical characteristics. It's a very technical business.

Nonetheless, we generally don't have to worry about most of that stuff. What matters is that they create stunning output and they're pretty affordable, typically running between $100 and $500.

I often run into people who are concerned about inkjet quality based on experiences they had with older printers from the late 1980s or early 1990s. But as I mentioned earlier, those fears are relatively unfounded. Inkjet technology has improved to the extent that there's almost no way to distinguish between a 35mm print and a quality inkjet print made on photo-grade paper. My walls are covered with digital images that I've printed, matted, and framed (see Figure 15-5). No one can tell the difference.

FIGURE 15-5 These pictures were printed on the Epson Stylus Photo 1270.

NOTE *You may see the term "bubblejet" when shopping for a printer. BubbleJet is the name that Canon gives to its inkjet printer line. Canon claims they made up the name because the company uses a slightly different ink deployment technology, but the bottom line is that it's just a name. Consider BubbleJets to be inkjets by every relevant measure.*

Dye Sublimation Printers

The smallest segment of the printer market is occupied by dye sublimation printers (also called dye-subs for short). Dye-subs work by spreading ink onto the paper from long rolls of heated, colored plastic ribbons. The results from dye-sub printers are nothing short of stunning—they typically look just as good as 35mm prints and even magazine photos.

The downside is that they're not much good for printing text, so your dye-sub printer will have to be a second printer almost by definition, which you only use when you're expressly printing photos. For me, a bigger disadvantage is that dye-sub printers typically only create 5x7-inch or perhaps 8x10-inch prints—nothing larger. Also, the selection of printer models is much more limited and much more expensive. You can find some printers in the $500 range, but full-page 8x10-inch prints require bigger printers that range over $1000.

Make no mistake, output from dye sublimation printers looks great. But given all the disadvantages, I think you're better off choosing an inkjet. And since pictures from inkjets look so good—just about as good as from a dye-sub—there's hardly a reason to choose otherwise.

Do You Need Two Printers?

I have two printers. I use an HP LaserJet 6P for routine text printing—I do a lot of that—and an Epson Stylus Photo 1270 for all of my image printing.

Do you need two printers? It might seem a bit decadent at first, but it's really not, depending upon how much printing you actually do. Both inkjets and lasers are reasonably affordable these days, but an inkjet alone will lead to slow and comparatively expensive routine printing. That's why I have one of each.

If you do have two printers, you can alternate between them by using a switch box. (Parallel port switch boxes are available at most computer stores.) If your printers connect via the USB port, you don't need to use a switch box. Or if you have two PCs in your home, you can connect one printer to each PC and then network the PCs together with a home networking kit. That allows you to print to either printer from either computer.

15

What to Look For

OK, so now you know you want to buy an inkjet printer. At least, that's the assumption I'm making. If you don't agree with me, you're shopping on your own. Actually, I'll talk about laser printers as well. I hope you're happy.

Where do you start? Walk into a store and all printers tend to look more or less the same. And in my humble opinion, salespeople are not particularly helpful unless you already have a pretty good idea of what you want. So use this checklist to help choose your printer:

- **Resolution**   Resolution is measured in dots per inch (dpi), and most laser printers are 300dpi or 600dpi. Keep in mind that 600dpi is four times higher than 300dpi. We're measuring the number of dots that a printer can pack into a square, so 600dpi in height and width is four times better than 300dpi. For a laser printer, the sweet spot is 600dpi. It's the highest resolution you'll find that's affordable. But if all you're printing is text, 300dpi is fine. In the inkjet world, resolution varies dramatically, though better printers will typically deliver 1440dpi.

- **Number of colors**   This is irrelevant for a laser printer, of course, but when inkjet shopping, look for a printer that uses a pure black cartridge instead of mixing all the other colors to mimic black. (The result is a muddy gray-brown instead of black, and these printers use up their ink exceptionally fast.) Better inkjet printers use five, six, or even seven independent ink colors to create more realistic photo prints.

- **Speed**   You should look for the printer's speed (measured in pages per minute, or ppm) and resolution. Slow laser printers run at 4ppm; the fastest are around 16ppm. Remember that inkjets print much more slowly; color is their selling point, not speed.

- **Eyeball the prints**   No matter what the specs say, a printer is only as good as the prints. Try out printers in the store before you buy. Most computer stores have demo models set up that spit out prints when you press a test button.

- **Ease of use**   Once you get the basic specs down, you might want to consider some less tangible factors like ease of use. Specifically, I think the easiest printers to use and maintain connect with a USB cable instead of a parallel port connector. Most good printers also come with status monitor software that lets you get important information about your printer—like how much ink is left—right from the Windows desktop. If you have a notebook PC or handheld computer, you might want to print directly to your printer via the wireless infrared port. Few printers have infrared support, however, so you'll have to shop around. My Hewlett-Packard LaserJet 6P, for instance, is one of just half a dozen or so printers on the market that can print via infrared.

- **Size and capacity**   Though most major manufacturers like Epson, Canon, and HP all make good printers that generate excellent results, they differ dramatically in terms of what kind of paper they can print on. You'll have to buy a wide-format printer if you want to create 11x17- or 13x19-inch prints, for instance.

Do You Need a PostScript Printer?

PostScript is a page definition language that is popular with users of the Macintosh and some high-end page layout and graphics programs. If you're a graphics professional, or if you want to work in Mac/PC hybrid workgroups over a network, then you should definitely consider PostScript. In general, however, you won't need PostScript and can save money by buying a printer that doesn't include it. Bottom line: don't let a salesperson talk you into buying a PostScript printer.

Printing Your Images

So you're all ready to print. You've downloaded your pictures from your camera to your PC. You have a printer connected to the computer. All you need to do is print. Let's talk about the things you need to ensure great prints.

The Right Resolution

The resolution of your image is one of the two most important factors that determine how good your pictures look when printed. Printers do vary, but in general you can use this rule of thumb:

Type of Printer	Resolution (in dpi)
Laser	150 or 300
Inkjet	150 or 200

Experimentation is key, though. Choose a high-quality image and sample it at several different sizes. Print each one and compare them to see where the quality threshold lies with your printer. In other words, what minimum resolution do you need to eliminate obvious pixels and jaggedness from your prints.

Let's assume that 200dpi is about right for your printer. Suppose you want to print an image on an inkjet printer. To determine how big your image should be before you print it, just multiply the output size (in inches) by 200. The following chart illustrates the minimum dimensions of your image for a variety of common print sizes with an inkjet printer:

Print Size (inches)	File Size (pixels)	Camera Resolution Needed
4x6	800x1200	1 megapixel
8x10	1600x2000	3 megapixel
11x17	2200x3400	6 megapixel
13x19	2600x3800	10 megapixel

15

Wow. Surprised? It takes a lot of pixels to make high-quality prints. So what does that chart mean—that you need a 10-megapixel camera to make a 13x19-inch print with a wide-format inkjet printer?

Well, yeah, that's exactly what it's saying. But there's good news: you can cheat. Many printers will still give you great results even if you feed them an image that's under-pixeled. In other words, suppose you have a 1600x1200-pixel image. You might still get quite decent results by printing it at 11x17 inches or perhaps even 13x19. Try it out and see.

NOTE   *Right now, digital cameras only go up to 6 megapixels. But if you have some 35mm slides or negatives, you can scan them into your PC at much higher resolutions than any digital camera is currently able to capture.*

Too Much or Too Little Resolution

As I already mentioned, a 4x6-inch inkjet print typically requires an 800x1200-pixel image to start with to avoid pixels and jagged edges in the final image. That's almost twice the resolution that a VGA-resolution 640x480-pixel digital camera can muster. So you can see the value in having a 2- or 3-megapixel camera. What happens if you print an image that doesn't have enough pixels for the size you want to achieve? You get something like Figure 15-6.

FIGURE 15-6   This happens when you try to print a low-resolution image too big.

If the output size isn't as important to you as having a sharp, quality print, then just print the image smaller. Cramming those pixels together on paper in less space will make the print sharper.

In reality, you can still get pretty good results printing even a 640x480-pixel image at 4x6, even though that only works out to 100dpi. If you look carefully at the finished print, you'll find that you can see jagged edges where there weren't enough pixels to fill in. For best results, pick a size that lets you print around 200dpi, or whatever resolution best matches your particular printer.

That's what happens when you print too few pixels for the size you're shooting for. What about too many pixels? Can an image that's too high-res ever be a problem? The answer is generally not. Too many pixels isn't really a problem, though it does make your image file bigger than it has to be, and it can potentially bog everything down. The bottom line is that if you pack more pixels than you need into an image—above 200dpi, for instance—odds are good that you won't improve image quality very much. Instead, you'll just make the file bigger, which takes more storage space on your hard disk and can slow down the printing process.

> **TIP** *Test your own printer by generating prints in high-quality mode at 100, 150, and 200dpi. Use these to figure out what the resolution threshold of your printer is, and strive to use that setting as often as possible.*

Of course, all this advice is specifically for someone who wants to know how much resolution an image needs to print well at a certain output size. If you just want to print an image and don't care how big it turns out, just print it. Most image editors have an option to let you print the image at full-page size or at the image's normal size. If you choose normal size, the image will print smaller than full page and probably look just fine. It's only when you force the image to print at a certain size that the image's original resolution becomes important.

Working with Paper

Here's a common scenario: you see great, photo-realistic prints in a computer store and think, "that's the printer for me. It's only $150 and it makes outstanding pictures!" So you buy the printer and bring it home. But when you actually get the printer set up and send your first few images to it, you're devastated. The output is horrible. The prints look flat and lifeless. The paper curls. What went wrong?

It's the paper. What you failed to consider is that the choice of paper is so important to the quality of your prints that it's essentially *more important than the printer itself!* There are a handful of printers on the market that can generate photo-realistic prints. But unless you use quality paper, they will all disappoint you.

Which Paper Is Best

Unfortunately, choosing paper isn't easy, even if you know that you want to get the best. There are a lot of choices, and it isn't generally clear which kind is best based on the name or description on the package. This is especially true for inkjet printers. I honestly don't know why paper manufacturers make this so hard; it would seem to be counterproductive to sales.

15

Paper for Laser Printers

If you have a laser printer, you may be wondering what kind of paper is appropriate for that printer as well. I suggest that you use ordinary 20-pound laser or copier paper that is at least 80lb bright. Decent laser paper shouldn't cost more than about $7 per 500 sheets (a ream). I'd be reluctant to buy really inexpensive paper ($3/ream or less) since loose paper fibers in budget-priced paper can, over time, clog your printer, affecting its performance and eventually even damaging it.

So where do you start? Let's begin with day-to-day use—plain paper, not photo printing. Even here, use quality paper, since cheap stock can plug the nozzles and decrease the effective resolution of the printer. For general-purpose printing, you can use the same stock that I recommend for laser printers. Of course, I'm assuming that the majority of what you print is just test prints, text, and other routine output. If every print you make is destined for the Louvre, then you might want to skip directly to the section where I talk about photo paper.

When you're ready to step up to some higher-quality printing, you have a number of choices on store shelves (see Figure 15-7). Here's a general overview of the various grades available:

FIGURE 15-7   With so many choices on the store shelves, it pays to experiment to find the paper that works best with your printer.

- ■ **Plain paper**   As I've already mentioned, this is good for general text and ordinary graphics printing. The paper is inexpensive, but the ink tends to absorb quickly into the paper and blur the image. The paper also curls and distorts.

- ■ **High-quality or coated paper**   This is one step up and embeds clay or some other ink fixture into the paper to stop the inks from spreading before they dry. For most printing you won't notice a big difference, but this paper improves photographic prints.

- ■ **Photo paper**   A variation of coated paper, photo paper is generally bright-white coated paper that's designed explicitly for photographs. If you're looking for paper in an intermediate price range that can give decent results, try this stuff.

- ■ **Glossy photo paper**   The best stuff around, this paper is expensive, generally costing about a dollar a sheet. Certainly you won't use it all the time, but if you plan to frame a picture or give your digital "prints" away to family or friends, definitely use the special photo paper. Note that you can only print on one side of photo paper; the back side looks like the back of a photograph and generally has a logo printed there (as you can see below). I don't recommend printing on the back of glossy paper, even on a laser printer.

Which Brand?

What brand of paper should you use? Should you use Epson in an Epson printer and Canon paper in a Canon printer, or should you buy paper from a company like Ilford—known in 35mm photography circles for their excellent paper—instead? This is a good question. Obviously, each printer company wants you to use their own brand of paper with their printer.

In truth, vendors like Canon, Epson, and HP go to great lengths to fine-tune their paper to match their inks so colors won't bleed and they'll be as vivid as possible. My own Epson Stylus Photo 1270 does best with Epson's Premium Glossy Photo Paper, and I use that paper exclusively now. When I first got the printer, I tried a dozen different kinds of papers, including paper from companies like Ilford and Tetenal, which came highly recommended by computer and photography store salespeople. After being disappointed with all of those other brands, I tried Epson's own Premium Glossy paper, and was blown away—the results were dramatically better. I've had similar

15

experiences with other printers, though I have to admit that they weren't as dramatic as with the Epson printer, which was clearly engineered with the specialty paper in mind.

So what should you do? If you have a few dollars to spare, buy a bunch of different paper packages and try them out. Print the same image on different kinds of paper and lay them out side-by-side in good light. Determine which one is best, and stick with that brand of paper.

Other Specialty Papers

In addition to ordinary plain, coated, and photo paper, printer manufacturers and paper vendors sell a variety of other specialty papers. You might want to investigate these papers, since they can be a lot of fun and enable you to do all sorts of things with your printer that you never imagined possible:

- **Greeting card paper** Greeting card paper and matching envelopes let you make your own greeting cards with your printer and some greeting card software.

- **Transparency paper** This clear film media is perfect for printing color overhead slides for business meetings. You can use this to print PowerPoint slides or any other kind of image or document.

- **T-shirt transfer paper** This special paper is really an iron-on transfer that you can run through your printer, then apply to clothing. When you print on T-shirt paper, be sure to use special T-shirt transfer software or just reverse your image before you print. (Create a mirror image of what you want it to look like.)

■ **Fabric sheets**   This unique kind of printing media is actually fabric that gives your prints texture. You can print on it just for its own sake or use the print to make cross-stitch designs and other craft projects.

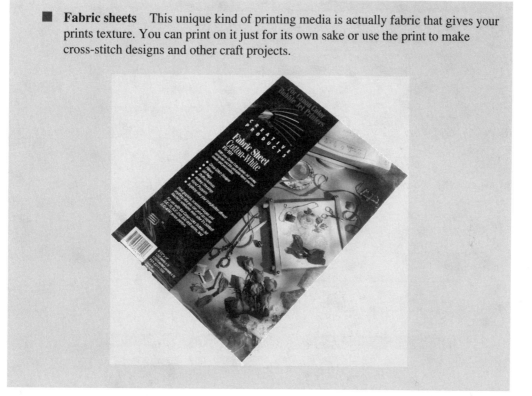

Making Your Prints

Now that you have all the parts in place, it's time to print. I'll show you how to make a print of a specific size in Paint Shop Pro; other programs use a similar method. Let's say we're going to make a print at 11x17 inches. Do this:

1. Load the picture you want to print in Paint Shop Pro.

2. Now we're going to select the paper size and orientation. Choose File | Page Setup from the main menu. You should see the Page Setup dialog box.

3. Click the Portrait or Landscape button in the Orientation section of the dialog box to get the image oriented properly.

15

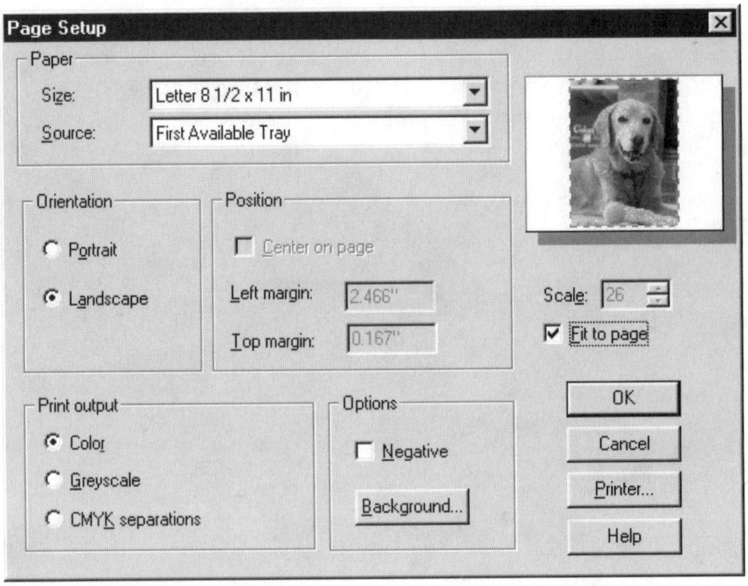

4. In the Size drop-down menu, choose US B 11x17 in.

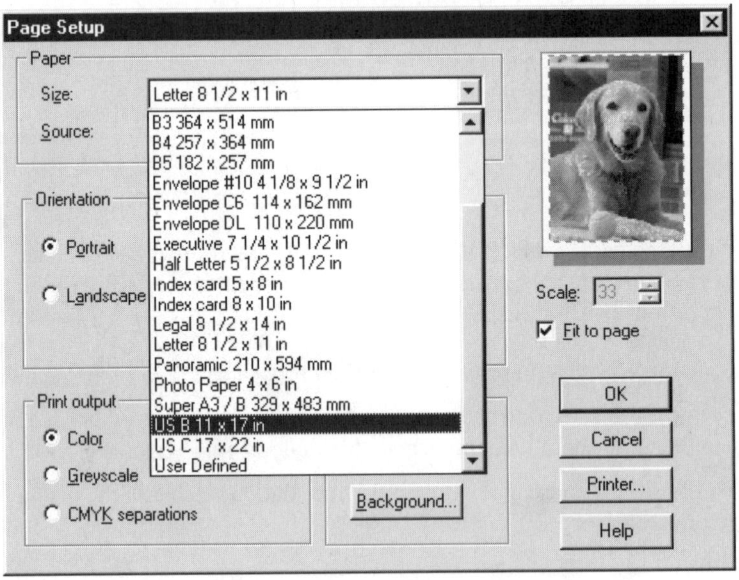

5. You can reduce the margins in the Position dialog box to squeeze more picture into the page. If the margin boxes are ghosted, uncheck Center On Page. Then enter a smaller number in the margins, such as **.15"**, shown here:

6. Click the Fit To Page box. You should see the preview of the image snap to fill most of the page.

TIP

If the image doesn't fill the page adequately, you can click OK on the Page Setup dialog box and crop the image so it better fits the page size you are trying to print to.

7. Click OK to close the Page Setup dialog box.

8. Select File | Print. The Print dialog box should appear.

9. Click Properties next to your selected printer. The Printer Properties should appear, though it will vary depending upon what kind of printer you have.

10. Select the correct type of paper. If this is going to be framed and hung on your wall, for instance, you probably want to select a glossy or premium paper.

NOTE

If you don't select the kind of paper you're actually printing with, the results will be disappointing.

11. Load the paper in your printer. Make sure that you put it in with the appropriate side set for printing, and only load a single sheet at a time.

12. Click OK to begin printing.

13. When the paper comes out of the printer, leave it there to dry for several minutes. Don't handle it until you're sure it's dry, otherwise you could smudge it.

Which Side Is the Right Side?

Often, it matters which side of the page you print on. Plain-old laser paper is the same on both sides, so if you print on a laser printer or you use plain paper in an inkjet, it doesn't matter. But if you print on specialty paper in an inkjet printer, make sure you load the paper the right way. Keep these tips in mind:

- Usually, the brighter or shinier side of the paper is the printing side. Sometimes it's also rough, like sandpaper.

- If you're printing on photo paper, the back will probably have a company logo on it.

- Many paper types label the paper with small marks to indicate the proper print side.

Be sure you look carefully at the print directions the first time you try a new paper. Ink won't adhere well—or at all—to the wrong side of specialty papers, and you could end up with a real mess in and around your printer if the ink runs everywhere.

Caring for Your Prints

All picture colors tend to fade over time, but inkjet photos tend to fade somewhat faster. In fact, inkjet inks are sensitive to ultraviolet light, and your images will fade faster if exposed to direct sunlight for extended periods. If you plan to frame pictures and leave them exposed to sunlight, consider using UV-shielded glass, available at some framing shops.

TIP   *Keep original image files on your hard disk or archived on CD-ROM so you can reprint them when the fading becomes noticeable.*

Some newer printers are marketed specifically as models that create prints with more *lightfastness* than older printers. You can probably guess that lightfastness is a print's ability to resist fading when exposed to light. A number of Epson models in particular offer a lightfastness of 10 or more years—some over 100 years. By comparison, 35mm prints tend to be lightfast for only about 50 years; so newer printers can create prints that last longer than traditional prints.

No matter what kind of printer, ink, or paper you use, you should protect your prints from fading from the moment you print them. Here are a few precautions you can take:

- Cover the print with glass or plastic as soon as it's dry. Contaminants in the air can fade a print quickly, but if you put it under glass or in a photo album, the print is no longer in direct contact with air and thus is protected. Some ink and paper combinations can cause a print to fade dramatically in a matter of days if left exposed to the open air.

- Keep the print out of direct sunlight, even when under glass. Hang the print where the sun doesn't shine directly on the wall.

- Avoid handling the print in such a way that you touch the ink with your fingers.

15

Working with Printing Services

Do you have a great picture that you'd like to print but can't get the results you want with your own printer? You can always enlist the aid of a print shop or service bureau. Such businesses are generally not cheap, but they may be able to take your image on disk and provide you with a very high quality image. And modern print shops aren't nearly as intimidating as they used to be, since local copy centers have started offering similar services.

If you want a print shop to make prints for you, shop around and find out a few important things before you decide which one you want to use:

- What are their rates?
- How does the volume affect the cost? (If you want 50 copies, it may begin to get a lot cheaper on a per-image basis.)
- What format do they require the image in?
- How can you submit files—on floppy, Zip, or email?
- What kind of paper do they use?

Most importantly, some local photo shops have started offering digital image printing. Visit your local photo finisher and see if they can make prints from digital images for you. Another alternative: some Web sites have begun offering this service as well. One site that I've tried and like is www.ezprints.com. This site can create prints as small as wallets or as large as 20x24 posters from digital images that you upload to the site.

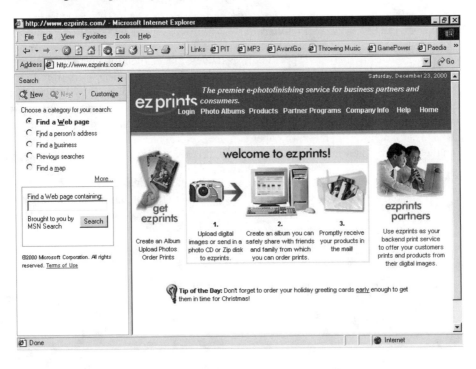

Chapter 16 | Sharing Your Pictures

How to...

- Send and receive images via email
- Choose the right file format for emailing pictures
- Compress images for email and disk
- Prepare images for display on the Web
- Choose a Web design program
- Store images on the Web without programming
- Show off pictures on a Palm handheld
- Display images on a digital picture frame
- Create a video slide show with your camera and a VCR
- Create a video slide show using PowerPoint on your PC

Taking pictures is one thing; actually sharing them with friends, family, and coworkers is something else entirely. Of course, this is one area where your digital camera has a leg up on 35mm cameras. To share traditional prints with someone, you need to physically give them a copy. That means visiting the photo finisher and having duplicates made. Or you could scan the images and distribute them electronically.

Digital camera images are electronic to begin with, though, and that makes everything a whole lot easier. Want to share your images? Email them. Or you can post them to the Web or show them off with a digital picture frame or a Palm handheld PC. In this last chapter of *How to Do Everything with Your Digital Camera*, I'll show you how to easily make your images available to other people.

Send Images via Email

Email is perhaps the most common way to share digital images with people who live far apart. Not only is email good for casually lending images to friends and family, it's also the medium of choice for professionals. When I create images for print in newspapers, magazines, and books, I typically send the files via email unless they are so large that email is not practical.

So how do you do it? Sending pictures within email is simply a matter of including one or more images as *attachments* in your mail message. Attachments are binary files—as opposed to plain text—that your mail program can deliver to another person's mail system.

Most of the time, attachments work just fine. Occasionally, though, you'll run into problems sending images as attachments. That's because the original Internet wasn't designed to accommodate the sending of binary files like pictures via email, and encoding schemes were "tacked on" after the fact. Here are some snags you may run into:

■ **Beware of sending files that are too big.** Most email systems can't deal with a single email file that's bigger than about 2MB. Personally, I'd consider 1.5MB to be your upper limit on file size. If you send a very large file to someone, it can get "stuck" in their mail server, clogging up messages that are trying to come in afterwards. Check the file size of your attachments (see Figure 16-1) before sending them.

■ **America Online can only receive a single attachment.** Even though most mail systems can accept multiple attached files in each email message, AOL doesn't quite know what to make of that kind of message. Usually, only one of the attachments will get to the recipient, and the others will simply disappear. Send AOL users one attachment at a time.

■ **Not all mail programs are completely compatible.** You can send a plain text message between virtually any two Internet mail programs in the world, but if you want to send an attachment, sometimes it won't work quite right. The solution? Your mail program may allow you to change the way your attachment is encoded. If that's the case, you may be able to experiment and send the file to the recipient anyway. The most common encoding schemes are called MIME and UUENCODE. If your recipient claims that an

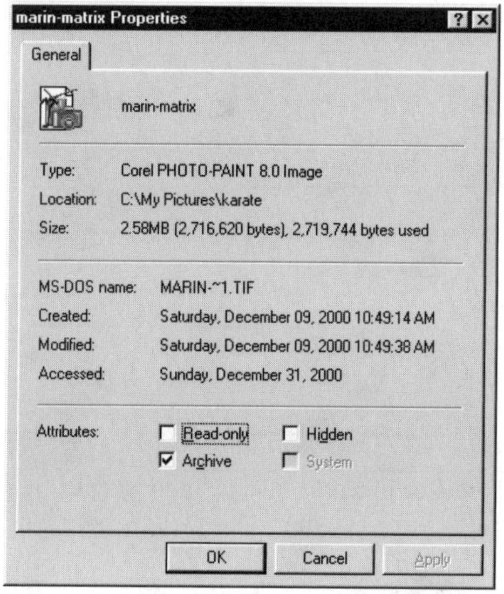

FIGURE 16-1 This 2.7MB file is simply too large to email effectively. Resize it so it's under a megabyte.

16

attachment came in all garbled—it looks like page after page of meaningless text instead of a picture—switch from MIME to UUENCODE or vice versa. Attachments should be icons you can actually click on to view, such as the one in Figure 16-2. If that doesn't work for other users, you can always switch back again. In Outlook, for instance, you can find these settings by choosing Tools | Options and clicking on the Mail Format tab of the Options dialog box (see below). From there, click the Settings button and change the format.

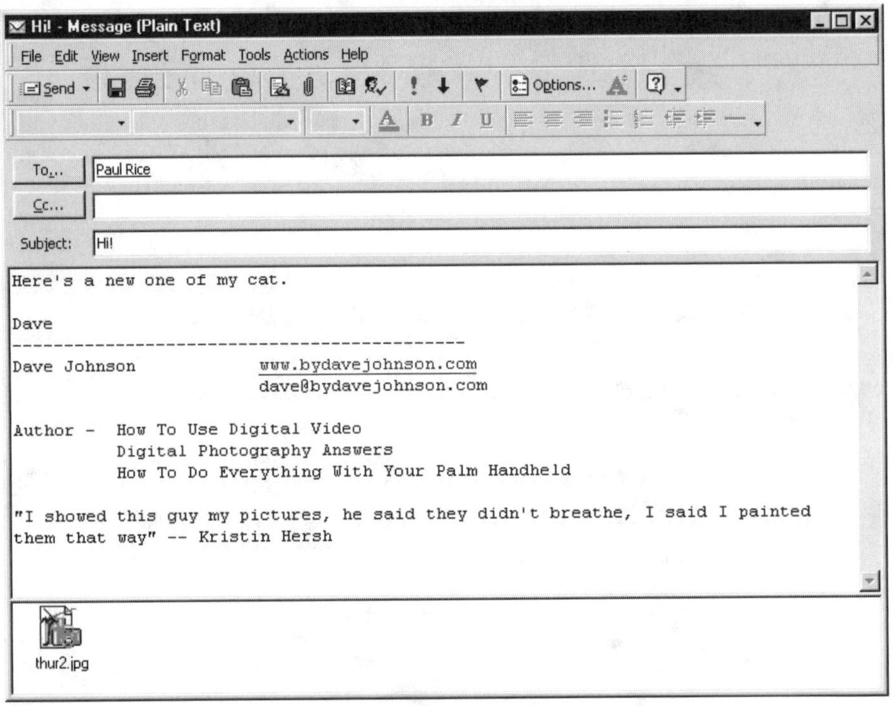

FIGURE 16-2 This is what an attachment looks like in most email programs; attachments that are decoded incorrectly by your mail program will instead turn out like gibberish.

Finally, there are programs around that create "multimedia email" messages for you. Sometimes you can get such programs with your digital camera or bundled with image editing software. Programs like Novita LiveLetter (www.planetweb.com/novita) help you create a complete multimedia experience with sound, graphics, and text, and then attach that to an email message and send it to someone else. The recipient merely double-clicks on the message to see the sound, picture, and text.

Attaching Pictures in Email

Though the process varies from one program to another, attaching one or more images to an email message really isn't hard. The basic procedure is this: drag and drop an image file directly into your open email message, or use a menu option to insert a file into the message. Almost all mail software uses the paperclip icon as a standard symbol to represent an attachment to your message, so look for that button and use it to specify files for inclusion in your email (see Figure 16-3).

16

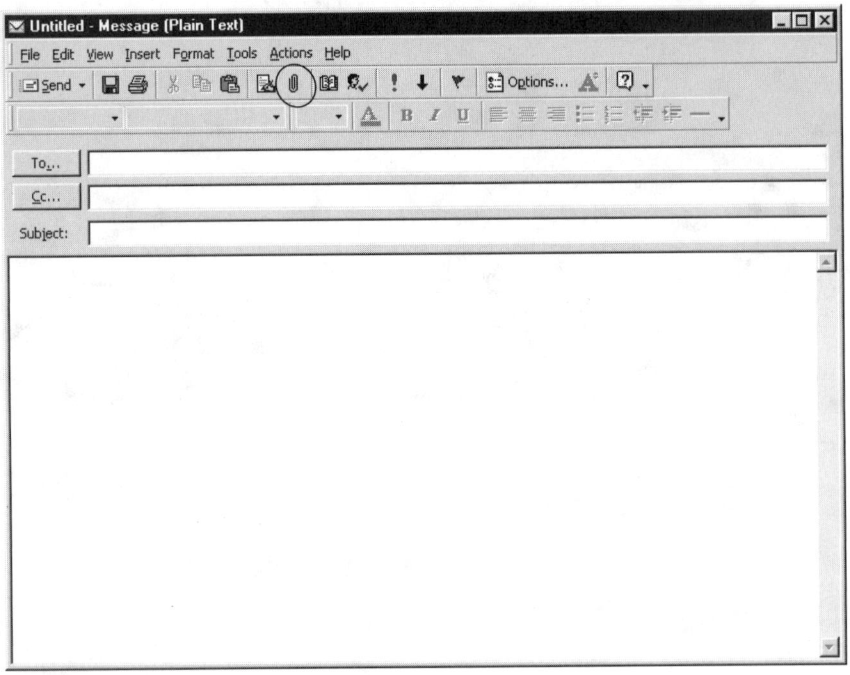

FIGURE 16-3   Use the paperclip to attach images (and other kinds of files) to your email.

How to ...   Send Email with Outlook 2000

If you're a Microsoft Outlook user, here's how to attach a pair of images to an outgoing message:

1. Click the New button in the Outlook toolbar to create a new mail message. A blank, untitled message should appear.

2. Address the email by typing the appropriate email address in the To box.

3. Add a subject by typing in the Subject box, seen below.

4. Enter some message text. It's generally a good idea to write a personal, specific note rather than sending a blank message with attachments—that way the recipient knows it's not some sort of virus.

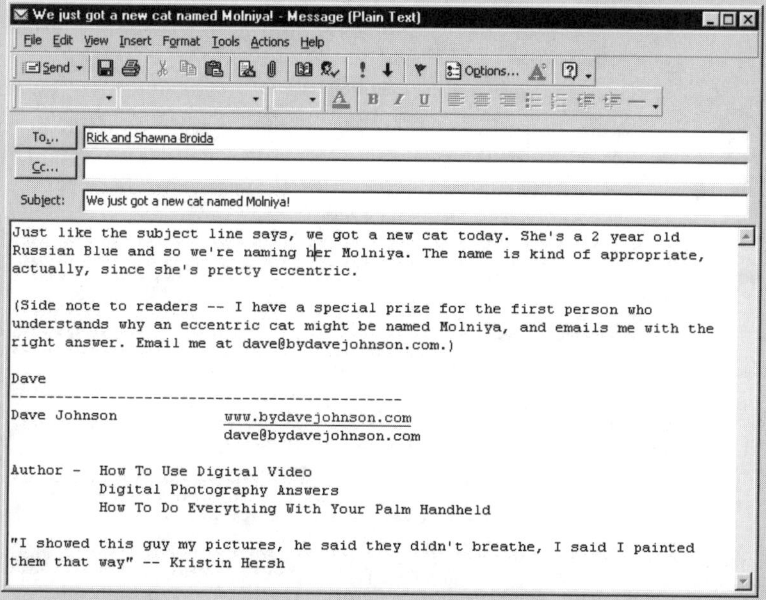

5. If you have a folder with pictures open on the desktop, you can drag an image file from that folder over the message window and drop it, as shown below. You should see an attachment appear in the message.

16

6. To add another image to the message, choose Insert | File from the message window's menu, or click on the Attachment button (shaped like a paperclip, which you should be able to see in the illustration below). You should see the Insert File dialog box.

7. Navigate to the appropriate folder and select the image file you want to attach. If you want to attach multiple files from the same folder, you can hold down the CTRL key while you click on each image file.

8. Click the Insert button to close the Insert File dialog box and insert the images in the message.

9. When your message is complete, click the Send button to send it to its recipient.

Viewing Images Someone Sent to You

In most email programs (like Netscape Messenger, Microsoft Exchange, Outlook, and Outlook Express), your attachment appears as an icon that you manipulate like any other file icons. Here are your most common choices:

- With the message window open, right-click and choose Quick View to see the image on the desktop without opening a large image editing program.

- Double-click the image icon to launch an image editing program and display the image.

- Drag and drop the image icon from the message window to the desktop or another Windows folder for permanent storage.

TIP *If you're sending an image to a Windows 95/98/Me user, almost any file format is fair game (but JPG is probably best since the files are so small). I recommend that you send Mac users files in TIF or JPG format, and Windows 3.1 users should get BMP or JPG files. Since JPG is a very efficient file format for sending photographic images, you're best off sending images in JPG format exclusively.*

Distributing Images on Floppy and Zip Disks

Since JPG images are so small, you can often copy a lot of images to a floppy disk and pass them around that way. After all, everyone has a floppy disk drive, right?

Even better, pretty much everyone can read PC floppy disks—even Mac users. The Macintosh floppy drive can read PC floppies. That means you can copy a few JPG images to a floppy and give it to a Mac user, and she or he will be able to read the images just fine.

One caveat, though—PCs can't read Macintosh floppies. So Mac users need to be sure the disk is formatted for a PC before doing the handoff. The same is true of Zip disks. A Zip disk made on a Mac cannot be read on a PC.

Strategies for Sharing Lots of Images

If you need to send someone a lot of images and the total file size is too much for email or floppy disk, you have a few ways to get the data to the recipient. Often, you'll need to combine these techniques. Here are some things you can try:

- Use a compression program like Zip (formally known as pkZip) to shrink the images down to a smaller size. You can see several images compressed into a single Zip file in Figure 16-4. If your image files are already compressed (such as if you use the JPG or compressed TIF formats), then Zip won't do much for your total file size. But if you are trying to send uncompressed images via floppy or email, this compression program can be a lifesaver. I suggest you get a version of Zip that has a friendly Windows interface, like WinZip (which you can download from www.winzip.com).

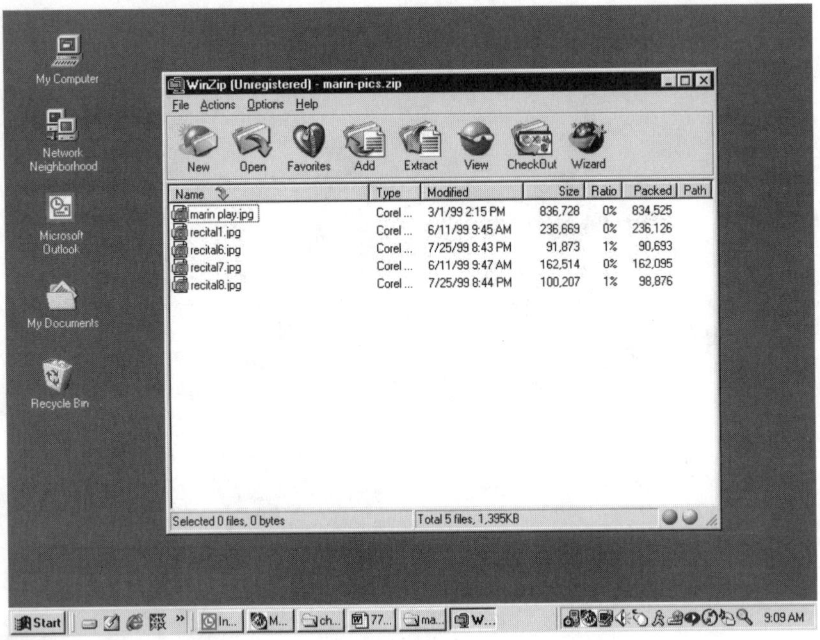

FIGURE 16-4   WinZip is a great tool for sending a bunch of images at once as a single, compressed attachment.

- Break the image collection into several email messages, with each message weighing in at less than a megabyte or so.

- Use the compression feature in the JPG format to reduce file size. With many images, you can compress the image significantly before you start to see any obvious degradation due to compression. This is great if you're just passing images around among friends, though I'd be more careful about images you are planning to print.

- Instead of email, mail a Zip disk. Since the Zip disk holds 100MB or more of data (depending upon which Zip drive model you own), you have an awful lot of room to work with. It's certainly more efficient than using the Internet.

Creating Your Own Web Pages

The Web is a great place to store and share your digital images. Your pictures are probably already in a convenient Web format—like JPG—and most of your friends and family probably already own a computer with Internet access. If you have a Web design program like FrontPage, FrontPage Express, or Netscape Composer, you can drag and drop your way to a nice little Web page with a minimal amount of effort. Figure 16-5 shows FrontPage 2000 being used to edit a typical Web page. The learning curve is similar to what you might expect from a program like Microsoft Publisher.

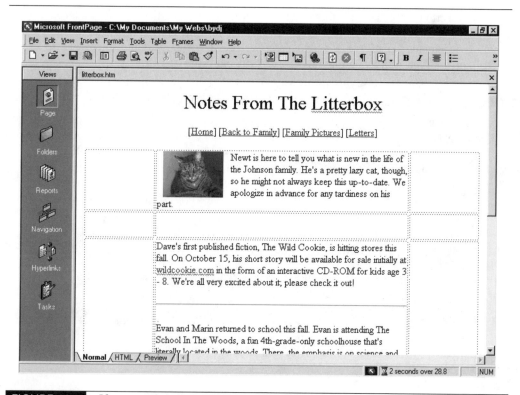

FIGURE 16-5   If you can handle Publisher, PowerPoint, or Word, you can probably slap together a simple Web site in FrontPage.

Using a Web design program, you can enter text, drag and drop graphics and pictures, and then edit and format the Web site's appearance with simple toolbar and menu controls. There are many good Web design programs on the market. Some are free and some are retail products. Here are some of the most popular editors:

Editor	Where to Find It
Microsoft FrontPage	www.microsoft.com/frontpage
FrontPage Express (free with Internet Explorer)	www.microsoft.com/Windows/ie
Netscape Composer	www.netscape.com
Adobe GoLive	www.adobe.com
Sausage Software HotDog	www.sausagetools.com
Softquad XMetal	www.softsquad com

Also, it's worth noting that you can create Web pages with some Microsoft products that aren't even designed specifically for the Internet. Publisher, for instance, has a feature that lets you publish documents to the Web. It's not a great Web design program, but it'll let you get pictures up on the Web with a minimum of fuss and with software you already own.

Choosing an Image Size and File Format for the Web

Many digital cameras take pictures in resolutions as low as 640x480 pixels, but this can be too big for a Web page. Not only does an image that big take a while to download, it consumes a lot of space on the screen. Instead, I recommend that you shrink your images down to about 500 pixels across. (Look back at Chapter 12 for details on how to do that.)

There are two file formats commonly used on the Web: GIF and JPG. CompuServe originally developed the GIF format, which stands for Graphic Interchange Format (making the term *GIF format* somewhat redundant). GIF is a compact file format that is commonly used in Web pages. The major disadvantage of GIF, however, is that it limits images to just 256 colors (or less, depending upon the settings you use when saving the file). That can affect the quality of the image on screen, though that's generally not real important.

Usually, Web designers like to use GIF format 89a. This is the newest version of the GIF format that supports three important features:

- **Transparency** Transparency allows you to specify a color in the image that will be treated as transparent. That way, you can make the image's background or border transparent. If you have an irregularly shaped image, like a diamond or oval, this feature can look really cool, as you can see here:

No matter what kind of background you use, a picture with a transparent background will blend in

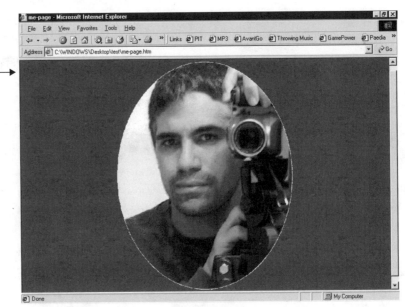

- ■ **Interlacing**   An interlaced image downloads to a Web browser first as a chunky, low-resolution image; then it increases in quality as more information is retrieved. Otherwise, the image would normally load a few lines at a time, so you'd see the top of the image display before the bottom. Interlacing isn't faster than the alternative, but it gives the viewer something to look at, and so it can seem faster. This is a good option to use when you know that people with slow Internet connections will be viewing your images.

- ■ **Animation**   An animated GIF is really just a sequence of individual images played one after the other. Not really fast enough to give a sense of cinematic motion with large images, animated GIFs are usually used to slowly display one image after another like a slide show.

The JPG format was created by the Joint Photographic Experts Group to be a scalable file format that could be compressed to yield low file size or be left uncompressed for higher quality. Unlike GIF, JPG images can display a full 16-million-color palette. Depending upon how much you compress a JPG image, however, the image quality can vary from nearly identical to the original all the way down to unrecognizable.

As we talked about in Part III of the book, you can specify the level of compression to use when saving a JPG file. Most programs default to a fairly low compression level, preserving image quality. In reality, though, you can often compress the image much more aggressively than the default and still get adequate quality for a Web page.

Sharing Images on the Web Without Designing a Web Site

Certainly, you can design a Web site that shows off your pictures to friends and family, and as I just mentioned, there are quite a few tools around to help you do just that. If you're not really thrilled by the idea of learning how to manipulate a Web design program, though, there's an easier solution—one that requires no programming, no eye for page design, and no real Internet skills. The solution? A photo-sharing Web site.

Which Is Best?

You can use whichever file format—GIF or JPG—that best suits your needs. It's perfectly all right to mix JPG and GIF images in a Web site, even on the same page. This chart should help you decide which is the appropriate file format:

Use JPG:	Use GIF:
To display full-color photographs compressed to very small file size	To use a transparent background
	To interlace the display of an image
	To display an image with just a few colors

Probably the fastest-growing kind of digital imaging service around, photo-sharing sites are fully automated, mostly free forums for posting your pictures online. These services take the arcane drudgery out of designing Web sites from scratch and posting photos to the Internet by allowing you to upload images to a commercial site via a simple interface. The site itself goes to the trouble of arranging your images into an attractive layout, complete with thumbnail views (which you can click to see a full-sized version of the image), captions, and even printing services that can print your favorite images and mail the hard copy directly to you. These sites are a convenient way to publish your images online for friends, family, and strangers to browse, and you don't have to learn anything about Web site creation.

There are more than a half-dozen photo-sharing sites around that all work more or less the same way. ClubPhoto.com, for instance, lets you arrange your photos into albums and display them for visitors (see Figure 16-6). The site lets you drag and drop images from your desktop directly to the Web browser—a very convenient way to upload images.

FIGURE 16-6   ClubPhoto arranges your uploaded digital images for you in an elegant manner.

Other sites abound. Zing.com is a well-organized site that also lets you upload images by dragging and dropping the files directly onto the Web browser. Visitors can watch your images individually or as part of a multimedia slideshow, complete with popular music that can be chosen from an extensive catalog of popular CDs. Another site, ememories.com, not only shows off your digital images, but also offers extra products like printed greeting cards and hardcover "coffee table" books made from your pictures.

Another option is ophoto.com. This site has a clever image editing tool built right into the Web page. You can crop, rotate, and even remove red eye from your pictures right from an ophoto.com upload assistant program (seen in Figure 16-7) that you can download and use to store images on the Web site.

Finally, there's PhotoLoft.com. PhotoLoft isn't completely free. You get 50MB of storage at no cost, and each 25MB after that costs $19.95 per year. You can upload images via the Web or by attaching images to email messages. The site also accepts a very wide variety of file formats, including BMP and PhotoCD. Most of the other sites accept just a few file formats like JPG and GIF. PhotoLoft also uses a special image viewer that lets viewers zoom in and pan around large images.

FIGURE 16-7   Some photo-sharing sites are so sophisticated that they let you crop and tweak your images as they're uploaded.

Here is a list of the photo-sharing sites:

photoloft.com

ophoto.com

zing.com

ememories.com

clubphoto.com

dotphoto.com

photopoint.com

shutterfly.com

TIP *Even if you maintain your own personal Web site, you can save yourself the time and trouble of arranging digital images on a photo page by linking from your own Web site directly to your album on a photo-sharing site. That's what I do; to see it in action, go to www.bydavejohnson.com and click on the Photography link to see how I connect to the ClubPhoto site.*

Showing Off Images on a Palm

A popular way to show off traditional 35mm pictures is by carrying them in your wallet. Wallet photos and digital imaging don't really mix that well—or at least they didn't, until recently. Now you can transfer images from your hard disk and store them on your Palm OS handheld (like the Palm III, Palm V, or Handspring Visor). Color handheld devices like the Palm IIIc and the Visor Prism work best; the Prism supports 16-bit color for more realistic images, though the Palm IIIc does an acceptable job with a palette of just 256 colors. A typical Palm device can store dozens of images, though the limited memory in these devices means your images compete for space with other kinds of data.

Applications abound for storing and displaying images on a Palm device. A popular image viewer is called FireViewer, and it is compatible with a conversion utility for transferring images from the PC to the Palm. In Figure 16-8, the image on the left shows FireViewer's main screen with a list of all the images stored on the Palm. The image on the right is a FireViewer image, complete with the pop-up menu for managing your images.

An even better solution, though, is called Album to Go, seen in Figure 16-9. This image viewer is designed expressly for displaying images as if your Palm were a wallet, so it has a slide show mode along with transition effects for switching elegantly between images. Album to Go works in two different ways:

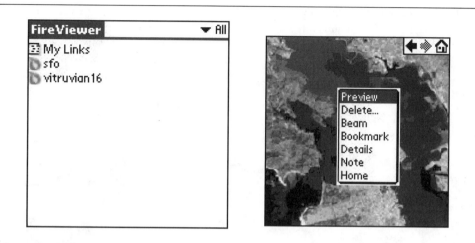

FIGURE 16-8 FireViewer plays images and videos on any Palm OS device.

■ Using the Album to Go desktop application (see Figure 16-10), you can drag images stored on your hard disk directly to the Palm. Note that for rectangular images that won't fit exactly in the Palm's square screen, you can move the image around in the preview window until it looks the way you like; then you can click Send To HotSync.

FIGURE 16-9 Album to Go's image list and viewer screen—the program can play your images in a slide show mode.

16

■ Alternately, you can download images from ClubPhoto.com directly to your Palm. To do that, visit a ClubPhoto album and click the appropriate Convert To Palm link in the left side of the screen (shown below). There are two links: one for the color Palm and another for grayscale Palms. After selecting the link, choose to "Open this file from its current location" on the File Download dialog box, and the image is automatically stored on your Palm at the next HotSync.

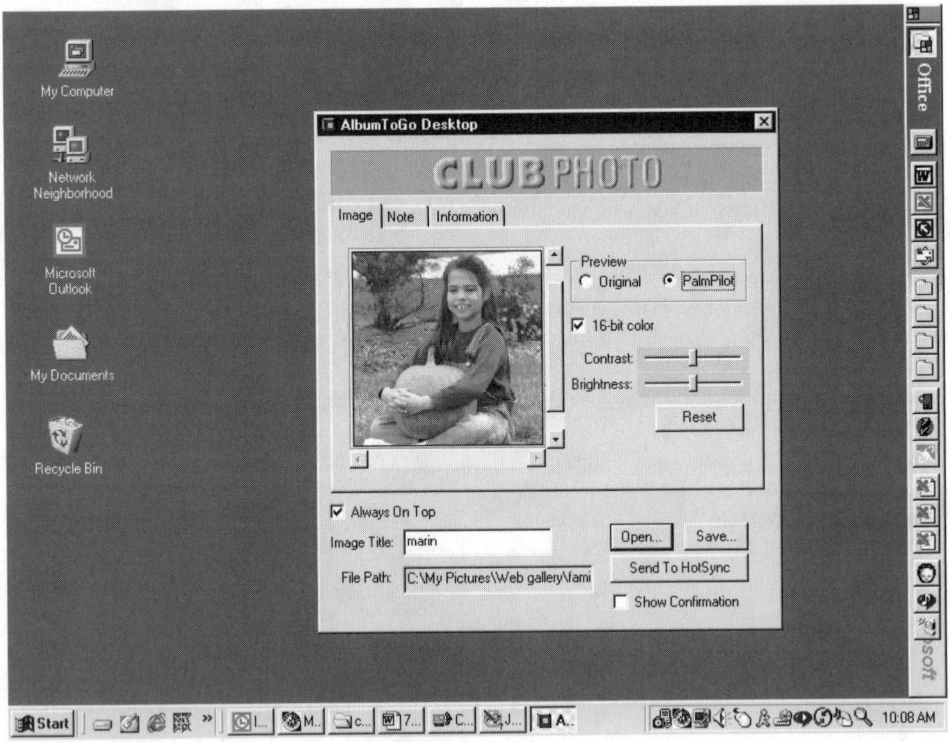

FIGURE 16-10 Album to Go lets you change the brightness, contrast, and cropping of the selected image before it goes to await the next HotSync.

Showing Off Images in a Digital Picture Frame

Another way to display digital images is in a digital picture frame. Digital picture frames are inexpensive LCD displays mounted in a picture frame shell. Equipped with a memory card, the picture frame can show digital images in a slide show format. Digital picture frames are readily available. Models include the Ceiva, the Digi-Frame, and Sony's Digital CyberFrame.

Sony's CyberFrame uses Sony's proprietary Memory Stick technology to display both still images and MPEG movies in a small LCD screen that you can place on a tabletop like an ordinary picture frame. If you already have a Sony digital camera that uses Memory Stick memory storage, the CyberFrame is a good choice because you can simply remove the memory card from the camera and insert it directly in the picture frame to begin displaying images. The Digi-Frame is a similar product, though it uses both CompactFlash and SmartMedia memory cards, so you can insert the memory card from most digital cameras to view your images.

16

The Ceiva, which you can see in Figure 16-11, is unique in two ways: in addition to a small cache of internal (nonremovable) memory, it also connects to the Internet via an ordinary telephone jack. Using a built-in modem, it regularly connects to the Internet and downloads images you've stored on the Ceiva Web site. With the ability to rotate among 20 images stored in the Ceiva's memory each day, you can have a constant supply of images on display with minimal effort. Likewise, Ceiva makes it possible to share images from your digital camera with other Ceiva picture frame owners. So you can establish a community of friends and family who exchange images among their picture frames via the Ceiva Web site (see below).

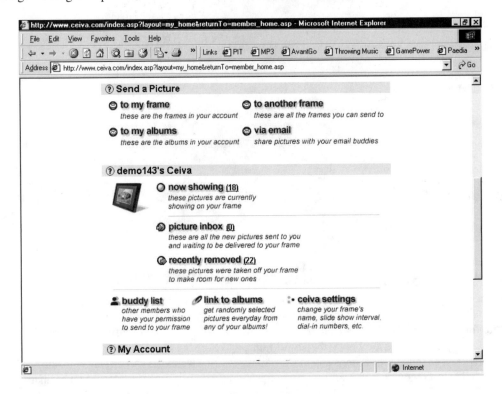

Here is a handy chart showing the digital picture frame makers and their Web sites:

Digital Picture Frames	Find It At
Ceiva	www.ceiva.com
Digi-Frame	www.digi-frame.com
Sony CyberFrame	www.sel.sony.com

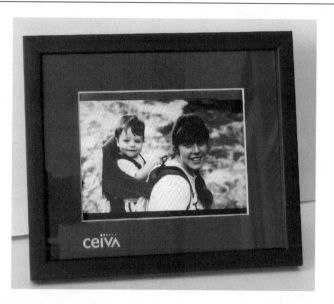

FIGURE 16-11 Digital picture frames let you show off an always-changing slide show of digital images on your coffee table.

Create a Slide Show on Videotape

Another way to distribute images is in a videotape slide show that people can pop into their VCRs. This is a convenient solution for folks who may not own a computer. For years, photography stores have offered video slide show services for a fee: they'd copy your old prints, slides, and negatives to videotape with a musical soundtrack. Now you can do it yourself.

Record Video Directly from the Camera

There are two ways to make your own video slide show, but if your camera has a video-out jack, you can do it quickly and easily without even using your PC. Here's what you can do:

1. Start by arranging the images you want to show off on your camera's memory card. Delete any images you don't want to show, for instance. You can also copy other images from your PC to the camera's memory card and then insert the card in the camera. Also, make sure that they're all oriented properly—sideways images taken by holding the camera on its side should be removed.

2. If your camera has the ability to display transitions between each image during playback, turn that mode on now.

16

3. Attach the video-out port of the camera to your VCR. If you want musical accompaniment, connect your CD player to the VCR as well, and queue up some music. Set the VCR on pause.

4. When your tape is ready to record, start recording, and start the CD player and camera's playback mode simultaneously. You should end up with a slide show of images with music recorded on tape.

Using PowerPoint to Make a Video Slide Show

Using the camera to create a slide show is easy, but it's fraught with compromises. There's usually no way to precisely time the transition from one image to another in your slide show, for instance, so you can't easily synchronize the images to music. Also, images tend to roll slowly onto the screen as they are read from memory. It might look cheesy, particularly if you're used to seeing pictures "snap" rapidly onto the screen.

Instead, you might want to try a more elaborate solution if you have the necessary gear. For this approach to work, you'll need a PC, a program like PowerPoint (which you may already have, especially if you use Microsoft Office), and a video-out port on your PC that you can connect to a VCR or camcorder. Here's how you can do it:

To create a slide show using PowerPoint, do this:

1. Start by making sure all of the images you plan to use are 640x480 pixels. If they're bigger, resize and save them using a different name. It's often easiest to create a special folder for all your slide show images, then delete that temporary folder when you're done creating the slide show.

2. Launch PowerPoint and choose Blank Presentation from the New Presentation dialog box.

3. We need to choose a slide style—it doesn't matter which one, so pick the blank slide from the very bottom.

4. Choose Insert | Picture | From File, as seen in the illustration. Find the image you want to add to the slide.

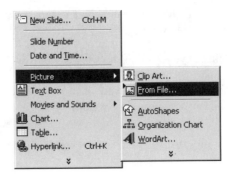

5. When the image appears on your slide, resize it if necessary so that it takes up the entire slide, from top to bottom and side to side, as shown below.

6. Now add another slide. Click the New Slide button option in Common Tasks, and then add another blank slide.

7. Add another image to this new blank slide.

8. Continue this process until you've created a complete slide show.

9. To add a common transition to every slide in your presentation, choose Slide Show | Slide Transition and select a transition from the transition drop-down menu. The Dissolve transaction is a good choice. To apply this transition to every slide in your slide show, choose Apply To All.

16

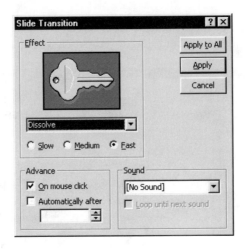

TIP *You can apply transitions to a particular slide or apply to all the slides at once. In my opinion, slide shows that use a different effect for every transition, however, have a decidedly unprofessional look. I suggest you stick with a subdued, single transition approach throughout the entire presentation.*

10. Save your presentation by choosing File | Save As.

11. When your slide show is complete, you can plug your PC into a VCR or camcorder and record the show to tape, using your own mouse clicks as timing for when to change slides. You can also add a CD audio source to the VCR to add a soundtrack as you record the show.

Index

INTERNATIONAL CONTACT INFORMATION

AUSTRALIA
McGraw-Hill Book Company Australia Pty. Ltd.
TEL +61-2-9417-9899
FAX +61-2-9417-5687
http://www.mcgraw-hill.com.au
books-it_sydney@mcgraw-hill.com

CANADA
McGraw-Hill Ryerson Ltd.
TEL +905-430-5000
FAX +905-430-5020
http://www.mcgrawhill.ca

GREECE, MIDDLE EAST,
NORTHERN AFRICA
McGraw-Hill Hellas
TEL +30-1-656-0990-3-4
FAX +30-1-654-5525

MEXICO (Also serving Latin America)
McGraw-Hill Interamericana Editores S.A. de C.V.
TEL +525-117-1583
FAX +525-117-1589
http://www.mcgraw-hill.com.mx
fernando_castellanos@mcgraw-hill.com

SINGAPORE (Serving Asia)
McGraw-Hill Book Company
TEL +65-863-1580
FAX +65-862-3354
http://www.mcgraw-hill.com.sg
mghasia@mcgraw-hill.com

SOUTH AFRICA
McGraw-Hill South Africa
TEL +27-11-622-7512
FAX +27-11-622-9045
robyn_swanepoel@mcgraw-hill.com

UNITED KINGDOM & EUROPE
(Excluding Southern Europe)
McGraw-Hill Education Europe
TEL +44-1-628-502500
FAX +44-1-628-770224
http://www.mcgraw-hill.co.uk
computing_neurope@mcgraw-hill.com

ALL OTHER INQUIRIES Contact:
Osborne/McGraw-Hill
TEL +1-510-549-6600
FAX +1-510-883-7600
http://www.osborne.com
omg_international@mcgraw-hill.com